CONTEXTUALIZED TEACHING
OF THE BIBLICAL DOCTRINE
OF SALVATION

Science and Art of Creating
Understanding of the Gospel

By

Paul M. Kamunge

CONTEXTUALIZED TEACHING OF THE BIBLICAL DOCTRINE OF SALVATION

Science and Art of Creating Understanding of the Gospel

Copyright 2004 by P. Kamunge

The scripture quotations in this book are taken from
The New International Version (NIV)

Published by

Western Seminary Library
5511 Hawthorn Blvd
Portland Oregon, 97215

ISBN: 978-9966-070-07-4

Printed by

Kijabe Printing Press
P.O. Box 40 – 00220
KIJABE, Kenya

2014

Dedication
To my dear wife (Mary Wambui Mwangi),
for her patience and encouragement along my academic journey,
and to our children, Aben, Joy-Faith and Darren who are a great
blessing from God.

CONTENTS

CHAPTER	PAGE

FIGURES

TABLES

ABSTRACT

Qualitative and quantitative field research was carried out in 2002 and 2003 among rural, Central Bantu Christians in Kenya, East Africa, seeking to learn and describe the population's mental models of salvation and certain related beliefs.

Historically, the Central Bantu peoples perceived salvation as a state of peaceful and harmonious relationship with God, with ancestors and with the living community. To maintain their salvation, people were seriously involved in their religious traditional practices. When AIM missionaries came in 1895, their message of salvation was not perceived by the Central Bantu to have the same meaning. To this day, Bantu Christians show evidence of a certain confusion of faith and practice.

This book highlights some cultural and traditional religious beliefs of the Central Bantu, highlighting their incongruence with the Biblical and Theological doctrine of salvation as taught by Evangelical Christians. Means are proposed for alleviating the fears that believers have concerning loss of salvation by helping them to understand that salvation is a gift of God to those who believe in Christ. Finally, contextual teaching of salvation is designed to train gospel workers who will reach out to the Central Bantu, nonbelievers and the church with a more scriptural doctrine of salvation, employing culturally-respectful methods of evangelism and teaching.

Chapter 1

INTRODUCTION

This book aims to enhance and to create understanding of the Biblical and Theological sound doctrine of salvation amongst the Central Bantu peoples of Kenya by formulating a transferable theology and proposing a contextual approach to teaching it. A review of historical, cultural views of salvation establishes a framework for presenting contextualized doctrines. It is the author's conviction that the Bible supplies absolute salvation concepts that must be contextualized for the Bantu in a meaningful Christian theology of salvation.

In this book, the contextual doctrine of salvation utilizes a narrative evangelism method that includes cultural tools such as story telling, parables and dynamic equivalents. Chapter one introduces the Central Bantu, the purpose of this study, its objectives, central problem, delimitations, and definitions of the terms. Chapter two reflects on early Central Bantu views of salvation prior to and after the coming of AIM missionaries in 1895. Chapter three exposes the Central Bantu concepts of salvation today as uncovered through qualitative and quantitative field research. Chapter four discusses a biblical basis of salvation from both Old and New Testaments. Chapter five discusses theological meaning of salvation and, six evaluates the Bantu present concepts of salvation, proposing some contextual methods of communicating the gospel to them.

The Central Bantu people comprise about 67% of the Kenya population, and include forty eight ethno-linguistic groups such as the Kikuyu, the Luhya, Kamba, Meru, Embu, Mijikend and Pokomo. Collectively, the Bantu people are categorized into three groups according to the geographical area where they live. The Central Bantu are the Kikuyu, Kamba and Ameru, who predominantly live in the Central province of Kenya.

Within the Kenya population (33,000,000), the Kikuyu people are about 6,146,000, the Kamba are over 3,829,000, and the Meru people are over 2,378,000 people.[1] In each tribe, there are other small sub-groups which are distributed in different geographical areas. These tribes share many similarities in their cultures such as language, traditional religion, and behavior.

Economically, the Central Bantu are angriculturalists and pastoralists. They grow corn, bananas, millet, beans, tea, and they keep cows, goats, sheep for daily products and meat. Unlike the other tribes of the Bantu, they are deeply rooted in their cultural practices such as circumcision, which according to their cultural worldview is a gateway for marriage, leadership and adulthood. They are religious in that many people are said to be "people of the church;" and those who do not belong to the church have their traditional religious practices. They are significant from other Kenyan tribes because they have similar language dialects, and they have no restrictions on inter-marring between groups. They have a common religious heritage, and today many people value God as their source of health and prosperity. Unlike other Kenyan tribes, the Central Bantu are clustered into social group such as clans, family and age groups, which can be helpful to the work of evangelism, especially when these groups gather for events.

The other groups of the Bantu people are the Western Bantu (Luhya and Kisii) who live in western part of Kenya and around Lake Victoria. The Coastal Bantu are the Miji Kenda who lives

---

[1] Kenya Census Report, 1999-2002.

around Kenyan coastal plain. Both of these groups are different from the Central Bantu in their language, culture and religious practices.

Though there are Christians from other Kenyan tribes that make up the Africa Inland Church denomination for example the Kalenjin, Boran, Maasai, Digo, the Central Bantu people are basically the majority. Since the Bantu still value their cultural religious traditions before and following conversion, many Christians are syncretistic in their form and faith practices. This was discovered through recent field research, conducted among the Africa Inland Church Christians. It is assumed that the same syncretistic Christian ideas are dominant in other Central Bantu church denominations in Kenya.

Chapter 2

EARLY CENTRAL BANTU'S VIEWS OF SALVATION

When the Africa Inland Mission workers came to the Central Bantu, they met people who were culturally and religiously rooted in their own tribal traditions, having their own cultural concept of God, spirits, life after death and salvation. When the missionaries presented the gospel of salvation to them, it did not make a lot of sense, because it was not contextualized, that is, it did not fit into their cultural thought forms. To this day, their view of salvation remains syncretistic, such that it retains cultural, moralistic ideas integrated with Biblical views.

This chapter discusses early Central Bantu views of salvation prior to and after the coming of the Africa Inland Missionaries in 1895. What an anthropologist would have recorded prior to that date differs from what would be recorded today. According to the research reported in chapter three, the Central Bantu still have a different perception of salvation from that of the Bible and sound Christian theology.

Central Bantu View of Salvation Prior to 1895

The cultural and traditional religious meaning of the term "salvation" among the Central Bantu prior to 1895 included enjoyment of a peaceful, harmonious relationship with God, including acceptance and favor with Him, with ancestors and with the living community. Thus, God (the Supreme Being) and the ancestors were important in the process of salvation.

The universal name that was used to describe God among the three tribes was *Ngai*. The name of the ancestors in Kikuyu was, *ngoma cia andu aria makuire tene*, the Ameru people called them - *irundu bia bajuju* and Akamba, *aimu*. The actual meaning of God (Ngai) will be discussed later but, the cultural euphemistic meaning of the ancestral spirits was, "the spirits of those who went ahead of us." The living community in Kikuyu and Ameru was, *andu aria me muoyo*, and in Akamba was, *andu ala me thayu* (those who are alive).

When cultural words that described the meaning of salvation are expressed in the languages of the three tribes, they are as: the Kikuyu people say, *guikarania na thayu* or *ngwataniro ya thayu*, (peaceful relationship), Ameru people: *ngwataniro ya ukiri*, while in Akamba: *kwikalany'a na muuo or thayu,* which respectively means the same (peaceful relationship). The term harmony in Kikuyu is, *uiguwano, rumwe*, Ameru is, *ngwataniro iinjega*, while in Akamba is, *wiw'ano, uumwe*. The term "acceptance" in Kikuyu and Ameru tribe is, *gwitikirika*, while in Akamba is, *kwitikilika* and the word "favor" in Kikuyu is, *kwendererwo, gwitikirika*, Ameru is, *kwenderua*, while in Akamba is, *kwonewa useo, kwitikilika*.

All the above salvation words were relational and culturally ritualistic, so that when people wanted to experience salvation, they had to offer sacrifices to God and to their ancestors. When all the cultural elements for salvation were in place, the salvific life of the people was observable. In his tape, "Ideas of Salvation in Africa," on the idea of peace, Adeyemo contributes that: "salvation is seeking God's mercy and peace in a ritualistic practice. This humanistic idea of salvation is also believed to make one happy."[2]

The three tribes perceived the idea of salvation through their senses and experiences, in the daily process of life. By using the term "perception," the writer means that the Kikuyu, the Ameru

---

[2] Tokunboh Adeyemo. *Audio Tape*, "Perception of Salvation in Africa"(Nairobi) March, 1983.

and the Akamba way of understanding salvation was through their daily acts, daily experiences and through the senses. Adeyemo too defines the term perception as: "it is the act, process or power of conceiving mentally, formulation of ideas. The ideas are perceived through observation by the senses."[3] The result of this perception was seeking God's, their ancestors' and the community's mercy, peace, reconciliation, harmony, and acceptance, which all contributed as well as made cultural salvation.

An anthropological question is: What is the relationship of these salvation terms? These terms describe an experienced calm, or a calm situation that people should experience, and anticipate experiencing in future. They all described an absence of calamity, epidemic, drought, physical attack, surprising deaths, famine, negative turning or any problematic human situations. These terms were used inter-changeably and carried with them a deep relationship between a person and God, with the ancestors and with the members of the whole community. For example, when they used the term "acceptance" they meant: "being gladly received or agreeable or satisfactory, favorable reception and approved worthy by God, ancestors and the community."[4] These terms were positive and were expected to exist simultaneously among the people who had a good relationship with God, the ancestors and with other people. These terms were known to have had permanent sequence among the people if this relationship was maintained and worked for. They all existed at the same time and therefore, one could not have one and leave the others. Breaking one of the cultural-religious requirements towards salvation meant losing all of them because they all made one, but only one situation which is "salvation."

The above salvation terms were applicable both to the people and their properties, and which included deliverance

---

[3] Ibid. 1983.

[4] Horndike Barnhart, *The World Book Dictionary A-K* (Chicago: World Books Inc, 1963), 12.

from illhealth and misfortune. More emphasis was given to God because He was perceived as the primary provider of peace, harmony, acceptance, reconciliation and favor; the ancestors were secondary providers of this "salvation." The participation of the community towards salvation was also needed for salvation, for it could not exist without their collective daily devotion to God, and to the ancestors.

To experience holistic salvation, people were expected to consistently involve themselves in cultural activities such as, worshiping God and the ancestors, avoiding sin against God, against ancestors and against other people in the community. In the process of salvation, people were also expected to be conscious of life after death, because if one was not living in the culturally expected standards, upon death he or she was not welcomed by the ancestors. This meant his or her salvation was not complete. To have complete salvation however, people were to persistently be in a ritualistic cultural environment that is, offering sacrifices to God and ancestors.

Salvation through ritualistic activities gave people the opportunity for airing their joy, gratitude, praises, as well as pouring out their tears and concerns as they struggled to maintain their salvation. Activities that one did towards "salvation" determined how he or she would spend life here on earth and thereafter. Salvation was therefore a continuous life, but broken and lost if one did not remain seriously involved in cultural-religious rituals.

Beside the general meaning of the word "salvation" and its components (peace, acceptance, reconciliation, harmony etc.), we need to specifically trace what each tribe would pronounce and say about the term "salvation" and what each tribe meant by it. The reason for doing so is to have a better understanding of the whole cultural salvation spectrum. Also, by understanding how they pronounce and write the term "salvation" in their mother tongues (which has its emic categories and comparisons), is going to provide insight into its background, interpretation, actual meaning, value and its reality.

The Gikuyu use the action verb *kuhonoka* (to save) from the verb *honoka* (save) implying either a person, an animal, an object or any kind of property has been saved, delivered or rescued from any sort of danger or disaster. When one is delivered from any danger, he will say, *nindirahonokire* (I was saved). In the early history of the Gikuyu people, this word would mean that one was delivered from the dangers of life and the savior (s) was or were either God, another person, group of people, clan, a family member or the ancestors.

The Akamba use the action word, *kutangiwa* (to be saved) from the verb, *tangiwa* (save). The word, *nimutangiie* (I am already saved) is mainly used by Christians which expresses the idea that someone has already been saved. To them, the term does not have a past aspect but has a continuous and future dimension, thus *nimutangiie*. This word expresses the idea of how one has been acted upon (rescued from danger) by another person. The word, *kuvonoka* which also means the same (to be saved) from the verb, *vonoka* is used generally in a more extra-Scriptural sense. For example, if Akamba is rescued from a burning house, he will say, *ninavonoka kuma mwakini* (I have been saved from fire). If one is saved from darkness he or she will say, *ninavonoka kuma kivinduni*. This means that the two verbs, *tangiiwa* and *vonoka* cannot be used inter-changeably by the Akamba, though in their early history before Christianity they only used, *kuvonoka* for save or rescue. The term *kuvonoka* is very old in the minds of the Akamba because in their religious ceremonies towards God and the ancestors, it was the only term that was used. They could ask either God or the ancestors to save them from famine, calamity, and jeopardy or from any disaster. The same term was also used when a person was or has been rescued from any life turning point. Rescuing an animal was another case where this term was used. In rare cases, the two words are contemporary and used by Christians expressing salvation in Christ. In order to refrain from their old known word for general salvation *kuvonoka,* the term *tangiiwa* was translated in their tribal Bibles as a functional substitution. The fact is that the two terms bring home the same meanings of rescuing, delivering, redeeming and saving which are synonymous in their thinking. These terms emphasize the present and future aspect of salvation.

On the other hand, the Ameru term for "salvation" is *umbonokio, mbonoka,* is "save" while the action verb is, *kumbonoka* (to be saved) which are expressed in both secular and spiritual realms. To say that, "I am saved," the Ameru will say, *nimbonoki* which communicates the idea of being saved either from any danger, or being saved from eternal damnation. This term has no universal meaning behind it, either secular or spiritual, but whatever the person expresses using it makes sense if he or she illustrates it. As used by the Ameru people, the meanings of these salvation terms are internal and individual and therefore, they have to be explained along with whatever is said so that people may understand and make sense out of them. Today, when the Ameru say that, *niambonoketie,* (he has saved me), this expresses an idea that, "I have been saved" and the quick contemporary interpretation is that, Christ has saved that person. Still the term does not indicate the Scriptural meaning of past, present and future.

If the Ameru word, *niambonokirie* (I was save or he saved me) which is just the same word used for "I am saved" is put in the past tense, it can bring a double meaning. It can mean that somebody delivered me from dangers of life such as disaster, famine, and any other drastic problem. The pronoun "he" has no specific gender, that is, it can be either a male or female who did the action. If one means that Christ saved him, he must mention that it was Christ who did the action otherwise it is very hard for the people to understand without specifying the person who did the action. The term excludes human participation, that is, what the person should do so as to be saved. This shows that the word "save" is only understood when the user expresses it clearly and says what he or she means with the term.

Simply, the three tribes used salvation words in their languages to mean any state of a turning point either in people's lives, animals' lives or in the well being of their properties. All these turning points were perceived to have been brought about by peoples' failures to fulfill the ritualistic requirements towards God and the ancestors. Again, the requirements were: worshiping God and the ancestors, avoiding sins against God, against ancestors and against one another. If this is not the case, peace, acceptance, harmony, reconciliation and favor with God, ancestors and other members of the community cannot be experience, hence, "salvation" will be thwarted.

The continuous life without experiencing the above components of salvation meant apostasy. Apostasy was the situation whereby, a person, family, clan, or the whole community was said to have completely gone astray against God, ancestors and even the other members of ones community. It was said about the person that he or could not be delivered nor could he be accepted any more. This was brought about by consistent failing to fulfill the above cultural values, though having been warned through those turning points of life.

To some people, families, age groups, or clans who were widely known to be good and respectable but sidetracked by failing to fulfill the traditional requirements, re-admission to salvation was said to be open to them. It was through their actions that they forfeited the opportunity of being in salvation and therefore, if they searched their lives and knew whom they had wronged, they were re-admitted. Re-admission was traditionally carried out through the religious traditional sacrifices and offerings to the wronged being. The concerned group or a person had to come to a personal realization of the state of numerous acts of unworthiness before the wronged person and that he or she was ready to be made worthy again. Including all the African tribes' perception of salvation, John Mbiti notes that:

> We cannot omit to mention that the notion of salvation in African Christianity addresses itself also to the social-political environment of contemporary Africa. Threats and dangers to human existence are plentiful and strong in the political realm, and Christians attempt in various ways to find the saving power of God in such situations.[5]

The perception of salvation in the thinking of the Bantu people was therefore; very humanistic and ritualistic in nature because one had to be involved in sacrifices, offerings, libations and oblations in order to actualize his or her salvation.

To summarize, salvation was having a peaceful relationship with God, being acceptance by Him, and having harmony and favor from Him and it included the belief in the the ancestral spirits. It was a daily sensory experience with God and the ancestors. One was to consistently avoid anything which might bring disharmony with God, ancestors and with fellow people. Salvation meant a successful and positive life which came as a result of people's sacrifices and offerings. The recipients of salvation were members of the community with their properties. Salvation was more physical than spiritual that, it meant experiencing material prosperity such as fertility of their lands, increasing the number of their animals, a flourishing economy and having a large number of children.

Sources of Salvation

In the process of attaining salvation, God and the ancestors were the two sources of salvation and people could not experience it without appeasing them with sacrifices and offerings.

---

[5] John Mbiti, *Bible and Theology in African Christianity* (Nairobi: Oxford University Press, 1968), 163.

The Supreme God

The perception of the existence of God among the Bantu is as old as the history of their existence. God is said to have been known through three vehicles: intuition, traditional beliefs and revelation. By intuition, the writer means through an inherent human capability. This is, as a baby is born knowing how to suck his or her mother's breasts, this is the same with the Central Bantu members who are born with areligious mind. It is not something which is taught but, as we have already defined the term "perception," it is something sensed. This is, "it is confidence or belief which springs immediately from the constitution of the mind. It is the knowledge of God which exists in the soul before sense is experienced."[6] Blaise Pascal contributes to the idea of intuition knowledge by saying that:

> We know the truth through our reason but also through our hearts. It is through the latter that we know first principles, and reason, which has nothing to do with it, tries in vain to refute them. Knowledge of the first principles, like space, time, motion, number, is as solid as any derived through reason and it is as such knowledge, coming from the heart and instinct that reason has to depend and base all its arguments.[7]

The second knowledge was through traditional religion, which was orally passed from one generation to another. This knowledge is said to be a traditional value system which was intentionally passed from one clan to another, one family to another, one age group to another, and one tribe to another. This knowledge was achieved through many experiences of life and it gave a holistic traditional perception of God and therefore, experience was another

---

[6] Cornelius Olowola, *African Tradition Religion and the Christian Faith* (Achimota: African Christian Press, 1993), 21.

[7] Blaise Pascal, *Pensees* (Baltimore: Benguine, 1966), 58.

factor of knowing God and it was the most emphasized.

The third knowledge of God was through general revelation (general manifestations), which we will not discuss in this project. His revelation was experienced through His creation, general phenomenon and through cultural specialists who we call actors in salvation. Some of these were prophets, medicine men and diviners. These specialists were traditionally believed to be God's appointed agents. When God revealed Himself in these ways, people took those different revelations as salvation because He was having peace with them, had accepted them, was in harmony and was in favor with them. Apart from those ongoing experiences, salvation was believed not to have been among the people.

Names of God
The Central Bantu had the same universal name, characteristics and the works of God. As traditionally perceived, the names of God expressed the idea of salvation and its source. Through cultural-religious knowledge of God's nature, His characteristics, His works, the people of our study were motivated to know how to handle and respect Him so that in return they would experience the expected salvation benefits from Him. The general belief was that, God was the primary giver of salvation and this was not an illusion, or imaginary, but was known, well understood and that was the reason He was highly respected, honored and worshiped.

In relation to the Central Bantu's concept of salvation, how did the names of God reflect their salvation? The three tribes' names for God expressed and acknowledged a Supreme Being and Sovereign creator of life and all that exists. "Practically, all African people associate God with the sky in one way or the other which indicates that God is One and great."[8] The three tribes recognized God as one and therefore, they were monotheistic in nature. The

---

[8] John Mbiti, *African Religions and Philosophy* (London: Heineman, 1969), 33.

most common and universal name given to Him was, *Ngai*. This name generally means a "Divider" and it communicated an idea of a supernatural Being who divided all the parts of the body as well as parts of natural phenomenon. The name *Ngai* describes God as a giver of life because He created everything. Whatever is visible and invisible was created by God. *Ngai* (God) was said to have divided all things and distributed them to different parts according to their likenesses. He divided all people according to their languages, hence He gave the three tribes one geographical location to cultivate and enjoy agricultural products. He also divided languages to all the people of the earth; hence He gave the three tribes language of similar dialects.

Among the Kikuyu and the Ameru, *Ngai* was distinguished from the ancestral spirits by being described as *Roho* (Spirit) but ancestors were described as *maroho* (spirits). He was perceived to be the creator of the universe and as the molder of all human beings, as a potter molds clay. He was described as the giver of all things, including salvation, to His creation.

Due to God's work of creation, the name *Ngai* was sometimes combined with another one, *Ngai-Mumbi* which means, "God the creator." Jomo Kenyatta writes:

> *Ngai* means to divide or distribute from the Kikuyu word *ugai*. He is the one who divided, divides and distributes everything to His children everywhere. This idea of *Ngai* motivates the Gikuyu tribe to turn to Him in prayer for all their needs including deliverance (salvation). The other name, *Mugai* is also used and means the same thing as *Ngai*.[9]

Concerning God as the creator and owner of everything, Jomo Kenyatta continues to say that:

---

[9] Jomo Kenyatta, *Facing Mt. Kenya* (Nairobi: Heineman Ed. Books, 1938), 233-34.

Ngai has no father, mother, or companion of any kind. He does His work in solitude. He love or hate people according to their behavior. He does live in the sky but has temporally homes on the earth, mainly situated on mountains, for example, Mt. Kenya, Mt. Longonot, and Nyandarwa ridges where he may rest during His visit.[10]

The Kikuyu and Ameru use another name for God, *Murungu* which seems to suggest the otherness, mystery, power, and mercy of God. This name was used during worship time. Thus, salvation actors were offering sacrifices and offerings. They (salvation actors) would address God as, *Ngai-Murungu*. The other name is *Nyene*, was also used at this time and it means that God is the ultimate great owner of everything.

Among the Akamba, the same name for God, *Ngai*, was used meaning that God is the "eternal cause of everything," that is, in heaven and earth, weather, people, universe and everything that exist on and above the earth. In this name, the concept of salvation is located in it because the aspect of God being the protector is the same as the deliverer. The Name also suggests that God is the great One over all living things.

The universal name of God, *Ngai* was commonly used during cultural-traditional prayer time, sacrificial days and during festivals. During this important communion with God, the Kikuyu Ameru people would address God as, *Ngai-Mwene Nyaga* which means the "possessor of brightness, beauty, majesty, glory and holiness."[11]

During their traditional worship, the Akamba would add another name to *Ngai*, which was, *Ngai-Mulungu*. This name indicated that God was the possessor of everything. God was believed to be a participant in community matters, which means that He was people oriented rather than being individualistic.

---

[10] Ibid., 127.
[11] Ibid., 127.

Individuals did not have direct contact or access with *Ngai-Mulungu,* because He had His residence above and beyond the universe which was called, *itune,* (heavens). This home of God, *etune*, meant that God had no specific place in the sky and therefore, He lived up and beyond the edges of the cosmos. He kept His eyes on every creature from the peaks of distinct mountains, *keema kio* and *keema kieo* (Mt. Kenya and Mt. Kilimajaro). These two mountains are the two places where He was believed to have been staying as He administered salvation to His creation.[12]

Another common name of God among the Akamba was *Mulungu*, which was similar to the Kikuyu and Ameru name of God, *Murungu*. *Mulungu* was only used without adding any other name. To the Akamba, *Mulungu* meant, the only Supreme Being who is the creator and provider of everything and every environment here on earth. He should be highly respected, honored, and worshiped by His creation. Since *Mulungu* was said to have fashioned every situation and environment, He was also said to be the giver of salvation.[13] They also had another common and significant name of God, *Mukunoku* which signified God's ability and mighty hand in doing things that men could not do. This name was associated with earthquakes and thunderstorms which were believed to occur when they failed to perform what was required for their salvation. God, *Mulungu* was said to be the primary cause of epidemics, calamities, bad omens, etc. for He was self-cause, cause of everything and self-existing. When He caused all these unpleasant things, it was believed that the equilibrium of their salvation was broken and therefore, they should seek ways of restoring it.

In this brief study of God's names, we can summarize by saying that His common name was *Ngai*. This was the name that

---

[12] Kivuto Ndeti, Elements of Akamba Life (Nairobi: E.A. Publishing House, 1972), 176.

[13] Gerhard Lindblom, The Akamba (Uppsala: Appelbergs Boktrycheri Aktiebolang, 1920), 244.

was used when the Bantu people were calling God to intervene in a pleasant or unpleasant situation for their salvation. It was the same name that was adopted by the early missionaries who brought the gospel to the three tribes of our study.

God's Characteristics

In this section, we are going to focus on selected attributes of God which often were featured in people's daily expressions and during their traditional worship.

Transcendent and Mysterious

The tribes of our study perceived God as being transcendent and mysterious. They understood Him as superior to both the ancestors and the human community. He was unknowable because He was said to be mysterious and somehow away from people. He was unlike the ancestors who lived together in their realm and who were always part of the community. One of the Kikuyu and Akamba proverbs says that, *Ngai ndariaga ngima* (God does not participate in eating traditional food). This is to say that God is very far from people and traditionally, He stays alone, cannot be known, is mysterious and He is impersonal. This was said to be a distinct characteristic which was not found in any human being or ancestor and therefore, it qualified Him as the giver of salvation. To understand God more on this characteristic, John Mbiti discusses it within the Akamba tribe:

> This concept means that God is made by no other; no one beyond Him is. There cannot be, and there is no beyond God: He is the most abundant reality of being, lacking no completeness. He transcends all boundaries; He is omnipresent everywhere at all times. He even defies human conception; He is simply the unexplainable. Ontologically He is transcendent in that all things were made by Him, whereas He is self-existence. In status He is beyond spiritual beings, the spirits, men and natural objects and phenomenon. In power and knowledge, He is supreme.[14]

---

[14] John Mbiti, *African Religions and Philosophy* (London: Heineman, 1969), 33.

In the above quotation, we can deduce that the meaning of this characteristic brings a picture of God being different from any creation, ancestors and people. He is great above all other existing beings and He was feared above all. He was feared beyond the traditional actors of "salvation" like witch-doctors, priests, prophets, medicine-men or diviners. He was perceived to be invisible and it was not known how and what He looked like and exactly where He lived.[15] It was said God alone is worthy to provide complete salvation to the human communities and to sustain harmony within the realm of both humans and the ancestors.

Even though *Ngai* was understood to be transcendent, He was also said to be immanent so that traditional people would actually have some contact with Him. In this regard, the community always acknowledged and involved Him in their many acts of worship and festivals. He was universally believed to be near so that through traditional mediators people would approach Him.

All Knowing

The Central Bantu believed that *Ngai* sees and knows everything. God is neither like the ancestors nor like traditional salvation actors who were said to be limited in knowledge and sight. God was perceived to be all knowing for it was said that He knows the past, the present and the future of His creation. It was said that there was no one who would hide anything or any thought from Him. The Kikuyu people would say, *Ngai oi kinya njuiri cia mitwe witu* that is, God knows even the number of our hair. This implied that His knowledge was perceived to have no limit. They also would say, *Wa Ngai nduri mugaruri na nioi rucio* (One cannot change the plans of God because He even knows what will happen tomorrow). John Mbiti elaborates on this attribute of God by describing all Africans:

---

[15] John Mbiti, *Akamba Stories* (London: SPCK, 1966), 14.

When the African people consider God to be omniscient; they are at the same time conferring upon Him the highest possible position of honor and respect, for wisdom commands great respect in African societies. In doing so, people admit that man's wisdom, however great, is limited, incomplete and acquired. On the other hand, God's omniscience is absolute, unlimited and intrinsically part of His eternal nature and being.[16]

Concerning the Akamba view of God as all knowing, Gehman notes that: "The Akamba believe that *Mulungu* sees and knows everything. Though one can deceive the *Aimu* (ancestors), no one can deceive *Mulungu*. God knows everything; we cannot hide anything from Him."[17] The knowledge of God was therefore, perceived as beyond people's understanding and that was the reason the Kikuyu people would say that, "God is over knowing" (*Ngai ni kimenyi yothe*).

All Present

This was a universal idea among the Bantu because they all agreed that God was present wherever people were. A Mukamba (Kamba person) never traveled without consulting God and after reaching the place, he would carefully thank Him for safety. This indicated that God was never left behind for it was believed that He would go with the people wherever they went. The Gikuyu believed that God was everywhere even in darkness (*Ngai ekundu guothe kinya ndumai-ini*). They contrasted Him with the ancestors and they would say that, *Ngai ekundu guothe kinya kuria andu aitu aria makuire tene mari* that is, God is everywhere even where the ancestors are. Among the Bantu, God was not limited to space and time like the way they were to their ancestors.

---

[16] John Mbiti, 30-31.

[17] Richard Gehman, *Africa Traditional Religion* (Nairobi: University Press, 1989), 199.

All Powerful

The three tribes believed that *Ngai* was all powerful. They held that there was nothing impossible to Him. The Akamba recognized the powerfulness of God by saying, the *Aimu* (ancestors) and *mundu mue* (a witch) can do nothing without permission from God. God will allow the *aimu* to kill or injure without necessarily approving the action. Wherever there is drought and famine, God also intervenes.[18] The Gikuyu also perceived God as being almighty. They described His mightiness as, *Ngai ni mwene hinya woothe* (God is all powerful), which means that there is nothing which can defeat him. The three tribes also expressed that God's power was above all existing powers by saying:

> *Ngai* (God) has no father, nor wife nor children. He is in all alone. He does not need any help from anybody for He does all things all alone. He does not need any hand from any created creature for He can do all things by Himself. There is no heavy thing for Him. He is the same today and all times. He does not die because He is more powerful than death. His power is beyond our ancestors and even our former and present specialists.[19]

They would vividly talk of God's power by expressing their confidence in Him by praying:

> O Lord, your power is greater than all powers. Under your leadership we cannot fear anything. It is you who has given us prophetical power and has enabled us to foresee and interpret everything. We beseech you to protect us with your mighty power in all trials and torments. We know that you are with us, just as you were with our ancestors, under your protection there is nothing that we cannot overcome. Peace, Praise you *Ngai*. Peace, peace, peace be with us.[20]

[18] Richard Gehman, 199.
[19] "Interview," May, 1998.
[20] Layward Shorter, *Prayer in the Religious Traditions of Africa* (Nairobi:

In regard to God's powerfulness, John Mbiti singles out the Kikuyu tribe and notes that:

> God's omnipotence is seen in His exercise of power over nature. The Kikuyu make sacrifices and prayers for rains, they address God as the one who makes mountains quake and rivers overflow. They also see God's omnipotence in terms of His being able to deal with, or control the spirits-these beings who are more powerful than men.[21]

Considering how the three tribes would describe God's omniscience and power, we can clearly deduce that they recognized His power over all things and over themselves. God was understood as being all powerful even over the spiritual realms where their ancestors were, over His natural phenomenon, over specialists like witch-doctors, traditional seers and even over the community. The Kikuyu in their prayer also recognized that it was through the power of God that some of them had been given prophetical powers to become seers. His power was perceived that it could protect them from their enemies. This perception of the powerfulness of God shows the significance of why the Central Bantu first traced their primary source of salvation from God. The ancestors, who were their secondary source of salvation, were also said to be powerful but not like God.

Spirit

The Central Bantu viewed this character of God as His eternal nature and therefore, He was said to be incomprehensible. They held that no one would know for sure what God was like (form) because He was only known through His visible activities over His people; hence, He was a Spirit. His invisible nature contributed to people's thinking that He was a Spirit Being. The Gikuyu and Ameru always would say that, *gutiri wanona Ngai*

Oxford University Press, 1957), 70.

[21] John Mbiti, 32.

kana agacemania nake: muraguri, murogori, murathi, ona kana ngoma cia aruna aitu. Ngai ndonekaga na maitho (no one has ever physically seen God: a diviner, witch-doctor, a seer, or one of our ancestors, God is invisible). This therefore, expresses the invisibility of God.

In relation to the perception of salvation, God's invisible nature was said to have contributed to the reality of salvation because it was given outside people's visible realm. The ancestors were once visible and lived among the people, but it was said that God never existed as a visible being. His eternal invisibility was viewed as being the first source of their salvation because He was the source of life and visible things.

Good, Merciful and Loving

In relation to the beliefs in salvation, the Bantu people believed that the goodness of God, His mercy and love were His general characteristics which contributed to their daily situation. They gave these general descriptions of God because of what He continuously did for them. The giving of rain, birth of children, multiplication of their domestic animals, making plants grow, protecting them from jeopardy, giving them good health, wealth, happiness, causing prosperity of their land and healing which a medicine-man could not do, all of these acts indicated the above characteristics of God. All of these positive situations were collectively described as "salvation." Among the Central Bantu, bad situations such as death of domestic animals, miscarriages, were mostly associated with the ancestors and other traditional spirits, who responded negatively if they were mishandled by some member of the community.

Due to the above attributes, the Bantu people never accused God of causing bad things to happen. The Akamba people would always say that, "God does no evil," which implied that God was only merciful, good and loving. They also referred to God as kind, taking pity on human beings. To them, the mercy of God was felt in difficult situations particularly when He delivered them from bad situations. God was always called by the Akamba to save (*kutangia*) them in all bad situations. Stressing on these attributes, John Mbiti notes that:

> To the Akamba, the mercy or kindness of God is felt in situations of danger, difficulty, illness and anxiety, when deliverance (salvation) or protection is attributed to Him, or He is called upon to help. Even when sorrows have stuck, *Ngai* may be called upon to comfort the people.[22]

Due to the above characteristics of God, the central Bantu collectively accepted that He was the key source of their salvation. Because of these characteristics, they were able to experience salvation through mediation by their traditional specialists. With these characteristics, in their communal prayers, a traditional priest would address God thus:

> Say ye, the elders may have wisdom and speak with one voice. Praise ye *Ngai*. Peace from God be with us. Say ye that the people and the flocks and the herds may prosper and be free from illness. Praise ye Ngai. Peace be with us. Say ye the fields may bear much fruits and the land may continue to be fertile. Praise ye *Ngai* the giver of peace. Peace be with us.[23]

These and many other characteristics of God would motivate the Bantu people to keep on trusting God for their traditional "salvation."

The Ancestors

The ancestors were also believed to be another source of people's salvation. Ancestors were believed to be their people who

---

[22] Ibid., p. 36.
[23] Jomo Kenyatta, 130.

died along time ago, and therefore they were not like God because they were His creatures. Their nature was said to be that of a man because once they were among the people here on earth, but the only difference was that they had become spirit beings. They were believed to have more powers than before they died, because were no longer physical but spirit beings. Due to their extra ordinary power more than the living people, they were perceived to have contributed a lot towards people's salvific life on earth and thereafter.

The Central Bantu people also associated their salvation with the ancestors because they were believed to have survived death and were living in the spiritual world. Though they were said to be spirit beings, they were perceived as always taking a lively interest in the affairs of their families, clans, age groups, and tribes.

The Akamba would call ancestral spirits the *aimu* (plural) and "iimu" (singular). The Gikuyu name for ancestors is *ngoma* and this word stands for both singular and plural. To distinguish whether one was talking of one or many ancestors, the Gikuyu could use "cia" (for plural) or *ya* (for singular) thus, *ngoma cia or ngoma ya*. The Ameru call them, *irundu bia bajuju* (plural) while singular is, *kirundu bia juju* respectively.

To become an ancestor, the only way was through death; that is, when one died he or she was believed to become an ancestor. When one becomes an ancestor, it was said that he or she was conscious and aware of what was happening in his family, clan, age group, tribe, and in his community. The person was said to continue demand great respect from the members of his or her community and if people failed to do so that ancestor would keep marring their salvation. Failure to respect the ancestors would mean they might in return cause disasters like misfortunes, calamity, and premature death within the family and in the community. S. Maimela notes the importance of ancestors by saying:

Undermining the ancestors, for instance, disposing of family fortune, or failing to care for one's immediate elderly family members provokes the anger of the founders of one's extended family or clan and this causes anger, curse and withdrawals of life blessings and support (salvation) from ancestors.[24]

All negative situations were associated with the ancestors; human beings were expected to keep good contact with them, hence to cultivate a conducive environment which they called "salvation." When members of the community were experiencing favourable situations, they would say that their ancestors were happy with them. The ancestors were regarded as part of the family and the whole community.

For their happiness, the ancestors were known to be very dependent upon the living. Not only did they like to be remembered but also to be treated as greater than the members of the living community. The ancestors were said to be subject to the same emotions as the living members of the community, and their moods were described as more constant than humans. Since sometimes they were said to be jealous or fickle, the living members were to be very careful not to offend them. If the ancestors were neglected, it was said they could become very angry and there after could demonstrate their feelings through some dangerous actions. When people experienced bad and dangerous actions, they would quickly sacrifice or give offerings to them to restore their relationship with them. These appeasements were to placate the ancestor who was offended, so as in return would hopefully deliver (save) them from chaos.[25] If the sacrifices and offerings were accepted, fellowship

---

[24] *Missionalia*, S.S. Maimela, "Salvation in African Traditional Religions", Vol. 13, No. 2, August 1985.

[25] James Mcveigh Malcolm, *The interaction of the Conceptions of God in African Tradition Religion* (Michigan: Xerox Company, 1971), 55.

and peace were rekindled and experienced again. How one became an ancestor, able to contribute toward people's salvific lives, was only through experiencing death. One must die so that his or her spirit will would become an ancestor and join other ancestors. The Kikuyu people talked about how one became an ancestor as, *roho wa mundu akua atuikaga ngoma ya mundu ucio* (when the person died, his spirit turned to be an ancestor). The Akamba also expressed the same idea by saying that, *veva wa mundu akw'a atwikaa iimu* (the spirit of a person became an ancestor upon death). These spirits of the dead were only remembered for four generations, and thereafter were forgotten. After four generations, they were believed to be forgotten in the families and communities because they were said to have turned into ordinary spirits who could no longer involve themselves in the family affairs, in the clan, tribe or in any community affairs. There were no sacrifices, offerings nor libations done to them because they would no longer participate in people's lives.

To be more specific on which ancestor was very important in people's salvific life, especially for the clan, the tribe or for the large community, it wasthe spitis of parents in the family, leaders of the clans, leaders of the age group and leaders of the tribes. For example, the spirits of the parents were said to have been directly communicating with the living children and giving them instructions and advice. They were to be highly respected and honored. Failure to respect them through the offering of sacrifices, inviting them during initiation rites and other important occasions would have caused them to negatively react, hence, thwarting their environment to "salvation." They could harshly punish their living children, tribe, clan, or other related people. They were also known to have given either a soft or hard discipline to those children who did not properly behave towards them, such as disrespecting and disconnecting them from family affairs. These spirits of the parents included also the grandparents who were regarded as the most important in the family.

A second category of ancestors were those of a clan. They were believed to have been very concerned with community affairs and were concerned with the welfare of specific clans. These spirits were once involved in these clans. They were said to be concerned with the prosperity, justice, behavior, and administration of that clan.

The third category of ancestor was those of the age group. They were believed to have been concerned with the well-being of their particular age-groups. If there was disunity in the tribe, they were called upon to unite the people.

These three categories of the ancestors were very important in the minds and lives of the Central Bantu people. When there was illness, premature death, death of animals, diseases or anything that hampered the well being of the people, through "salvation" actors, they were consulted with sacrifices and offerings. For example, they would consult a traditional diviner or a medicine-man in the village to determine the cause. After casting lots and finding out what spirit or spirits had marred their salvific life, the actor would determine what sort of appeasement was to be offered. People's harmonious relationship with their ancestors, peace, favor and reconciliation with them was always expected to be in a consideration.[26]

Practices in Salvation

We have seen that the belief in salvation among the Central Bantu was tri-dimensional, and that the members of the community were supposed to be actively involved toward it. This "salvation" was experienced by the community when its people committed themselves to the required religious traditional rites such as: worship of God and the ancestors (sources of salvation), avoiding sin against God, ancestors and each member of the community,

---

[26] Jomo Kenyatta, 268.

and being conscious of one's destiny after death. It was said that the effective worship of God and the ancestors motivated the other two involvements.

Worshiping God

In the Bantu tribes, worship of God and the ancestors was the first major activity to follow in their daily lives. To maintain salvific life, one was to live a life of worship of God and his ancestors. Religious worship was both a positional and a progressive activity. It was positional in that, one was to realize at once the reality and need of starting to worship God and the ancestors, as orally taught and passed on by the members of the community. It was progressive in that, it was expected to be a life time exercise. Deviating from it meant that one had completely lost his or her "salvation" from God and from the ancestors, which would have affected his or her whole family, property, clan, age-group, or even his or her tribe. Worship was taken seriously throughout one's life time, so as to continue having a peaceful relationship with God and the ancestors.[27] The following diagram illustrates Bantu traditional worship:

Figure 1. Positional and Progressive Worship

As we discussed the Bantu concept of "worship," for their salvific life, the writer continues to use this term for the spontaneous act of expressing profound adoration and giving honor to God and ancestors. This word in this section denotes all the religious activities of members of the Central Bantu towards the two sources of salvation, God and the ancestors. With the same idea of worship, John Mbiti, defines worship as: "worship broadly defined means man's act or acts of turning to God or his ancestors."[28] Blaji Idowu defines it as:

> Worship is an imperative urge in man. Its beginning may be traced back to the basic intricate which was evoked in man by the very fact of his confrontation with numinous. Man perceived that there was a power other and greater than himself, a power which dominated and controlled the unseen world in which he felt himself enveloped. This worship in its rudimentary form originated in spontaneous and extempore expression of revelation which evoked in him an active response.[29]

The Gikuyu referred to "worship"as, *guthathaiya*, which literally meant "to beseech God" and there was a different word for the worship for ancestors. The worship of the ancestors was *guitangira* or *guthinjira ngoma*, which meant, "to sprinkle beer or something else to the spirits or to slaughter an animal for the ancestors." Worship of either God or the ancestors was very specific; when it was mentioned, people were able to know who was being worshiped. During the worship of God, the ancestral spirits were always invited. As well as when the ancestors were being worshiped, God was also requested to delight in that worship.

In the process of worship, it was either an individual act

---

[28] John Mbiti, *Concept of God in Africa* (London: Heineman, 1970), 178.

[29] Blaji Idowu, *Olodumare: God in Yoluba Belief* (London: Clower and Sons, 1962), 107.

or a communal one though; the emphasis was mostly expressed and sensed in a communal way. The traditional worship was both ritualistic and liturgical, and was done differently by the three tribes. The Akamba never worshiped God individually but only in a communal way. Their acts of worship were never regular but sometimes were done two to three times a year. Sometimes they worshiped God before the rains and after the harvest. Worship before the rains was through prayer and sacrifices, asking God to give them rain. After the harvest, they worshiped God in a form of sacrificing an animal and thanking Him for the good harvest. They never went to the traditional shrines for nothing, nor did they see the need of bothering God unless there was an immediate need like famine and community problems.[30] If there was an individual problem like sicknesses and death in the family, the ancestors were consulted through a traditional salvation actor, for example a medicine-man.

Worship among the Gikuyu and Ameru was performed both in an individual and a communal way. In the families, worship involved all the individuals in that family throughout their life time. The most common occasions when worship was done to God was mainly during birth, initiation, marriage, and death. During these occasions, the whole family pledged its interest in the life of the person who was involved.[31] "That was the time when communion was established on the individual within the family."[32]

Another occasion which was equally important for worship among the Kikuyu and Ameru was during the rite of second birth especially among the Kikuyu tribe, that is, *gucokia mwana ihuini*.[33] This rite was done when a child was between two and a half to

---

[30] Richard Gehman, *Ancestor Relations among the three African Societies in biblical Perspective* (Fuller University: Microfilms International, 1984), 203.

[31] Jomo Kenyatta, *Facing Mt. Kenya*, 226.

[32] Ibid., 226.

[33] M. N. Kabetu, *Kirira kia Ugikuyu: Customs and Traditions of the Kikuyu people* (Nairobi: E. A. Literature Bureau, 1966), 11.

four years of age. The rite communicated the idea of incorporating the child into the communal family spirits. Failure to worship God and the ancestors during these important occasions was calling for trouble in the family. The inflicted troubles might be extended either to the clan, age-group or the whole tribe and therefore, worship of God and the ancestors was taken seriously.

Content of Worship

Among the Central Bantu, there were three common contents of worship: sacrifices, offerings and prayers. Each of these helped worshipers obtain peace, acceptance, harmony and favor with God and with the ancestors, hence, maintaining their "salvation." Sacrifices were tokens given either to God or to the ancestors; blood was shed, such as edible domestic animals like a sheep or a goat. Offerings were gifts given to God or ancestors, and involved no blood shed; for example, foodstuffs, alcohol, water, milk or honey. Prayers were utterances that were voiced to God or to the ancestors, and most were spoken along with sacrifices or offerings. About the importance of sacrifices and offerings, John Mbiti notes:

> Sacrifices and offerings are acts of restoring the ontological balance between God and man, the spirits and man, and the departed and the living. When this balance is upset, people experience misfortunes and sufferings or fear that those will come upon them. Sacrifices and offerings help, at least psychologically to restore this balance.[34]

Sacrifices, offerings and prayer were very important to people's holistic life. Sacrifices and offerings were also said to be man's best way of maintaining and establishing a relationship

---

[34] John Mbiti, 179.

between himself and his object of worship.[35] They were acts and occasions of making and renewing contact between God and people and people and ancestors.

When sacrifices, offerings and prayers were directed toward God and the ancestors, they were a symbol of fellowship, recognition that God and the ancestors were valuable for both their existence and salvation.[36] Those rituals were also intended to bring a pleasant situation to those who were victims of the oppressive or sinful human conditions. They were offered to save and preserve the situation, the individual, the family, the clan and the community from impending danger, thus ensuring their future maintenance and security.[37]

On the purposes of sacrifices, offerings, and prayers, Idowu contributes: "The basic purpose of sacrifices, offerings and prayers is right relationship between man, deity and his ancestors; the more urgent the need for the maintenance or restoration of that fellowship the higher the condition man is prepared to fulfill."[38] Tokunboh Adeyemo lists five popular sacrifices and offerings made among the African tribes: "meal and drink offerings, gifts of thanks, appeasement sacrifices, mediatory sacrifices and substitutionary sacrifices."[39] Sacrifices and offerings were there to enhance the act of worship among the people and to involve God and the ancestors for their salvation.

Also, sacrifices were offered to end (save) situations like an epidemic, famine, drought or serious illness among the people. An animal or animals were offered for the sacrifices so as to appease God or the ancestors. Concerning this way of appeasement,

---

[35] Tokunboh Adeyemo, *Salvation in African Tradition* (Nairobi: Evangel Publishing House, 1979), 33.

[36] John Mbiti, *Concept of God in Africa* (London: SPCK, 1970), 179.

[37] Missionali S. S. *Maimela, 13, No. 2,* August 1985.

[38] Blaji Idowu, 120.

[39] Tokunboh Adeyemo, 33.

Kenyatta notes that: "sacrifices to God are made when rains fail to fall at the usual time, when people, after preparing their fields for planting see that the rain has failed and the drought is prolonged."[40] The animal which was sacrificed was black, brown or white. It should have no spot, no matter how small. The owner was thoroughly investigated so as to make sure that he was of a good reputation, that it was bought through his cultivated crops, honey or rightfully owned land.

Among the Kikuyu community, sacrifices were done under a traditional fig tree called *mugumo* or traditional sycamore tree called *mukuyu*. These trees were known to be sacred and natural (not planted by anybody) and were associated with God. To accompany any sacrifice, there was traditional beer, or milk from a ceremonial cow. Milk, honey and beer were poured for the ancestors, and meat was spread on the ground ready to be offered to God. The conducting priest would pray the following to God:

> We praise you *Mwene-nyaga* in the same way our forefathers used to praise you under this very same tree, and you heard them and brought them rain. We beseech you to accept this, our sacrifice, and bring us rain of prosperity. The elders chant the chorus: peace, we beseech you, *Ngai*. Peace be with us.[41]

Among the Kikuyu community, if the sacrifice was to beseech God to give them rain, a traditional priest would sacrifice, praying:

> Reverend Elder (God), who lives on *Kirinyaga* Mt. Kenya), you who make mountains tremble and rivers flood; we offer to you this sacrifice that you may bring us rain. People and children are crying; sheep; goats and cattle are crying. *Mwenenyaga*, we are going to sacrifice to you. Refined honey, milk and beer we have brought for

---

[40] Jomo Kenyatta, *Facing Mt. Kenya*, 133.
[41] Ibid., 137.

you. We praise you in the same way as our forefathers used to praise you, under this very same tree, and you heard them and brought the rain. We beseech you to accept this, our sacrifice, and bring us rain of prosperity. Peace, we beseech you *Ngai*. Peace be with us.[42]

When this sacrifice was offered, the priest expected rain to start pouring, or pour after a few days. Rain was an indication that God had heard and accepted their worship in that form of a sacrifice.

Since worship was progressive, after the rain, the same elders used to go back to the same shrine with the same type of a sheep to sacrifice for thanksgiving. After the sheep was killed and certain other ritualistic acts were performed, the priest would stand as usual facing Mt Kenya and say the following prayer in chorus:

Mwenenyaga (God), you who have brought us rain and have given us good harvest, let people eat grain of this harvest calmly and peacefully. Do not bring us any surprise or depression. Guard us against illness of people or our herds and flocks; so that we may enjoy this season's harvest in tranquillity. Peace, praise ye God, peace be with us.[43]

After the harvest, the sacrifice and prayer were followed by other traditional rituals to purify the grains. The first time they asked God and the ancestors to provide an environment conducive for their existence, existence of their children and their property. After they received rains and the harvest was ripe, they would offer sacrifice and beseech God to let them continue experiencing a pleasant time. This was a life long salvific process.

---

[42] Aylward Shorter, *Prayer in the Religious Traditions of Africa* (Nairobi: Oxford University Press, 1975), 69.
[43] Jomo Kenyatta, 258.

When the Akamba faced the same unpleasant environment, that is when their salvation was marred, a significant traditional elder among them would take a black bull under a *Mumbu* or *Mukuyu* tree and sacrifice it. The elder would first pour milk and honey to appease God and the ancestors, and then sacrifice the bull. After the sacrifice, the problem was believed to be solved. They would repeat the same sacrifice, but this time to thank God for the way He helped them in solving their problems[44].

Beside sacrifices, tokens of offerings were also part of worship. Things that were commonly offered were fruits, traditional foodstuff, milk, eggs, tobacco, beer and honey; these were the best products from people's farms. Sometimes these tokens were not taken to the traditional shrines but were offered wherever the person was, especially in the house before meals. It was observed that before the Akamba man went for a journey or hunting, he would always offer tobacco and food to *Ngai-Mulungu* and would asked Him to bless his journey, bows and arrows. He would also, through libation, talk to one of his supreme ancestors and asked for blessings. These offerings showed how the person was desperately dependent on God and his ancestors.[45]

On a daily basis, the Kikuyu people would offer different things at different times, particularly to their ancestors. Libation was always done before one took anything, for example before taking tea and food at breakfast. Small libations were offered to the ancestors by the side of a fireplace or by the center pole of each house. God was only intreated during the big occasions.

The Meru people were also sacrificing to God and to their ancestors, but differently than the Kikuyu. They always offered food to God and the ancestors before eating anything, and would ask for blessings and prosperity. All the activities that were done in their offerings were to appease God and the ancestors, to secure good good time in their lives.

---

[44] Interviews July 18, 1998.
[45] Ibid., July 18, 1998.

The third form of worship was prayer. Among the three tribes, purposes for prayer were petition, intercession, thanks giving, praise, asking for blessings, laments or asking for forgiveness. With all prayers, offerings and sacrifices had to accompany them. The Bantu believed that one should not go to God in prayer empty handed, and therefore offerings and sacrifices were carried out during prayer. Prayers always stressed the necessity of the worshiper being in peace, acceptable, being in harmony and in favor with God and with the ancestors. An example of petition and thanksgiving prayer is like what the Akamba would pray when a child was born, "O creator, *Mwatuangi*, (divider) who does all human beings create, thou hast on us great things and worth conferred by bringing us this little child."[46]

Being guided by a traditional seer (*mugwe*), the Meru people could protectively pray cursing an evil doer who distorted their salvation: "The uncircumcised man who hates another, may he perish. Who hates these people of mine, may he perish. The man who curses another, who say: "may he perish"; he will die on the spot, curse with the curse of the back."[47]

Mugwe was also responsible to pray for the prosperity of the living community. Since prosperity was one element of what traditionally was perceived as "salvation," *Mugwe* would pray:

> God, owner of all things, I pray thee, give me what I need because I am suffering.... I beg thee for life, the good one with things (rich life); healthy people with no disease, may they bear healthy children, and also to women, who suffer because they are barren, open fully the way by which they may see children. Give goats, cattle, food, honey and many things also the troubled other lands that I do not know....[48]

---

[46] John Mbiti, 1969, 195.

[47] Aylward Shorter, 54.

[48] John Mbiti, *Prayers of African Religions* (London: SPCK, 1957), 60.

In the above example of prayer that was basically addressed to God, *Mugwe*, who was a traditional seer, would beg for those components of salvation such as: life, riches, health, children, and fertility of women, cattle and food. It was a prayer of concern particularly for those women without children, so that God would open a way for them to have some. He would also ask God for a universal prosperity, praying that God would remove all the troubles of the other lands which he did not know. It was noted too that many times *Mugwe* would have his own individual prayer that he offered to God before he represented others. He required his own individual deliverance so as to have enough strength and protection from the evil spirits. His prayer was:

> *Ngai*, you created me and you gave me strength. Every little thing in its entirely is of *Ngai*. Instil strength into me, give me all things: millet, sorghum, beans, goats and lambs. Guard me from going to any resting place with bad spirits, because bad spirits are they who trouble sleeping man.[49]

In his prayer, *Mugwe* would ask God to protect him from bad spirits, which meant protection from those ancestral spirits who died being very demanding, disturbing the living community. Those spirits were also of those bad people who died and were believed to be continuously disturbing people.

Another example of prayer was asking God for blessings after completing building a new homestead. An elder would pray,

> You, the great elder (God), who dwells on the Kirinyaga mountain (Mt. Kenya), your blessings allow homesteads to spread. Your anger destroys homesteads. We beseech you, and in this we are in harmony with the spirits of our ancestors; we ask you to guard this homestead and let

---

[49] Aylward Shorter, *Prayer in the Religious Traditions of Africa* (Nairobi: Oxford University Press, 1975),

it spread. Let the women, herd and flock be prolific. Peace, praise you *Ngai*. Peace be with us.[50]

This type of prayer was done after a libation of beer or milk had been poured from a horn over the foundations of the new house. The traditional seer would first ask for his own peace and reconciliation from God and from ancestors and second ask the same for his family, property and for the new homestead. Addressing prayer to the ancestors, John Mbiti notes from Kikuyu traditional priest:

> Today we have cooked (a feast) for so and so, today we have given him meat; let the people have good health. Let the people have health, lions and leopards, let them be killed; be killed; be killed; be killed.... Let the women have good childbirth; may the food crops germinate. Evil things that are in the homestead, the setting sun, let it take; . . . .[51]

Where offerings of food and drink were placed before the ancestors, those offering gave people an opportunity to tell the departed that their names were not forgotten, and therefore they would ask them for favor.

Harmony with God

To keep harmony with God, one was to consistently avoid sinning against Him. Among the Central Bantu, sin was any act which could cut their friendship and relationship with God, with the ancestors and also with one another. It was also the destruction of the stability of the community, the refusal to love and have fellowship with God and one's fellow neighbors. It was anything that undermined life within the community.

---

[50] Ibid., 68.
[51] John Mbiti, 1957, 104.

Whatever a person did to distort the balance of life was a taboo, and it was referred to as "sin."[52] Sin was either a personal or a communal act. To know what was sinful and what was right was determined by the governing traditional laws, customs, norms of behavior, regulations, taboos, which constituted the moral code of each community. Some of the governing rules were believed to have been instituted by God or by the old ancestral leaders before they died. Those rules were there to facilitate the process of salvation. Whoever broke one of those requirements was termed a sinner, and was punished either by God, ancestors or members of the community.[53]

Among the Gikuyu tribe, murder, theft and adultery were considered to be offences against God, and it was believed they would destroy their harmonious life with God. Stealing somebody's cow or chicken and beating of wives were offences against members in one's community. A person was to make all his effort to avoid getting involved in immoral behaviors, so as to sustain self-fulfilment in life.

Punishment for murder was from the community, but more was expected to come from God and sometimes from the ancestors. This was done to keep a harmonious relationship with God and with one another. Punishment from God and from the ancestors because of murder or adultery was considered to be very severe, and was believed to sometimes be extended to the members of the family and extended family. Repayments or restitutions were only given if the offence affected a single individual.

Like the Kikuyu community, the Ameru and the Akamba had the same categories of sin. They took offences like theft, killing, adultery and murder as sins against God and the ancestors. Stealing one's property, witchcraft, and trespassing on somebody's property were said to be offences against a person in the community.

---

[52] Renison Githige, *Christian Religious Education* (Nairobi: Longman Kenya Limited, 1988), 146.
[53] John Mbiti, 1969, 205.

Punishments of these two categories were also different. Sin which was done against God and the ancestors was said to have been punished by God and the ancestors. Sometimes members of the community could punish the person concerned. Punishment from God and from the ancestors was believed to have been carried from one generation to the other, and therefore people were very careful. Any punishment either from God, ancestors or from the community was administered to discourage the undermining of salvation among the people. Concerning the two categories of sins and how each was punished for the betterment of people's harmonious life, John Mbiti notes:

> Moral evil pertains to what man does to his fellow man. Natural evil are those experiences in human life which involves sufferings, misfortunes, diseases, calamity, accidents, or chance; it must be all be caused by some agents, either human or spiritual.[54]

The Central Bantu's concept of sin and the fear of it helped people to retain their sense of relationship with God, with the ancestors, and with one another. Knowing what was sinful and avoiding it was seen as a way of retaining their "salvation."

Conscious of Life after Death

Consciousness of what will happen to a person after death was another important aspect in people's lives. Thinking about life after death influenced how people lived and behaved before God, ancestors and the living community. It determined how the person would be welcomed by the ancestors, because it was believed that the final destiny of one's life was death, and thereafter to join the ancestors. The individual was very preoccupied with the future, apart from material security. Their

[54] Ibid., 215.

mind focused on one question: "What will happen after death?"[55]

The belief in life after death was clearly confirmed by the Central Bantu's belief in the existence of the ancestors, who were considered to be members of the community and one of the sources of "salvation." A person was believed to be completely saved when he or she peacefully joined the ancestors and became one of them, and continued giving a pleasant life to those left on earth. Being accepted by the ancestors and becoming part of them after death depended on one's life in the living community. Consciousness of life after death was also guided by the idea that if one was a good person by following cultural norms; he or she would exist in the life to come. To qualify the continuous existence after death, Tokunboh Adeyemo notes:

> Life does not move in a straight line; rather, it is compared with the circumference of a circle. In other words, there is no break between life and death, but continuity between the two. The death constitutes the invisible part of the family, clan or tribe, and this invisible part is the most important.[56]

The deceased person was still counted as part of the family in all the diverse ways as he used to be. He was trusted to continue giving some instruction like he used to do while living among the living members of the family. He was also superior to the living community, he was an immortal being, he was in the intermediary position between human beings and God and other ancestors, and could punish members of the family for not carrying out particular instructions.[57] Being in the spiritual realm, the person could undermine their salvation if they did not sufficiently care for the other ancestral spirits. Being in this status was perceived to be of great importance.

---

[55] Tokunboh Adeyemo, Audio Tape "Salvation and Destiny" March, 1983.

[56] Tokunboh Adeyemo, 63.

[57] John Mbiti, 162.

Consciousness about life after death helped people to become patient in difficult situations, such as in times of drought and illness, to behave properly and to long to be an ancestor. It was believed that those who died unpleasantly, that is whose spirits were not welcomed by the ancestors, went straightaway to be in the realm of evil spirits, never to be remembered. It was said that God and the ancestors did not give them salvation, that they did not deserve favor, peace and harmony from either God or ancestors.

Meaning of Death

Death was viewed as a pathway from living, to becoming an ancestor, and from mortality to immortality. It was the actual separation between the living and the ancestors. Death was a transition into another form of life where one was believed to go to complete salvation. Death was said to be the last breath after being called home by the ancestors. It was believed to be a temporal departure, from the land of the living to the spiritual realm. It was said to be temporal because the spirit of the departed could continue as part of the living. It was also "a transformation of the living in order to play a different role in the community."[58]

The Gikuyu and Ameru term for death is, *gikuu* from the verb *kuua* (carry) which means, "to be carried away." The Akamba word for death is *kikwuu* from the verb *kwita*, (call) which means "to be called." When one dies, the Gikuyu and Ameru will say, *niakuua* which means that the person "has been carried away or has been called home." Instead of using the above words for death, the Central Bantu people use different euphemism expressions such as, Kikuyu -*niaratutigire, niaretirwo, niarainukire*, which means, "has left us, has been called, has gone home." These euphemistic expressions imply that the ancestors have participated in carrying

---

[58] Kivuto Ndeti, *Elements of Akamba Life* (Nairobi: E.A. Publishing House, 1972), 174.

or calling the person to leave the living community and be with them. At death, it was believed that the person was carried by the ancestors.

The Akamba euphemism expressions of death are like, "going home, being summoned, being called, has passed away, has gone back and has followed his father's company." All of these imply that the ancestors who have powers over the living have fully participated in calling the person to themselves.

Though the ancestors could carry or call living people to themselves, there were many other causes of death, such as witchcraft, magic, sorcery, diseases, curses from the senior people, or breaking a traditional taboo. These and many others were traditionally believed to be brutal vehicles that could carry people to the ancestors. Concerning these vehicles, Tokunboh Adeyemo contributes:

> The commonest causes of death are magic, sorcery and witchcraft. This is found in every African society, though with varying degree of emphasis; and someone is often blamed for using this method to cause the death of another. The living dead and the spirits are another cause. The fourth cause of death is God, especially for those for whom there is no other satisfactory explanation; an example would be death through lighting, or from old age.[59]

Including all African tribes, John Mbiti, adds to the causes of death:

> One or more causes of death must always be given for virtually every death in African villages. This means that although death is acknowledged as having come into the world of ancestral spirits and remaining there ever since, it is unnatural and preventable on the personal level

---

[59] Tokunboh Adeyemo, 66.

because it is always caused by another agent. If that agent did not cause it, then the individual would not die. Such is the logic and such is the philosophy concerning the immediate functioning of death among human beings.[60]

Actors in Salvation

The worship of God and ancestors was to be mediated; a person who was not traditionally designated to offer sacrifices would not attempt to do so. The traditional priests, medicine-men, and prophets had a significant role in sacrifices, offerings and prayers. In the time of sacrifices and offerings, these agents in people's salvation were called to lead in worship, to harmonize, to reconcile, to rekindle peace between the people and God, and between the people and the ancestors. People would not approach God or the ancestors without consultation from those agents.

Traditional actors were distinct people, because in the case of any unpleasant situation, they would stand between people and God as well as between people and their ancestors, consult either God or the ancestors and do what was necessary and required that is, through sacrifices and offerings. When people had problems in their day to day lives, they came in to rescue them, hence they acted as mediators. The following diagram illustrates this idea.

---

[60] John Mbiti, 1969, 156.

Figure 2. General Mediation

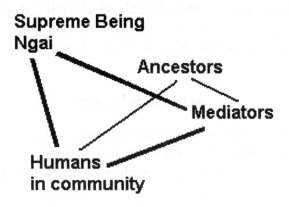

Priest

As it can be observed in the above diagram, a priest was a mediator between the community, God, and the ancestors. The Kikuyu people called him, *muruti igongona*, (the one who offers sacrifices), the Akamba called him, *muthambi* or *mundu wa ng'ondu*, (the one who sacrifices sheep) and the Ameru refer to him as *muthinjiri* (the one who appeases through slaughtering). His main work was to offer sacrifices on behalf of the community and individuals. According to people's problems, a priest would also offer prayers, offerings and ceremonies. Many times he would consult God for help but on a few occasions he would consult the ancestors. If at times he consulted the ancestors, it was also for the benefit of the community. The priests were much respected for their moral character; trustworthiness, devotion to their religious traditional duties towards the community, supreme being, and the ancestors. "However, the priest had to undergo a period of apprenticeship to make him knowledgeable in religious matters."[61] After his oral training, he was commissioned by those from whom

---

[61] Renison, Githige, *Christian Religious Education* (Nairobi: Longman Kenya Limited, 1988), 158.

he inherited the priesthood. His major duties were to prepare and make sacrifices and offerings during all the religious ceremonies, community matters, and to intercede for people before God. The following diagram illustrates a single mediation of a priest.

Figure 3. Mediator-Priest

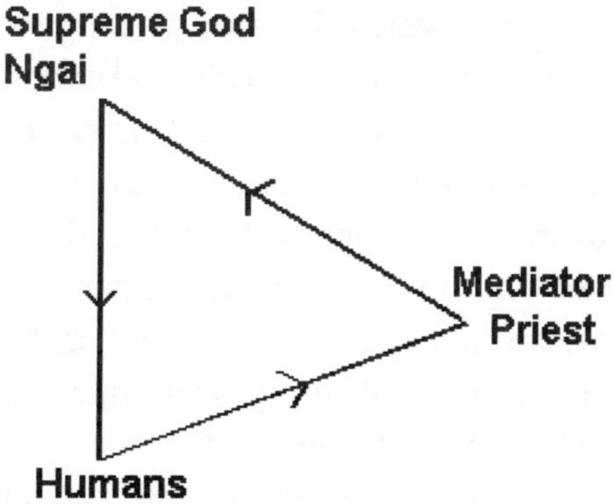

Medicine-man

The medicine-man, called in Kikuyu *mundu mugo*, the Akamba, *mukimi wa miti,* and the Ameru, *mureguri* or *mugaa* was another agent in people's salvation life. He was a person known to be gifted with the knowledge of traditional herb medicines. His herb profession was said to have been inherited from his forefathers, who had already joined the ancestors. He only mediated between people and the ancestors, and was also consulted for the herbal medicine. He never consulted God for any help especially when he cured different diseases in the family, clan or in the large community. A medicine-man was culturally known to have possessed high qualifications of trustworthiness, moral uprightness, friendliness, able to discern people's need and ready to serve the community.[62] He was the last person to consult, after sacrifices and offerings would not solve the problem. As an agent who would help people to have a pleasant life, a medicine-

---

[62] John, Mbiti, 1969, 167.

man would use several elements from plants or trees to cure any disease. He used herbs, tree leaves, tree roots, fruits, barks, grasses, dead insects, bones, different types of powders etc. He could not neglect prayers in his own religious traditional style.

Beyond curing diseases and sicknesses, a medicine-man would provide protective measures against magic, witchcraft, sorcery, evil eye and bad words. He also would give aid to increase productivity of crops in the fields, animals, and children. A medicine-man could give hope for the society by promising good health, prosperity, and security from bad and destructive spirits, through the required religious traditional rituals. He advised people on how to protect themselves from misfortunes, for example, by giving them protective charms. He could purify people from their social conflicts, purify and dedicate crops for planting, consecrate animals and homes from impurities which were thought could cause misfortunes. It was also his duty to eradicate witches, detect sorcery, and cleanse people from curses. The following diagram illustrates a single mediation.

Figure 4. Mediator – Medicine-man

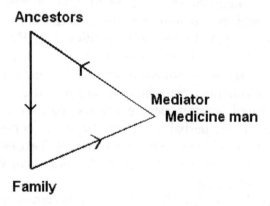

Prophet

The religious traditional prophet, called by Kikuyu people, *murathi*, the kamba people *muoni* and *mugwe* for the Ameru, was another agent in people's salvation. He performed religious duties in the community which were beyond the realm of a priest or a medicine-man. In other words, he would communicate with supernatural beings on behalf of the people. Unlike the priest and medicine-man, a prophet did not undergo any training, but he was thought to possess his prophetic power from God, or spirits, or both. As a religious prophet, he was known to be sober, kind to all, and happy in marriage. He acted as a judge and he could also pray for the people, blessing or cursing those who deserved it. He was believed to be a mediator between people and God. He was also known to have power for foretelling things to come. He was thought to be a man with a continuous knowledge of communicating with the spiritual world on behalf of the community. The following diagram shows the single mediation of a prophet.

Figure 5. Mediator-Prophet

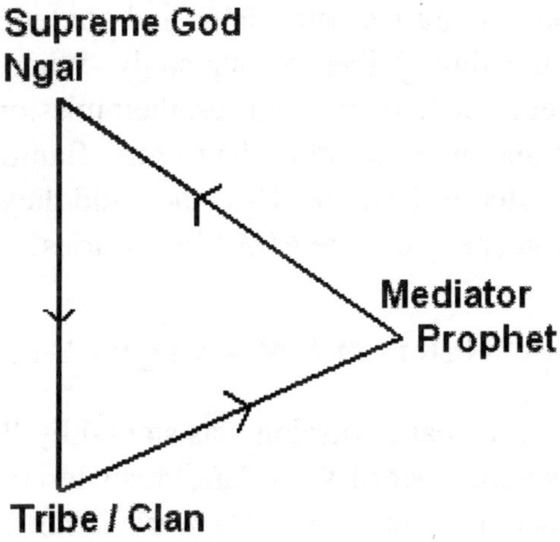

Supreme God
Ngai

Mediator
Prophet

Tribe / Clan

Having historically described the Central Bantu's model of salvation before 1895, we can sum up this chapter by noting that their perception of salvation was centered on what a person would do to God and to others. It was physical because people were only looking forward to having a peaceful relationship with God, ancestors and other members of the community. People also would strive to have a harmonious relationship and reconciliation with God and the ancestors. Thus, salvation was through self effort.

Central Bantu Perception of Salvation after 1895

Before the Africa Inland Mission missionaries came, there were other missionaries who had come in Kenya but worked around the Coastal province. They would not have moved inland because of wild animals and the hostility of the Maasai people who were neighbors of the Kikuyu, Akamba and Ameru. Peter Cameron Scott, under AIM, managed to penetrate into the interior region of the country in 1895 and was followed by other missionaries including Fredrick Kriger in 1897. Methodist missionaries who were AIM contemporaries came later and started their mission work among the three tribes of our study. When some of the missionaries returned to their countries, their missions would send others to the same mission field. The Central Bantu people heard the gospel in different fashions. How then, did they perceive and respond to the gospel from the AIM Missionaries?

Brief History of AIM among the Bantu

The Africa Inland Mission was started by Peter Cameron Scott who was a member of West Park Presbyterian church in the state of Philadelphia. Peter's parents were committed Christians who were under theological influences of their day such as, pre-millenialism and the holiness movement.[63] In 1889, Scott is known to have been converted under the Keswick movement,

---

[63] Catherine S. Miller, *Peter Cameron Scott: the Unlocked Door* (London: Parry Jackman Limited, 1955), 15-25.

and his strong desire was to go to Africa as a missionary. Though his parents could not understand his call to Africa, he joined the New York Missionary College but he did not finish the three year course. He claimed to have been carried away by the spirit and was told to pack and go to Africa and preach the gospel. Since he could have not gone without being sent by a mission agent, he joined Simpson's International Missionary Alliance which promised to support him. Being enthusiastic for mission, he and his brother sailed to Africa and after a few months, both of them were attacked by malaria. John, Peter's brother, died. At the same time, Peter went back home very sick.

After Scott recovered from his illness, he went back to Africa in 1895 and landed in the coastal province of Kenya. Some miles away in the interior part of the country, Scott was able to introduce and establish himself to some Central Bantu people like the Akamba from Kangundo and Kilungu.[64] It is said that many other missionaries from his mission joined him in 1896 and helped him to start a new mission station, evangelize people through building them small schools, providing medicines and teaching a few Bantu how to do better farming. It was during this time that many AIM missionaries were attacked by malaria and went back home. Scott and others continued, and two Swahili boys were converted to Christianity. The missionaries embraced those boys aiming that they were to become their helpers in diverse ways.[65] Scott died from malaria during this year and was buried in Machakos, where he had already started a mission station and a Bible training center for the Bantu church leaders. After Scott's death, his mission sent Charles Hurlburt to continue with the mission work but, under new policies. Hurlburt and other missionaries continued with the work, expanding their mission to different regions of the Bantu such as the Kikuyu of Kiambu and Meru.

---

[64] *Hearing and Doing Magazine*, Jan. 1896, 3-5.
[65] *Hearing and Doing Magazine*, June 1898, 6; Sept. 1898, 7.

In 1901, AIM expanded their mission by establishing Kijabe as their mission headquarters where they built a medical clinic, a training school for Bantu evangelists, a mission school where they taught people how to read and write, and a church. The other regions of the Central Bantu such as Machakos, Kangundo and Kitui were still under AIM, for many other missionaries had joined in.[66]

As the missionaries continued evangelizing the Central Bantu and their neighboring tribes like the Maasai and the Kalejin people, they encountered many cultural rites which they felt were threatening their work. One of these rites was female clitoridotomy which indeed caused alarm between the missionaries and the Bantu people.[67] Female circumcision was a rite of passage which moved a girl from childhood to adulthood, it was a gate for marriage and it was physical badge that expressed self-identity. A boy or a girl who would refuse (though it was not common) to undergo it was an outcast. Without any biblical basis to support their argument against it, the missionaries could not convince their converts why it was a bad practice. Many of them opposed it on the medical ground and argued that there was a high possibility of dying at child birth.[68] Since this was part of the people's culture, the missionaries did not consider substituting it with a scriptural dynamic equivalent, and that is why many Kikuyu and Ameru people strictly opposed them.[69]

The tension between missionaries, their converts as well as non-Christians_continued for many years. The missionaries made a rule for their convert that, whoever circumcised his or

---

[66] *Hearing and Doing Magazine*, March - April, 1903, 12.

[67] R. Mcpherson, *The Presbyterian Church in Kenya: An Account of Origins and Growth of Presbyterian of East Africa* (Nairobi: The Presbyterian Church of East Africa, 1970), 105-115.

[68] Carl G. Rosberg and John Nottingham, *The Myth of "Mau Mau": Nationalism in Colonial Kenya* (Nairobi: Transafrica Press, 1985), 111-25.

[69] Jomo Kenyatta, 130-154.

her daughter was given harsh discipline.[70] Girls who were forced by their parents to undergo circumcision could run away to the mission station where missionaries cared for them, even taking them to school. Due to that crisis, missionaries were continuously accused of causing disunity in the families and thwarting their cultural rites, as well as taking people's lands by force. This caused many converts and non-churched people to fight and accuse one another. Many of those who left the church were among the Kikuyu and Ameru who were strictly for the rite.[71] They formed their own independent churches that were cultural and contextual as well as comfortable with the female circumcision rite.[72] The circumcision controversy and church discipline continues in AIM churches even to this day.

Missionary Methods of Communication

In order for the missionaries to communicate the gospel, they had diverse strategies and methods that they thought might help in doing the work. One of those methods was to build mission stations where they would stay as they did their work. They taught skilled farming to the Bantu people, introduced medical facilities and started mission schools where they taught people how to read and write.

In 1895, Cameron Scott and his companions were able to establish their first mission station at Nzaui in the Kamba region which was not far from Mombasa. Though they were at first highly opposed by the nationals, they persisted and finally they

---

[70] Dick Anderson, *We Felt like Grasshoppers: The Story of the Africa Inland Mission* (Nottingham: Crossway Books, 1994), 88.

[71] Virginia Blakeslee, *Beyond the Kikuyu Curtain* (Chicago: Moody Press, 1958), 191.

[72] John Middleton and Greet Kershaw, *East Central Africa Part V: The Kikuyu and Kamba of Kenya (2nd)* London: International African Institute, 1965), 371-73.

would invite people to the mission station to teach them how to read and write as well as to tell them the story of Jesus. After one year (1896), other AIM missionaries joined Scott and in unity, they established other mission stations in Kilungu and Kangundo, which were in the Kamba territory. They would convert people to Christianity when they came to the station, and the converts attended their mission church.

After building mission stations, they also constructed their own houses which were made of wood and bricks, and they helped the Kamba people to do the same. As they did so, the nationals were very happy because they could move from their traditional houses which were made of mud and roofed with grass to the new. Many of the national houses leaked when it rained, and therefore the technology of using bricks to build houses encouraged many who later befriended the missionaries, fostering a good opportunity for evangelism. Along with building houses, the missionaries started industrial missions: they would provide the Central Bantus with new and healthy seeds for their farms, showed them how to plant, to weed and to care properly for their domestic animals.[73] With the new farming technology, the missionaries hoped they might win some of the people, who would form a distinct and different type of Christian life style.[74] This also helped the missionaries to evangelize the people, and to procure milk and other daily products from their converts.

Missionaries did help the national Bantu with medicine when they suffered from different sicknesses such as pain, colds and sores which their traditional medicine-men could not cure. This too was another method of communicating the gospel. Before the missionaries helped a person, they would use their body language to communicate the story of Jesus. They would use their hands,

---

[73] Margaret Scott, "*A Descriptive Sketch, "hearing and Doing*" (Aug. -Sept. 1897), 8.

[74] David B. Barret (ed.), *Kenya Churches Handbook: The Development of Kenyan Christianity, 1948- 1973* (Kisumu: Evangel Publishing House, 1973), 33-36.

because they had not yet learned the verbal language of the people.

Educating national converts was another type of evangelistic method that the AIM missionaries used. They decided to educate the Central Bantu evangelists both in formal education and Bible knowledge. Scott also noted that the missionaries could not reach everybody in their scattered areas and regions of the Central Bantu and therefore, the solution was only to train the nationals whom they assumed would do better in reaching their own people.[75] Education was also used as an evangelistic tool. The AIM missionaries also decided to give formal education to the children with the aim that they would possibly be the best gospel propagators among their tribes. Along with education, they aimed at converting them to Christ. "*Hearing and Doing*" records this aim as:

> If we can win the children to Christ, they will be the best propagators among their own people.... Our hope is first, to get the boys and girls to come to the station for about two hours daily for a time, to receive instruction in reading and writing their own language, and memorizing scriptural verses. Then, afterwards, we will endeavor to gain the father's consent to some of the children, the young people, especially, remaining with us and living on the station, being prepared by teaching, to go out and tell the blessed evangel to their friends in heathen darkness and superstition.[76]

The missionaries hoped that in the process of educating the children some of them might accept Christ as their Savior and thereafter go home and talk to their families about Him and their new life in Him. By educating the children, the missionaries estimated highly that the ability of the children to reach their parents with the gospel through their discussions on how they were

---

[75] *Hearing and Doing Magazine* (July 1896), 5.
[76] *Hearing and Doing Magazine* (July 1897), 7.

doing in school. It was in 1896 that this new strategy of evangelism moved in that direction under the young AIM missionary lady by the name of Miss Margaret Scott. The instruction at school was given in Kiswahili, for Miss Scott had known some, but could not fully communicate in that language.

Under the leadership of Margaret Scott, missionaries did not contextualize education or the gospel message so as to fit the context of the students, but they taught it the way they had learned in their home country.[77] In doing so, the missionaries faced a lot of problems with their Central Bantu students, especially from the Kamba tribe. Many of their students did not understand what they were taught, nor did they like staying in the mission station. According to Mogonko's report, many of the students would only go back to their ordinary village life and wait for either initiation rites, look after domestic animals or get married at early age.[78] This strategy for evangelism did not work out well.

Responses of Bantu Tribes

Though there were very many prevailing problems between the nationals and the missionaries from 1900 to 1903, the missionaries had many Kamba converts, especially from Kangundo, who were those who had accepted Christ through revival meetings.[79] It is not known whether they were converted to missionary life or to Christ, because many liked to stay with the missionaries. Due to the missionaries' work on constructing roads, the evangelistic work at Mbooni flourished and there were

---

[77] John Anderson, *The Struggle for the School: The interaction of Missionary, Colonial Government and Nationalist Enterprise in the Development of Formal Education in Kenya* (Nairobi: Longman, 1970), 1-10.
  Hearing and Doing Magazine (Dec. 1900), 2.
[78] *Hearing and Doing Magazine* (Nov. - Dec. 1906), 3.
[79] John W. Stauffacher, "*History of the Africa Inland Mission*" (Un Published Manuscript, n.d., Billy Graham Center), 12-45.

as many as 300 or more people who could attend church worship every Sunday.[80]

On the side of the Kikuyu and Ameru, they were more receptive to the gospel than the Kamba. Under Hurlburt, many mission stations were established in Kikuyu land, especially at Kijabe where in 1903 (when Kijabe Mission was opened) many Kikuyu would attend Sunday worship. It was in 1904 that the missionaries baptized the first converts.[81] The numerical and qualitative growth of Christians was also in other areas like Kambui and Matara where there were other mission stations. By 1907, many of these mission stations had many converts who were propagating the gospel in their families and their neighborhoods.[82]

Bantu Perception of the Gospel

The missionary methods of communicating the gospel were not very relevant to the people of our study. Many people did not like the way they were presenting the gospel, for example asking people to renounce their traditional rites. The missionaries hid some of the Bantu girls whom they thought should not undergo traditional circumcision. They did not immediately seek a dynamic equivalent to communicate the gospel. Reflecting on the issue of circumcision of girls, Elizaphan Machaga, who was born in 1911, and got married in 1933 and was a missionary convert, notes:

> We did not like the teaching of missionaries on marriage and circumcision of girls. They created a lot of controversy for they did not tell us why they were forbidding this cultural rite of passage. Due to lack of misunderstanding, this issue caused enmity between girls and their parents as well as their extended families. I wish they told

---

[80] Hearing and doing magazines (Nov. - Dec. 1906), p. 3

[81] John W. Stauffancher "History of the African Inland Church" (published manuscript), p. 12-45

[82] *Hearing and Doing Magazine* (April - June 1909), 18.

us why this rite was not good in the culture and substitute it with something else to accomplish its significance.[83]

When Machaga was asked whether he was taught the meaning of salvation at that time, he responded:

> As a young boy, I was taught the word of God by the AIM missionaries. It took me three years in catechism class before I was baptized, for the missionaries could not baptize young kids. One was to pass catechism class before is baptized. Baptism meant that one has salvation and is fully a church member.[84]

Commenting on missionary teaching of what salvation meant, Margaret Wanjiru who was born in 1918 and later became a Christian, says:

> In schools, we were told to throw our traditional clothes and we were given some missionaries' ones to wear. We were taught how to read the word of God and even to write other things. After knowing how to read and write, the missionaries would issue us a certificate. Some of us would read the Bible very well. ...Before one was allowed to attend catechism class, his or her traditionally pierced ears had to be stitched. The missionaries and those who had accepted Christianity before could not believe that one would claim to be saved and yet with pierced ears. Most people gauged salvation by looking at the outside appearance.... My ears were stitched, I attended catechism class, was baptized in 1937 and I was declared saved. Through a Christian revival group of 1954, I came to understand that salvation is repenting of ones sins before God and when I testified of that, I was de-fellowshipped from the Kijabe Mission church.[85]

---

[83] Interview, "*Testimony of Elizaphan Machaga Gicheru,*" March 7, 2003.

[84] Ibid., March 7, 2003.

[85] Interview, "*Testimony of Margaret Wanjiru Duncun,*" March, 9, 2003.

Worse came to worst when the missionaries started building good houses for themselves and gardening with high technology tools. They not only took national farms and possessed them but they also hired Bantu people as their slaves. They began doing so with a motive of self-support, but later it became enslavement. The farming activities were good for the missionaries' survival, but it was not the best way for evangelism and winning people to Christ. When the missionaries tried to present the gospel of salvation to the nationals, it was very hard for them to fathom because they would not relate or reconcile what the missionaries were calling the "Good News of salvation" with their lives of being "slaves."

By the missionaries snatching girls from their families to keep them from circumcision, the people were confused as to how that meant salvation. The people too were confused whether salvation meant to separate oneself from unchurched members of the family, which was encouraged by the missionaries.[86] Due to this sort of teaching, many Bantu people from the three tribes resisted the gospel.

The most outstanding obstacles that the missionaries created were cultural misunderstanding and scriptural salvation ambiguities. They first thought the natives were greedy, saying, "They were creatures of appetite."[87] For sometimes the Bantu people would ask missionaries for material help, and because to them "asking for help" was part of the culture. This misunderstanding caused the Bantu people to resist the gospel. Since material prosperity was perceived to be one element of people's salvation, the missionaries condemned it and asked people to give it up for the glory of God, hence people were more confused about the biblical doctrine of salvation. The missionaries did not appreciate the legitimate economic ambition which their few converts had. They discouraged the material blessing which people had and as

---

[86] Interview, "*Testmony of Elizaphan Machaga,*" March 7, 2003.

[87] *Hearing and Doing Magazine* (May 1896), 2-3.

a result, a few of the Kikuyu converts composed related songs such as: "*mburi na ng'ombe na mbia itiri na bata, kindu kiria kina bata no riri wa Jesu*" (goats, cows and money are worthless or useless, what is important is the glory of Jesus).[88] Due to this misunderstanding and ethnocentrism, many the Central Bantu people did not want to join the missionaries' religion and those who joined them did not really understand what salvation was.

The other obstacle was how the missionaries emphasized human sinfulness. According to the Central Bantu's concept of sin, no one could be called a sinner unless he or she had violated the cultural norms or expectations, the social and religious taboos. The missionaries addressed sin as moral guilt that is caused by sin and would say that it was only Christ who would remove it. The concept was good but, they failed to use a better method of explaining it. Convicting the Bantu people how sinful they were before God did not make any sense, and therefore many of them did not accept the gospel. Those who were converted to Christianity followed practices which they could not really explain. Most of converts did not know the meaning of salvation, thus they integrated their cultural beliefs with Christian ones.

Despite the missionaries' commendable efforts at reaching the Central Bantu with the gospel, to this day, many Bantu Christians place high value on their traditional religious beliefs. Although many talk about their faith in Christ, most do not exactly understand the biblical basis and meaning of salvation. Some define salvation by what they eat and what they do not, the type of clothes they wear, the kinds of people they mingle with and who they do not mingle with. Some of them even consult traditional practicianers to mediate for them.[89] Some fear they might lose their salvation, which is the subject of chapter three.

---

[88] Interview, Feb. 16, 2003.
[89] *Sunday Standard,* "This is the Job I was Born for," June 28, 1998.

Chapter 3

CENTRAL BANTU'S CONCEPTS OF SALVATION TODAY

This chapter sheds light on the present understanding of salvation among the Central Bantu Christians, based upon field quantitative and qualitative research. Only the methods of quantitative research, findings and recommendations are discussed in this chapter.

This chapter also discusses the meaning of salvation as held by the Central Bantu Christians, measuring four psycho-metric variables: knowledge, attitudes, behavior and values. This chapter has stated the purpose of this study, goals and objectives and it has described the implications relative to the beliefs and fears of the Central Bantu, in relation to God and their fear of losing salvation. That leads to a hypothetical framework of causes and effects of the Bantu tribes' misunderstanding of Biblical view of salvation.

Quantitative Research

The purpose of this research was to measure the prevalence and strength of beliefs about salvation as perceived by the Central Bantu believers of the Africa Inland Churches by measuring four variables: their knowledge about salvation, attitude, behavior and belief system. The finding will: help the writer in creating a relevant pastoral guide for teaching the biblical doctrine of salvation and its theological meaning. It will help me to effectively educate the Central Bantu's pastors in training, pastors who are already in the field and all believers on the biblical doctrine of salvation. It will motivate Africa Inland Church's pastors in carrying the gospel of salvation to their own social networks. The finding will reveal the conflict between the cultural and religious traditional beliefs of the Central Bantu of Kenya in their notion of salvation and the biblical meaning of the doctrine.

This research seems significant, for it both contributes to general scholarly knowledge and to mission and evangelization. Theological scholars have written nothing about the present view of salvation among the people of our study and, therefore, this work will serve as a bridge in solving the long existing misunderstanding of the Biblical view of salvation among the Bantu Christians. We can also utilize the principles that will be used to solve the problem by applying them to other communities of the world, so, it will provide a significant strategy. The findings may also contribute to the sensitivity of carrying Christ's salvation to any religious traditional community of the world that seeks to produce Bible believing churches.

Question and Objectives

The research question then is this: What are the prevalence and strength of beliefs about salvation as perceived by the Central Bantu believers of the Africa Inland Churches in Kenya?

The variables for the research include:

1. The Central Bantu believers' knowledge about salvation and related concepts.
2. How the Central Bantu believers behave in relation to their belief in God.

3. How the Central Bantu believers behave in relation to their belief in salvation.

4. Their attitudes toward God and ancestors

5. Their fears about loss of salvation

6. What Central Bantu do to achieve salvation or forgiveness

Many writers have discussed the perception of salvation among the Africans as relating to God, ancestors and their fellow communities. Some think that salvation is seen from three focuses because the Africans think of past, present and future. Most of these writers generally agree that the African view of salvation evolves from God and some selected ancestors. In his book, *Eschatology*, Mbiti contradicts others by stating "that Africans only think of the past (*zamani*) and present *(sasa)* in their salvation." This clearly shows how we desperately need to bridge this knowledge gap by this quantitative study specifically among the people of our concern. This research will be the best standard, because the writer is from among these people, is born in one of the tribes, knows and understands their languages and has been actively involved in different leadership capacities for ten years among these people.

Methodology

This section explains the procedure applied to collect, analyze and interpret the data.

Design

The design of this quantitative study was that of a survey which aimed to measure the present cultural understanding of salvation. The survey was conducted among lay-people of the ruralized AIC churches. The researchers were third year students of Moffat College of Bible, and the writer.

Sample

The sample selection was multi-stage, for we did not go to the population directly but went in different stages. The selection took place in three major ruralized, dominant Africa Inland Church denomination regions, where the Moffat Bible college students come from and work during their practical ministries, during their internships, and upon their graduation. The three regions were the Kitui West, Kijabe and Central.

From the three church regions, the researchers asked each region executive secretary to give us the names of all churches and each local church member's register, categorized by gender and age. The number of churches was 107. Since we wanted to see that each church had a chance to be included in the sample, we used "Rotary" probability program which selected six churches which first we wanted to identify. From six churches, we entered all the names of Christians (youth and adult) and used the same program to choose 144 names who became our sample group. This was to ensure that all Christians in those churches had an equal chance of being chosen to participate in the sample group. To administer the questionnaire, we designated six Sundays, and each Sunday we administered questionnaires according to the names represented in each church. Sample members would meet after Sunday worship and fill out the questionnaires. They did that either in the church building or in the church compound. We helped those who could not read and write.

Instrument

Before we administered the questionnaires to the sample group, the writer shared the research information and soon after trained the researchers (January 6th -16th, 2003) on how to conduct the research. Second, I clearly explained why we were conducting that research. I explained the questionnaire questions and items, and the researchers had enough time to familiarize themselves with them and their variables, and translated them into two target languages (Kikuyu and Kikamba). We also pretested the translated questionnaires with some people outside the sample to see whether they were comprehensible.

The instrument was developed by the writer and it consists of 37 items which are grouped under 14 questions and are are related to the research purpose. Variables are distributed throughout, to avoid the temptation to write the same answer, and biases. The 37 items that seek to measure knowledge, belief, behavior or attitude are random, and widely distributed. The data are as follows:

The first data position is the serial number, and is there to help us to itemize the instrument. The second variable is the age group, which is attributive in nature. It helps us to compare and contrast the age group and their beliefs concerning salvation. The third variable is the gender, which is independent. The forth is the tribe, which is independent. Researcher, date and place are all independent variables.

Questions number one and two seek to measure the Bantu knowledge about salvation, and their data type is ordinal. It is a dependent variable, and its indicators show the belief system that one has about salvation. Questions three and four are attitudinal, measuring people's attitudes towards salvation, that is, how they feel. Their data is ordinal.

The data type of question five is ordinal, and the indicators are expected to be shifts in behavior and sound biblical doctrines. Its indicators are ability to demonstrate change in life, and ability to express knowledge that has been taught. Question six, seven, eight and nine are behavioral, which are dependent, and can serve as intervening variables with ordinal data type. Their indicators are behaviors and the ability to demonstrate sound biblical doctrine.

Questions ten to fourteen measure people's belief about salvation and how they value it. These questions require an individual point of view of what the person is saying about his or her relationship with God. Their data type is ordinal.

Procedures

From three Church regions, the following is the way we came to the specific sample group: From six local churches, each pastor gave us the names of his local church members and entered them in the Rotary Probability program. The sample was of lay-people who have never undergone any theological training and are permanent in their ruralized churches. Those who were chosen to fill out the form did it voluntarily, confidentially and individually.

In Kijabe region, we had two churches: AIC Kamangu where we administered 24 questionnaires on February 2, 2003, and AIC Kijabe Town, where we administered the same number of questionnaires on February 23, 2003. In Central region, we administered 24 questions at AIC Magumu on March 2, 2003 and at AIC Kirenga we administered the same number of questionnaires on March 17, 2003. In Kitui region, we administered 24 questionnaires at AIC Kaluluni on February 16, 2003 and the same number of questionnaires at AIC Kivani on the same date. Each day we administered questionnaires, researchers would supervise the exercise and collect questionnaires and hand them over to me the same day.

Training

Before the 24 researchers administered the questionnaires, I trained them on how to administer the questionnaires in the tribal language of the sample group. For example, if a sample is from Kikuyu tribe, the researchers were Kikuyus who would read and understand the research instrument, understand the culture, and answer any related questions. It was also so to the Kamba. I trained them how to explain about the survey to the sample, for example, how to correctly fill out the questionnaires, and how to assist those who do not know how to read or write. I also demonstrated to them how they should show the sample to record the answers, and how to keep the destroyed questionnaires. I gave each research team a bag in which to keep the questionnaires.

Before they went into the field, all of them were confident in their abilities to administer the questionnaires because they were involved in small groups under my supervision, where they would demonstrate what should be done in the field. As the research consultant and supervisor, I was always there when each person of the sample group filled in the questionnaires. Many times I would first preach in the local church and thereafter explain about the research, and also answer any related question.

Statistical Choice

The data collected for the research is ordinal. The basic techniques employed to summarize and analyze the data are frequency tables, bar and pie graphs. The focus is to look for relationships among the variables, differences between social groups (men and women from the youth, adult and older). Hence, Chi Squire will fulfill this.

Validity

The writer designed the survey only to the Central Bantu people who are ruralized, and the survey questions reflected on their salvation beliefs. The survey dealt with four measured variables which enhanced validity of the findings. The findings were valid and reliable, because the targeted sample members were able to fill in the questionnaires. The research was internally accurate (valid) because each group understood questions that were translated into their mother tongue. Those who did not understand the questions would ask researchers to clarify to them. The trained researchers knew what to do in the field, especially how to answer questions asked by the sample members. However, there were four threats that could mar the accuracy of this research. First, questionnaires were administered on different days, and some members who filled the questionnaires first could have shared the research information with those who would fill it later. Second, there was the possibility of a researcher's influence on those he or she helped in filling the questionnaires. Third, there was no equal representation of gender and social groups (youths, young-adults and adults) and this could not represent accurately the larger gender of each tribe. Forth, many sample members did not know how to read or write, and therefore they might have interpreted questionnaire items differently. The quantitative study was triangulated by the qualitative one because the Bantu people are more comfortable in expressing their belief verbally than writing them down.

Findings

The most threatening finding of this research which the Chi Squire statistical test has already identified is that, there is no significant effect from social groups (men and women or their ages) on the four variables that were measured. A good example is the Chi Squire table below (Table. 1) which tests the difference between social groups with the question whether salvation is a gift from God. About 85% of the population very strongly or strongly value salvation as a gift. Within this analysis, 53 were men and 65 women of the ages 51 and above. About 13% of the sample group do not believe so and others are those who are not sure whether it is a gift or not. Those who answered a "little" carry 5% of the sample group.

With the above description of the findings, there is no great significant difference that can be identified. Thus, this fact allows social groups to be treated together in the following analysis. However, along with the descriptive report, the findings of this research will help in reflecting and understanding the Bantu cultural background of what they presently know, believe, value, and behave toward salvation.

Table 1. Salvation As a Gift

Chi square: 12.004, df 4

Y / X	1 Man	2 Woman	n / %
1 Very Strong	43 66.2% 51.8% 29.9% 00.8	40 50.6% 48.2% 27.8% 00.7	83 57.6%
2 Strong	10 15.4% 28.6% 06.9% 02.1	25 31.6% 71.4% 17.4% 01.8	35 24.3%
3 A Little	3 04.6% 42.9% 02.1% 00.0	4 05.1% 57.1% 02.8% 00.0	7 4.9%
4 Nothing	3 04.6% 25.0% 02.1% 01.1	9 11.4% 75.0% 06.3% 00.9	12 8.3%
5 Not Sure	6 09.2% 85.7% 04.2% 02.6	1 01.3% 14.3% 00.7% 02.1	7 4.9%
n / %	65 45.1%	79 54.9%	144 100.0%

Cell contents: cell frequency, % of column, % of row, % of total, cell chisquare

In this section therefore, the writer has organized it around the four major objectives that measured the Central Bantu knowledge, attitude, behavior, and values about salvation. No effort is made to present results for all 37 items in the questionnaire. However, the entire result is to be found in Appendix D.

Figure 6. Sample Group Age

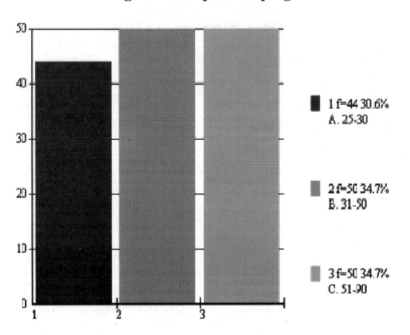

Figure 7. Sample Group Gender

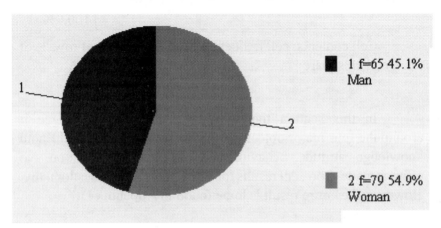

In the above charts (fig. 6 and 7) which represent the age and the gender of our sample group, out of 144 people whom the questionnaires were administered to, 44 people were between ages 25-30 which is 30.6% of the whole population, 50 people were between ages 31-50 which is 34.7% and the other 50 are between 51–90 years which is 34.7% of the whole population. Out of 144 believers, 79 (54.9%) of them were women and 65 (45%) were men. Distribution of gender was not equal because most of the Central Bantu AIC churches have more women than men and sometimes there were no men in the church. In many churches, the ratio of women to men is generally observable as 30:3 or 100:20.

The sample group was made up of two tribes, that is, the Kikuyu who were 98 (68.1%) and Kamba were 46 which was 31.9% of the whole sample. Since the researchers could not administer questionnaires to the Meru people, we assumed that believers from the Kikuyu tribe could represent them because they share the same salvation beliefs, knowledge, cultural values, behaviors, attitudes, worldview and language. This exclusion caused the researchers to administer more questionnaires to the Kikuyu believers.

Knowledge

According to the graphs shown below (fig. 8, 9 and 10) which reflect knowledge about salvation among the two tribes, the knowledge variable is dependent and its indicators are beliefs about what believers experientially know and say about salvation in relation toGod. One's Knowledge of God is presumed to facilitate one's concept of salvation. About 80 people hold strongly and very strongly that salvation means to have peace with God and this number is 99% of the sample population. From the whole population, 57 men and 67 women strongly and very strongly agree on that. Both of these genders are people between ages 51 and above. This frequence that indicates "peace" is very high and though the writer will culturally define it later, the question remains: which kind of peace are they talking about? To the two tribes of our study, "peace with or from God" has a different concept than the one that is acquired by a person who accepts Christ's death for salvation.

Those who strongly and very strongly hold that salvation is having peace with people are 45.1% of the sample. 41.7% is those hold a little or nothing and 13.2% are not sure about that belief. About 43% of men and 37% of women strongly and very strongly agreed that salvation is having peace with people. They are equally from ages 31-50 and 51 and above. About 23% of the whole sample holds strongly and very strongly that salvation is having peace with the ancestors, and some among them are not sure.

Figure 8. Peace With People

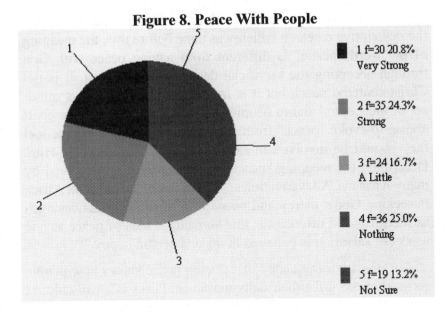

1 f=30 20.8%
Very Strong

2 f=35 24.3%
Strong

3 f=24 16.7%
A Little

4 f=36 25.0%
Nothing

5 f=19 13.2%
Not Sure

Figure 9. Sacrifices to God

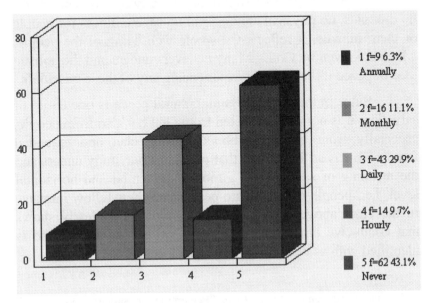

1 f=9 6.3%
Annually

2 f=16 11.1%
Monthly

3 f=43 29.9%
Daily

4 f=14 9.7%
Hourly

5 f=62 43.1%
Never

Considering the general cultural meaning of salvation, and the descriptive research which was done before this, the meaning of the word "peace" is different from having peace with God through accepting the sacrificial death of Jesus Christ. It is not Christ centered peace but it is from the cultural-religious mind-set of the Central Bantu people. As shown by the sacrifice chart above, to evoke "peace" from God, about 47% of the people feel they should be involved in sacrificing a goat or sheep to Him. Describing the meaning "peace" and the way it is perceived by many Africans, Adeyemo notes: "The ideas of salvation in Africa is seeking God's mercy and peace in a ritualistic practices such as sacrifices and offerings ... this humanistic idea of peace as one aspect of salvation is believed to make a person happy."[90]

The high frequency of valueing peace shows how people seriously need it for their daily existence. Peace is a real cultural need which expresses the desire for conducive and pleasant environment among the people of our study. Its main indicators are life without calamities, not dying at early age, no epidemics, no droughts, no physical attacks, and no severe illness for people or their animals. It reflects the whole well being of the people, which are given by God.[91] Many believers understand the holistic idea of peace if they are not experiencing any of these mischiefs.

Since in the Central Bantu cultural peace is one entity of salvation, it is not only expected from God but also from people, especially from one's neighbors, family, clan and extended family. This is an indication that people of our study understand the meaning of salvation in a more experiential and horizontal level, i.e., people can facilitate peace with their fellow humans. In the chart above (peace with and from God), clearly shows that conducive environment which is called "salvation" and is identified with as well as associated with peace.

---

[90] Tokunboh Adeyemo, *Audio Tape*, "Perception of Salvation in Africa," Nairobi: 1983.
[91] Ibid., 1983.

The questionnaire number 2 under the item 11 measured the believers' knowledge (cognitive) about salvation. Its data is ordinal, and it is a dependent variable with indicators that show beliefs in salvation. Concerning whether God can forgive one's sin, 95% of sample population collectively answered "very strong" and "strong." About 59 men and 77 women strongly and very strongly agreed with that, and they are from ages 51 and above.

Considering the previous study and qualitative research, sin in the two cultures means "doing anything that is forbidden by God or community, not fulfilling the Ten Commandments in the Bible, anti-social behaviors that mar the social order or social equilibrium of the people which also means any act against God's expectations.[92] The chart does not holistically convey the idea that sins are forgiven on the basis of people's faith in Christ but, it might have multiple meanings as well as reflecting on their daily ritualistic activity towards God's forgiveness. Whether ancestors forgive sin, the research revealed that 69% of the researched population does not believe so. Those who are not sure, and those who strongly hold that ancestors do, are 26% of our sample group.

[92] Renison Githige, *Christian Religious Education* (Nairobi: Longman Kenya Limited 1988), 146.

Figure 10. People Forgive Sins

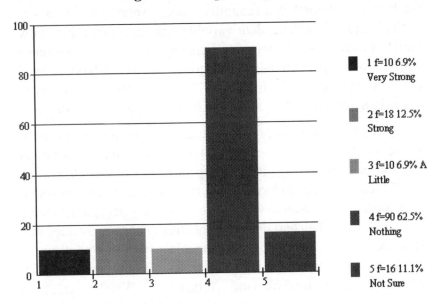

The above graph (10) shows that 63% of the sample population holds that people cannot forgive sin so as to have salvation, while 20% strongly as well as very strongly hold that people do forgive sins for salvation. About 11% are not sure whether people do forgive sins, while 7% hold that people can do so a little. Comparing with the historical cultural religious concept of our people who believed that people could forgive sins for salvation,[93] we can clearly deduce that there is a great shift of knowledge as well as in their belief system which the gospel has caused in people's Christian lives. They no longer highly value people or ancestors as a primary source of forgiving their sins for salvation.

---

[93] John Mbiti, *Prayers and African Religions* (London: SPCK, 1957), 215.

Attitudes

Figure 11. Sins Are Forgiven

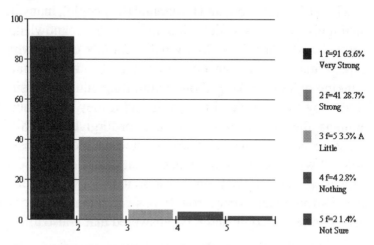

The above graph (fig.11) shows that the Central Bantu believers who very strongly and strongly agree that their sins are already forgiven carry 93% of the sample population. About 7% agree a little and others not sure. The attitudinal questions which are culturally relevant to the people of our study are why sins are forgiven and how. According to the qualitative report, when many believers talk of their sins being forgiven, they don't clearly express that human beings are sinners by nature but they refer to the practical aspect of sin like what John Mbiti lists as, breaking the moral code of his or her family and community, breaking a taboo, violating some rules, or doing whatever is forbidden by God in His holy Bible.[94] This view of sin corresponds with what many believers repeatedly expressed when they said that, "salvation is fulfilling the ten commandments which are absolute Word of God."[95]

---

[94] John Mbiti, *Prayer of African Religions*, 205.

[95] "Reflection of Qualitative interviews," January to March 2003.

Though the Central Bantu believers feel that their sins are forgiven by God or by other fellow humans, when most of them talk about the forgiveness of sins, it is an integration of the cultural way of thinking and the Christian view. Since the forgiveness of sins is vertical (by God) and horizontal (by people), many believers distinguish the sins which God forgives by acknowledging the one he or she has done. Many believers talk of sins which they experientially know, but not which are already committed, like thinking evil or thinking about committing adultery. If sins affect God, they ask Him for forgiveness and if they affect their fellow humans, they ask the wronged party for forgiveness. This idea of sin corresponds with what many people answered in questionnaire item 37 which asked about whether the sin of stealing can affect God as well as people. From question item 37, 78% of the sample group strongly and very strongly answered that when one steals, that act affects people and 85% answered that it also affects God.

To the Central Bantu believers therefore, sin which one asks for forgiveness is basically when it is committed and identified, but sin is not clearly understood as the intrinsic nature of human beings. Some sins are said to make God angery while others only affect fellow humans. The following graph (fig. 12) shows people's attitude of sin and their perception on how it causes God's anger.

Figure 12. Sin causes God's anger

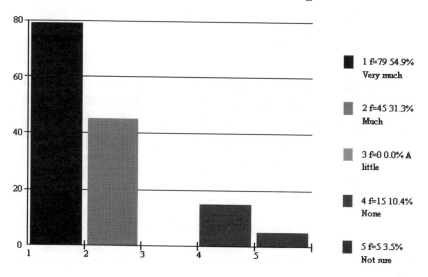

Legend:
- 1 f=79 54.9% Very much
- 2 f=45 31.3% Much
- 3 f=0 0.0% A little
- 4 f=15 10.4% None
- 5 f=5 3.5% Not sure

Behavior

Whether God forgives sins, about 98% of the sample group feels that it is important or very important to pray to God. As indicated in the appendix D, other response frequency and confidence intervals show that praying to the ancestors or to people is not important. This is because beside the ancestors, in the Bantu culture, God is regarded as a superior object of prayer for He holds nature and exercises His power over it. It is also God who is said to be able to make mountains quake and rivers overflow, and He is the only Being to be prayed to.[96] Many believers also feel very strongly that prayer should be a daily and hourly activity of believers.

About 95% of the people hourly and daily stop their activities and pray. Within this percentage, 65 men and 75 women are the ones who stop their daily activities either hourly or daily and pray. Their age is between 51 and above. All prayers are

---

[96] John Mbiti, *African Religions and Philosophy* (London: Heineman, 1969), 32.

offered to God in a form of worship which might be expressed either in petition, intercession, thanks giving, praise, lament or asking for forgiveness.[97]

Values

    This section analyzes the value of salvation as perceived by the Central Bantu believers. From the chart below (fig. 13), we can clearly deduce whether the Bantu believe in assurance of salvation and security of believers' salvation or not. Chart 14 shows whether they believe salvation is a gift or a reward which one should seek to earn.

Figure13. Salvation As a Gift

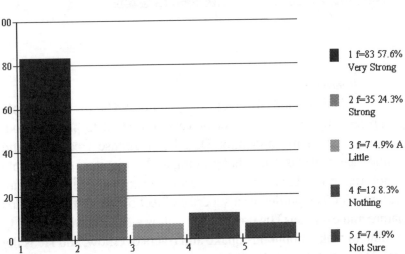

1 f=83 57.6% Very Strong

2 f=35 24.3% Strong

3 f=7 4.9% A Little

4 f=12 8.3% Nothing

5 f=7 4.9% Not Sure

    In the above chart (fig. 13), about 82% of the whole population strongly and very strongly believe or value salvation as a gift. Within this percentage, 53 were men and 65 women of the ages 51 and above. According to chart figure 15 below which

---

[97] Ibid., 195.

shows how people answered about whether a believer can lose his or her salvation, about 30% believe that unbelief can cause them to lose their salvation and 55% believe that sin can. In the percentage, 54 men and 65 women answered strongly and very strongly that a believer can lose his or her salvation. Their age is between 31-50 years. About 9% believe that people can do so. Those who believe that nothing can cause them lose their salvation is only 4% of the whole population while 2 % are not sure.

According to this analysis, it seems right to say that many Central Bantu believers do not have a biblical assurance and security of their salvation. Some 9% believe that other people can cause them lose their salvation hence, ending their life in hell. However, though the percentage of those who very strongly believe that they can lose their salvation is high, according to the Chi Squire statistical test of social groups that is, gender, age and language, there is also no significant differences or relationships (whether men or women or tribe) in that answer.

Conclusion

The research question asked, what are the prevalence and strength of beliefs about salvation as perceived by the Central Bantu believers of the Africa Inland churches in Kenya? A baseline survey was conducted to collect data. The data clearly reveal that the Central Bantu believers desperately need to be reached with a biblical view of salvation which is both relevant to their culture and theologically coherent. The data also reveal that the people of our study need to be taught a biblical basis and theological meaning of salvation, the object of salvation, and a biblical view of assurance of salvation and security of believers' salvation. Specifically, the Central Bantu need a contextualized gospel of salvation, which will amend their spiritual outlook.

Hypothesis

The confusion and syncretic salvation beliefs among Central Bantu Christians, derive from their wide experience with cultural and traditional religious beliefs before and following conversion.

Chapter 4

A BIBLICAL UNDERSTANDING OF SALVATION

In view of the research results of chapter three, this chapter seeks to lay a biblical basis for understanding biblical salvation, in response to the following questions: What are the biblical reasons for salvation? How is salvation based in the Holy Scriptures? What are the Hebrew and Christian concepts of salvation? And, what is the biblical way to attaining salvation?

In answer to these questions, the chapter adopts a general, narrative, evangelism method,[98] that is, story-telling, an effective Central Bantu cultural means of communicating a message. This method allow a teacher or leader to capture the attention of an audience, communicate a central point and theme, and elicit responses by addressing the cultural knowledge, attitude, behavior and belief system, which were measured and described by field research. As a result of so teaching of the doctrine, these cultural variables can be expected to shift and so have a desired effect in the lives of Bantu people.

Biblical Reasons for Salvation

The Central theme of the Bible is God's mission to the

---

[98] This is a method used to narrate events sequentially such as in the Bible to make one story. Examples are like the event of creation, rebellion of Adam and Eve, judgement and God's plans for redemption.

human beings so to bring them to receive and experience His saving grace. The book of Jonah vividly declares that "salvation comes from the Lord" and the book of Psalms also says that, "from the Lord comes deliverance."[99] These two verses and many others in the Bible affirm that the work of salvation belongs to God and it is not from human beings.

The Bible clearly shows that the basis of human salvation is God's ultimate love for sinners, their sinful condition that needs to be taken care of, and His final act of salvation through the death of Christ. As we will later highlight, terms like reconciliation, peaceful relationship and harmony with God are the key concepts that surround the whole Bible, that is, God calling people for repentance and to obey so as they may receive His salvation. Blessings, prosperity, peace, settling in the land, were the result of the Israelites' obedience to God and these elements are components that make up God's salvation in the Old Testament. The Bible does not only indicate present salvation but also it promises salvation for the future.

The following table gives biblical reasons why human beings need God's salvation and how it became a real need of all people. It indicates God's original purpose of creating Adam and Eve who later willingly violated that purpose. Their deliberate disobedience caused them to move away from God's presence, from His fellowship and from His ultimate relationship.

---

[99] Psalms 3:8 (New International Version)

Table 2. Human Estate Before and After Salvation[100]

Before Sin	Were holy Before God (Ps. 26) Created in God's image (Gen. 1:26-28) Were very good (Gen. 1:31 Had dominion over all creatures ((Gen. 1:28) Fellowshiped, communed, communicated with God and Had peaceful relationship with Him (Gen. 1:28, 2: 16-19)
After Sin	Became disobedient to God (Gen. 3:1-7) Were under God's curse (Gen. 3:15-19, Rom. 3:19, Jhn. 3:36) Became sinners by nature and practice (Ge. 4:1ff, 6:5-6, 11, Jer. 8:4, 10, 11 Became under physical and spiritual death (Gen. 3:19, 3:2, 5:5, Rom. 5:12 Became sons of the devil (1Jhn 3:8-9, Jhn 8:44 Were alienated from God and no fellowship (Gen. 3:1-11, 22-24) Became God's enemy (Romans 5:1-11) Communication was marred (Gen. 6:1-ff) Were sinners before God (Rom. 3:9-10, 22-23, Eph. 2:6, Ps. 14, Isa. 53:6 Became hostile (Eph. 2:16)

---

[100] Design Borrowed from: Enoch Wan, "Practical Contextualization: A Case Study of Evangelizing Contemporary Chinese" CATW, March 2000.

Benefits of the New relationship with God through Christ's death	Made new creation (2Cor. 5:17)
	Image of God restored (Eph. 4:24)
	Declared righteous before Holy God (1Cor. 6:3)
	Made God's children (John 1:12-13)
	No longer under God's condemnation (John 3:18)
	Walk with the Triune God (John 3:21)
	Have ultimate peace with God (Eph. 2: 11-12)
	Love of God is demonstrated to us (Rom.5:8, John 3:16)
	Given the Holy Spirit (John 14: 15-16)
	Put in the body of Christ through baptism (1Cor. 12:13, Eph. 4:3-5)
	Given spiritual gifts (1Cor. 12, 14, 15, Eph. 4: 11-12)
	Saved from God's wrath (John 4:14, Lk. 19:10, Acts 2:2 and we are Godly(Rom. 5:6)
	Christ become a brother (Heb. 2:14)
	Christ became our ultimate mediator (1Tim. 2:5, Heb. 8: 6)
	Christ was united with us by God (Heb. 2:10-11)
	Sin and guilt removed(1Cor. 5:7, John 1:29, Eph. 5:2 Will be with God forever in heaven (Rev. 21)

If we closely follow the above table, we can understand how the original fellowship and communion between human beings and God was thwarted. Genesis 1:26-27 records vividly how Adam and Eve were created in the image of God which means that their personality, attitude, consciences and morals were good before His eyes. After He created them, He pronounced that it was good! By giving them freedom of choice, God intended to continue having fellowship, communion, peace, and harmony with them (Gen. 1:28-30, 2:16-17). God had also trusted them to obey and abide with the basic regulation that He had given them. The commands that God gave them were to facilitate their relationship with Him (Gen. 2:17). To further His relationship with them, God had given them dominion over all other created things. God only required them to keep a harmonious relationship with Him by fulfilling those commands. Due to their curiosity of wanting to know and experience what God had forbidden them, Adam and Eve deliberately rebelled against God and ate the forbidden fruit (Gen. 3:1-5) and immediately they were under His judgement. Their rebellion alienated them from the presence of God, it brought disharmony between God and themselves and both spiritual and physical death (Gen. 2:17, 3:3, 3:19, 5:5, Rom. 3:12-24). Thus, they experienced total separation from God. Not only did God alienate Adam and Eve from Himself, but they also alienated themselves from Him and each from the other (Gen. 3:8-10).

After Adam and Eve rebelled, they started hiding themselves from God because first, they did not want to face the holy God, second, they were guilty and they knew that they deserved punishment (Gen. 3:10-25). Due to their willing rebellion, God rejected them. Hence forth, they did not have their original wholeness and would never regain it by any self effort. They also experienced alienation from each other because Adam immediately started blaming Eve and Eve did the same (Gen. 3:12-13).

Through Adam and Eve, human rebellion against God resulted in three ways: "there was alienation in relation to self, to each other or others and to God."[101] Toward self, sin brought guilt, condemnation and corruption (Gen. 3:8-11; Mk. 7:21-23; Jer. 17:9). It also brought enslavement from Satan so that people became subtle, cruel and evil (Jn. 8:34, Rom. 7:14). Sin made all people limited in their ability to love, which would have enabled them to continue having a good relationship with God and their fellow neighbors.[102] Adam and Eve and their generation became sinners not only by nature but also by choice and practice (Gen. 4:1ff, 6, 11, Jer. 8:4ff, 10, 11, Rom:5:12-18). On the other hand, God cursed their environment such that, they did not continue ruling the earth. They were no longer at peace, in fellowship or have harmony and reconciliation with the created order. Hoekeman describes the result of the fall: "Adam and Eve wanted to be higher than God. After the sin had been committed, the second perversion of the self-image occurred, this time in a downward direction. Adam and Eve felt ashamed of themselves and their self-image became negative."[103]

Adam and Eve and their generation needed a solution as to how they could rekindle their relationship with God. God's ultimate desire was not for them to be at a distance from Him, and therefore He did not completely block them from His face. He gave them a solution (Gen. 3:15). The solution was that, after appeasing Him with sacrifices and offerings, He would rekindle His love, fellowship and peace with them. He consistently kept going to them by way of making covenants with some of them, for example with Noah, Abraham and Lot (Gen. 9, 15, Ex. 3). The covenant was done through sacrifices and those sacrificial systems and covenants were to strengthen His relationship with them (Exod., Lev, Numb., and Deut).

---

[101] Reuel L. Howe, *Man's Need and Gods Action* (Greenwich: The Seabury Press, 1954), 38.

[102] A. Hegre, *The Cross and Sanctification* (Minnesota: Bethany Fellowship, 1969), 26-27

[103] Anthony Hoekeman, *Created in God's image* (Grand Rapids: Eerdmans Publishing Company, 1988), 104.

After the fall, the only way people (patriarchal and Israelites in general) could approach God was through sacrifices and offerings. Levitical offerings, like the burnt offering (Hebrew - olah - Lev. 1:3-17; Judg. 13:16), fellowship offerings or peace offering (selamim - Lev. 3:1-17; 7:11-21) and sin offering (hattat - Lev. 4:1-6:7; Numb. 6:12; 1 Samuel 6:3-4) were given to God as an appeasement for people's sin so they could experience His salvation.[104] Those offerings and sacrifices were done in the way which God had instructed them as:

> 1. An unblemished animal, signifying moral perfection, was presented at the door of the sanctuary by the offerer. 2. The offerers placed their hands on the animal's head, denoting identification with the victim and the transfer of sin's penalty to the substitute. 3. The animal was then slain, signifying death as the requisite punishment for sin. 4. The priest sprinkled blood of the victim on the altar, the blood representing the life of the victim (Lev. 17:11). 5. The offering, in part or in whole, was burned on the altar of burnt offering, its fragrance ascending to God as a pleasing aroma. Repeatedly, the scriptures indicate that the purpose of these sacrifices was "to make atonement" and provide forgiveness for the offerer (Lev. 1:4; 4:20, 26, 31, 35; 5:13, 16; 6:7; Numb. 5:8; 8:12; 15:25). Without doubt, these sacrifices and offerings anticipated the vicarious sacrifice of Christ.[105]

The above sacrifices and offerings were always repeated as many times as it was required. They could not eradicate sins but they would temporally cover or hide them from the face of God.

Since all sacrifices and offerings were repeatable, the only permanent alternative that God finally provided was the ultimate and unrepeatable sacrifice of His Son Jesus Christ (Jn. 3:16). The death of Christ effected a permanent cleansing that

---

[104] Bruce Demarest, 169.

[105] Ibid., 169

did not require day-to-day repetition (Heb. 9:26; 10:10). When He died, He sacrificed once for all (Heb. 108-10). His death was the only absolute way that God would have reconciled Himself with human beings as well as human beings being restored in their fellowship with Him, with one another and with the created order. Jesus Himself became the Good News for the human beings in that; through repentance they would continue experiencing peace and harmony with God and with one another. Christ took upon Himself all human sins so that they may be made righteous before God (2Cor. 5:21). He provided salvation for all such that, through His death, "God was reconciling the world to Himself in Christ."[106] It was through the death of Christ that forgiveness of sin was possible, thus,

> The death of Christ, by which He bore sin's condemnation as an essential divine forgiveness is at the same time a demonstration of the immensity and the holiness of God's love. The fact that God has Himself met in the death of His Son the requirement of His holy judgement of sin in the final manifestation of His love.... It is a love that Has its action in the atonement of Christ's death.[107]

Through Christ's death, the eternal death that was upon human beings was overcome (Rom. 5:18). Through His death and resurrection, human sins are removed (1Cor. 15:17).

For a sinner to receive salvation, which is to be reconciled with God, to have a peaceful and harmonious relationship with Him, he or she has to repent and have faith in Christ. After one becomes aware that he or she is a sinner, repentance should follow (Lk. 5:35).

The reason for salvation was therefore out of the human problem that is, rebellion against God. Sin in human beings needed to be solved so that they could continue in fellowship with

---

[106] 2Cor. 5:19 (New International Version).
[107] H. D. McDonald, *The Atonement of the Death of Christ* (Grand Rapids: Baker Book House, 1985), 31.

their Creator. Human beings needed to go back to God so that they could continue fellowshipping and communing with Him.

Old Testament Salvation Themes

Affirming that the Good News of salvation (Christ's life, death, burial resurrection and appearances) was divinely in the economy of God, Paul repeatedly confirmed to the doubting Corinthians that the gospel which Christ brought with Him was, *kata tas graphes* (1Cor. 15:3-5) that is, it was according to the Scriptures. To verify this, he indirectly alluded to the book of Isa. 53:1-12; Ps. 22 and Isa. 7:14 where he also indicated the subject of the gospel was Christ. Affirming Christ's mission on the earth which was to atone for human sins, W. Norton repeatedly used the phrase, "according to the Scriptures" to show us that there was nothing that Jesus did, especially His death on the cross for our salvation, which was not prophesied in the Old Testament.[108] Thus, Isa. 7:14 and Isa. 53:1-12 are Old Testament salvation themes that reflect God's ultimate intention of bringing sinners back to Himself. In His discussion about the atonement, Grudem feels that to accomplish salvation for sinners, Christ came as a human being and died according to the Old Testament prophecy, that is, "atonement is the work Christ did in His life and death to earn our salvation according to the Scriptures."[109] This shows that without Christ's life and death there is no salvation at all.

In this section therefore, the writer briefly discusses two Old Testament themes that help us to understand Christ's salvation. In Isa. 7:14, it is Christ's life (incarnation) for salvation and in Isa. 53:1-12 is His death that culminated His mission on earth. How then do these two texts relate to the rest of the biblical facts of the sacrificial death of Christ for humans' salvation?

---

[108] Will Norton, "Class Lectures," Christology of Mission - The Glory of the Living Word, June, 2002.

[109] Wayn Grudem, *Systematic Theology*, (Grand Rapids: Zondervan Publishing House, 1994), 56.

Immanuel

Isaiah 7:14 is one of the Old Testament Messianic themes which, reveals the intention of God for salvation. According to the brief information that is given by this passage, Syria and the Northern Kingdom of Israel (Ephraim) had arranged to fight against Judah because of her refusal to join them in standing against powerful Assyria. They had an intention of conquering Ahaz, replacing him with their own king who could do their desires and cooperate with them. Fearing the invasion of his neighbors, Ahaz inclined to call on the aid of the Assyrian conqueror. Socially, Judah was always at war with her enemies, and therefore there was a need for a permanent Savior.

Before the Immanuel verse, there are three verses (vv. 10-13) that help us to understand how the promise came to be. In Hebrew Bible, v.10 reads, *Yosef Yahweh daber va el Ahaz le amor* (Again the Lord spoke to Ahaz). Due to Ahaz's disbelief of God's deliverance (v. 7-9), God continued to speak through Isaiah to him, saying, *seal leka ot me im Yahweh elohim ka* ... (Ask your God for a sign ...v. 11). Isaiah asked Ahaz to ask God for a confirmational sign. This sign was something to do with the deliverance (salvation) of Judah from the peril of their enemies. It was a proof that God determines what will come to pass and that it was His will that Judah would not suffer from the armies of Ephraim and Syria, but very soon their armies will leave Judah without being molested at all. It is an event which should be a pledge for the fulfillment of the prophecy, the genuineness of a promise, the reality of an experience.[110] It may be given as a token that something really will happen in the future or as a reminder that something previously predicted has now actually happened. A sign might be an ordinary event or an extraordinary miraculous nature which might be a wonder.[111]

---

[110] George, Buchanan Gray, *A Critical and Exegetical Commentary on the Book of Isaiah* (New York: Charles Scribners Sons, 1912), 121.
[111] Ibid, 121.

Lindblom feels that the "sign" was "something to occur that would point to and warrant the salvation of Jerusalem from the attack of the Assyrians."[112] Whether Ahaz agrees or not to ask God for a sign, God in His divine will promised that He would give a sign. God's sign would not be Ahaz's choice. It will not be miraculous like that offered to Ahaz and rejected, but God's power will uniquely extend to the physical, *haemaq sealah o hagebbehha le maelah* (deep down as well as heights above).

Verse. 12 reads *Va yomer Ahaz lo eseal ve lo anasseh et Yahweh* (But Ahaz said, I will not ask; I will not put the Lord to the test). Ahaz would not willingly test God by making Him prove His power (Exod. 17:7). Though Ahaz was reluctant to ask for God's "sign" hence, not to test God (v. 12), Isaiah continued pronouncing (oracle) what God intended to do in the house of David and his dynasty, *bet David ha meat mikkam haleot ... taleu*, "hear now you house of David (v.13).

In verse 14, la ken yitten Adonay lakem ot hinneh hu ha alemah harah ve yoledet bben ve qarat simo Immanu-el (Therefore, the Lord Himself will give you a sign. The virgin will give birth to a son and will call him Immanuel).[113] In this verse, we clearly see God offering His own sign after Ahaz refused to accept God's offer (v. 11). God chooses a sign which is not to take place. There are four words, laken, ot, ha alemah and Immanuel (therefore, sign, virgin and Immanuel) that are descriptively used in this verse which vividly explains what was to happen.

Therefore (Laken)

After Isaiah denied Ahaz to test God's patience, he connects v.13 and 14 with the Hebrew particle *laken* (therefore). This word may be clarified by phrases such as "since this is so," "for these reasons," and "according to such conditions."[114] This connection

---

[112] Ibid., 18.

[113] Hebrew Bible, (Transliteration.)

[114] Brown, Driver, and Brings, *A Hebrew and English Lexcon of the Old Testament*

was used by Isaiah to introduce a divine pronouncement or declaration. Concerning this (laken), Young says that, "the mere presence of the particle does not itself insure that the declaration to be one of doom but of blessings."[115] Young also feels that this particle serves to introduce a "sign" of a different character from that which had previously been offered.[116] Ahaz could have chosen any sign (wonder) to attest God's message of hope as delivered by Isaiah, but he refused and "therefore" God will choose His own significant sign to give to Ahaz. His "sign" was to be so significant that it was more unique than the normal wonder. The particle draws attention to a change but as the emphasis shows, it is a change of the person who chooses the sign (the Lord).

The context in which verse 14 fits is thereby unified with the transitory word, "therefore." Since Ahaz could not trust in God, the prophet Isaiah assured him that Yahweh was to give (*la yitten -natan*) him a sign that will arouse and command his trust. The house of David that was to be destroyed also needed some confidence, and to trust in God's maintaining the throne of their father David for all generation. This was through the sign of Immanuel who commands their confidence in God.

The prophet (Isaiah) had a message of hope to Ahaz but instead he gave him a sign of both impending doom (to Judah) and ultimate and extraordinary hope (to the throne of David). About this sign, Webb states that "the Immanuel sign contained a promise as well as a threat. For Isaiah and his followers it meant the promise of God's protecting presence and the eventual fulfillment of God's good purpose for his people....117

Sign (Ot)

The *Interpreter's Bible* declares that: "Sign: a signal,

(Oxford: University Press, 1907), 486.

[115] E. Young, *Studies in Isaiah* (Grand Rapinds: Eerdmans, 1954), 156.

[116] Ibid., 156.

[117] Barry, Webb, *The Message of Isaiah* (Leicester: InterVasity Press, 1996), 63.

communication ... it may be a natural event which becomes a sign because it is predicted, or an extraordinary or miraculous happening: a wonder."[118] Lindblom also notes that, "in Isaiah 7:10ff. "Sign" means a warranting sign in a proper sense, whereas the word in 7:14ff means "wonder," a wonderful action by Yahweh, pointing to His power."[119] In the Old Testament, the word in Hebrew, *ot* refers to something addressed to the senses, to at least the existence of divine power. Often, it is said that extraordinary events were given as a sign to assure faith or to demonstrate authority.

After considering the immediate context of this verse (14), Alexander has given a moderate view of the term sign, of which he says that," It is not necessarily a miracle but more of a pledge of the truth of something."[120] The *Interpreter's Bible Dictionary* also points out that, "the usage of the "sign" in Isaiah 7:14 is one of assurance."[121] We should note that this important sign was given by Yahweh. Isaiah uses this word "sign" to emphasis the Lord's omnipotence.[122] It is therefore, only Yahweh who can give a sign whether in heaven above or here on earth.

The sign in this verse is directed to "you" *lakem - la* -preposition and *kem* which is plural and is different from "you"-*nu* in verse 9 which is directed to Ahaz. "You,"(*lakem*) here is referring to the house of David. Since the context tells us that the dynasty of David is what is at stake in the impending invasion, it would seem proper to so interpret the plural "you" as the "house of David which is the recipient of the sign."[123]

Two questions can be asked: what is so significant about the sign to the "house of David?" What is the significance of the "sign?"

---

[118] *Interpreter's Bible Vol. 5* (New York: Abingdon, 1958), 217.

[119] Lindblom, 18.

[120] J. A. Alexander, *The Earlier Prophecies of Isaiah* (New York: Wiley and Putnam, 1970), 111-12.

[121] *Interpreter Bible, Vol. 5,* 32.

[122] Young, 157.

[123] Ibid., 158.

The passage provides us with the answer to the first question, for Rezin and Pekar were seeking to eliminate the Davidic dynasty by placing the son of Tabeel on the throne which could have thwarted the promise of God that "David's Kingdom will be forever." The sign was to prevent this problem and to seal the promise. Answering the question, of the significance of the sign, A. Simpson in his book on Isaiah, provides the following answers based on the view that the "sign" is a prediction of Christ who is the Savior of Israel. He says it is significant because:

> First, the prophetic announcement and fulfillment; second, demonstration of God's interest in human affairs; third; indication of the supernatural character of Christianity; fourth, moral significance of humility; fifth; sign of God's own character and will; and sixth, incarnation is a pledge of the Second Advent.[124]

Simpson's devotional comment shows that the sign is eternal, that Christ will come to restore the Davidic kingdom. This kingdom will be everlasting and, it will also be sealed in people's hearts through Christ.

Virgin (Ha Alemah)

After promising a sign, Isaiah turns to describe that sign, "ha alemah," which is translated "maiden" or a "young woman" will be with a child and will give birth to a son and will call him Immanuel." The term *alemah* refers to a girl or a young woman above the age of childhood and sexually mature whose sexual emotions awaken and becomes potent. It asserts neither virginity nor the lack of it; it is naturally in actual usage, often applied to women who as a matter of fact certainly or probably are virgin.[125]

As we continue with this verse, it is important to underline the question: according to the theme of Christ's salvation, who is

---

[124] A. B. Simpson, *Isaiah* (Harrisburg: Christian Publications, n. d.), 89-102.
[125] George Bushanan Gray, *A Critical Commentary*, 125.

ha alemah? The KJV bible says,"shall conceive and bear a son," and NIV says, "Will give birth to a son." The Hebrew verb *yoledet* (bear), which is a participle feminine singular, carries with it a future event which is either distant or infinite. Some theological scholars view the verb "bear" as present tense, "bearing."

If the term alemah is well handled, the implication is that a mature girl will be pregnant and a son will miraculously be born without a father. Alexander points out that, "if this word Alemah means virgin, then it implies only a state of present virginity, not that she will always remain a virgin."126 If the verbal action were future tense, there would be no guarantee that the virgin who would (in the future) bear a son would still at that time be a virgin, and not a wife. But if a "virgin maiden" is with a child and is obviously both a virgin and a mother, we cannot escape the conclusion that this is a picture of a virgin birth.127 Birks understand the term alemah to signify the damsel of the race of David through whom the Messiah would come.128

God with Us (Immanuel)

In verse 14d, *ve qala' t semu Immanu-el* (and will call his name Immanuel). It was not Isaiah to call the son Immanuel, but the mother. The description of the child is that, his name will be "Immanuel" which means, "God with us." According to Isaiah's description, the name indicates what the child is or will be in the reality of what he represents, rather than his proper name (God with us). If the name, "God with us"(NIV), "God is with us" or "with us is God" is taken today in our messianic traditional way, it may imply two things; first, that he is personally among us and second, if taken as a promise of blessing, He is with us in the sense

---

Alexander, 116.

127R. Kittel, *Great Men and Movements in Israel* (New York: Macmillan, 1929), 270.

128 T. Birks, *Commentary on the Book of Isaiah* (London: Church of England Book Society, 1878), 52.

that He blesses us through some great individual.[129] Vine connects the Immanuel passages in Isaiah to the actual birth of Christ when he writes:

> An outstanding feature of Old Testament prophesies is that they connect events chronologically separated. Conditions more immediately relating to Assyria were developed under subsequent powers successively, culminating in the Roman, under which Immanuel was born. The circumstances depicted by Isaiah as prevailing in the Land continued up to and in Immanuel's day.[130]

The gospel of Matthew quotes this page for one or two reasons. It is to reassure his readers that the announcement of the angel to Joseph is in accord with the O.T. prophetic scriptures, or it is a quotation of the angel's message to Joseph's trust in what he has told him. In either case, it must be admitted that the quotation of Isaiah 7:14 is for the purpose of confirming Jesus' incarnation as the direct plan of God's for human salvation.[131] In support of Immanuel as the promised Messiah and Savior as the gospel of Matthew mentions, Edward Hindson also notes:

> To deny that Matthew has given us a proper interpretation of Isaiah is to deny that Jesus knew what He said of Himself as He instructed His disciples "in the prophets" concerning Himself. It is to deny His ability to "open their understanding that they might understand the scriptures."[132]

Hindson supports a single fulfilment of the Immanuel passage of Isaiah, and suggests that Matthew alluded to what was prophesied about Jesus' birth as the Son of God (God with us).

---

[129] Ibid, 52

[130] W. E. Vine, *Isaiah's Prophecies, Promises, Warning* (London: Oliphants, 1953), 35.

[131] Edward E. Hindson, *Isaiah's Immanuel* (USA: Presbyterian Reformed Publ. Comp. 1-78), 86.

[132] Ibid., 86.

After Isaiah's description of Immanuel, he attributes Him with distinct qualifications (Isa. 9:1-6) that only fit Jesus Christ and that, is why Matthew sees Jesus as the fulfillment of the Scriptures. Both in Isaiah and Matthew, it seems likely that Immanuel is a wonder-child and wonder-King; thus, we are justified in speaking of Isaiah's correct prophecying of Messianic ideas in connection with Immanuel, who is Jesus in the gospels. When Matthew described Jesus as the Immanuel of Isaiah 7:14, He refers to Him as God, because of what was written in the scriptures about Him.

Isaiah 7:14 describes Jesus as God incarnated for the sake of human beings; so in that context, He may permanently provide everlasting salvation His people Israel and also to whosoever will accept Him. Jesus' death reconciled the sinner to God; the broken relationship between them is restored. Without His incarnation, there is no fulfilment of salvation which God promised, no fellowship, reconciliation or peace between human beings and God.

Suffering Servant

The suffering servant of Isaiah 53:1-12 is another Old Testament theme that eludes toGod's intention for sinners' salvation. This text is mostly aluded to by the gospel writers because it reflected what was predicted to happen to Jesus. When Paul was explaining the meaning of the gospel to the Corinthian Church (1Cor. 15:3-5), he also said to by saying that the death of Christ happened "according to the scriptures." The passage reflects how the servant would die in substitution for His people or "in place of His people." Scripture says, "he took our infirmities, carried our sorrow, was pierced for our transgressions, was crushed for our iniquities and He was punished on our behalf." Since the death of the servant is sacrificial and a ransom for sinners, the thesis of this text is: "The Death of the Servant is meaningful and significant because it brought an ultimate hope of salvation and eternal life for the sinful humans."

This passage is Isaiah's "Servant's song" and its theme is the death of the Messiah. It describes the meaning and the significance of Christ's death that brought ultimate hope for a sinful world. The passage is a prophetical song that consists of five stanzas, and each stanza has three verses. The first stanza starts with chapter 52:13-15 and 2 - 4th stanzas are in this passage (v.1-12). Reflecting on our human hopelessness that was caused by sins, this passage provides hope for salvation.

Sad Story

The second stanza (vv. 1-3) emphasizes what happened to God's Servant that is, His rejection. The message of hope and salvation that He was giving to His people was rejected. This verse reminds us what the gospel of John tells us, "He came to His own but His own did not receive Him. Yet to all who received Him, to those who believed in His name, He gave the right to become the children of God...."[133]

Christ is referred to us as God's Servant because He entirely submitted and obeyed to God's directive will for salvation for the world. He never desired to fulfill His own will but God's. He denied all of His glory and took the nature of a human being (Phil. 2: 5-11), and He entirely obeyed God right through death on the cross. Christ humbled Himself before God as well as before His persecutors, just as a servant would do. He took an inferior place in human nature. Through His obedience, He became a mediator between humans and God. With the idea of mediatorship, Vigeveno describes Jesus as: "Jesus is the mediator between God and man. He is God-became-man for the purpose of mediation. He unties the tragic knot with His bare hands. He brings peace through His cross."[134]

---

[133] John 1:11-12 (New International Version).
[134] H. S. Vigeveno, *Jesus the Revolutionary* (Glendale: A Division of G / L

In His human nature (v. 2-3) which is His incarnation, Christ did not display His divinity, for He completely identified Himself with humans. His mission was to die, to provide forgiveness of sin, and in so doing reconcile sinners with God. Instead of people accepting Him and the freedom from sin that He was offering, they rejected Him and also rejected the hope that He gave through His death. The final result of rejection was that He was crucified (v.3).

Death of the Servant

The third stanza (v. 4-9) is describing the servant's main mission, which was to provide freedom from sin. Isaiah affirms that the Servant came willingly to "suffer for us." Isaiah says that the Servant "took up our infirmities and carried our sorrows" (53:4) and this is also alluded to in Matt. 8:17. The Hebrew verb *Nasa* means "lift up" or "bear" and *sabal* means, "carry" or "transport" and together communicate the idea of substitution.[135] In the whole song, Isaiah ten times says that Christ: "Came for us." He came for us, not for His own sake. "Us" means: the whole world, the whole human Race. It was a sacrificial death that He faced. Isaiah affirms in another passage that as the Servant was undergoing terrible physical and emotional pain the Messiah neither resisted nor shrunk back (Isa. 50:5). He records that the Servant will endure all the sufferings so as to save His own people (53:6-7). Specifically, in verse 6, Isaiah says that, "the Lord has laid on Him the iniquities of us all" Hebrew - *paga* means "cause to fall on"[136] which means that God divinely caused our sins to fall on the Servant who is Christ. Isaiah added that the Messiah "was numbered with the transgressors," anticipating Christ's crucifixion among common criminals (Isa. 53:12) which Luke alludes to in 22:37, 23:33. He was given an unfair trial, and His life was cut off

---

Publications, 1966), 154.

[135] Bruce Demarest, *The Cross and Salvation* (Wheaton: Crossway Books, 1997), 172.

[136] Ibid., 172.

by a violent death (Isa. 53:8). Isaiah also describes Him as a "man of sorrows and familiar with suffering" (Isa. 53:3).

Since Christ was the prophesied Messiah who will substitutionally die for the sinful world, that is in place of all sinners, as a Servant (Hebrew, *ebed*) He was with a mission: to Israel His people (Isa. 49:5-6, 52:5-6), His accomplishment was still future (Isa. 42:4, 49:6, 53:11) and the work that He will perform will be extraordinary (Isa. 42:6-7, 53:11-12).[137]

The death of the Servant was to take away our infirmities which means, to forgive our sins which had separated us from God. Our harmonious relationship with God was thwarted by sin, and the only solution was for Christ to die so that His death would restore us back to fellowship with God. We were spiritually sick and therefore, we needed a healer. His death healed our relationship with God, and with others. When we were alienated from God as well as alienated from Him, His death acted as a good medium for our restoration. The stanza reveals more about the condition of our hearts: "we have followed our own ways" (gone astray) and "we have chosen to live in sin." Sin has caused us to be spiritually sick with no hope of being healed. Due to this severe condition of human lives, Isaiah declares that Christ's death was to carry our sicknesses.

Christ became our Substitute by carrying away our sins. For God to forgive sins in the Old Testament, there was a requirement for a scapegoat which did not have any blemish, and it would carry the sins of the people, so that they could retain their relationship with God. The scapegoat was believed to have carried all the iniquities, transgressions, and infirmities of the people, and that is why Isaiah prophecied the Servant with that type of a mission.

Through His death, Christ became our substitute like that scapegoat. All human sins were placed on Him, and forgiveness

---

[137] Ibid., 172.

of sins was announced to those who believe and accept His death. He brought hope, peace with God, reconciliation, healing, to those who accept Him but to those who refuse and do not accept the forgiveness of their sins, there is future judgement from God.

Isaiah affirms that the Servant did not only suffer, but also died and he was buried, "He was assigned a grave" (v.9). Christ did not resist his persecutors but he obeyed, knowing what was ahead of Him and what He wanted to accomplish.

Triumph of the Servant

The fourth stanza which is the conclusion of this song affirms that the Servant died oby God's choice, and not by accident. Verses 10-12 represent Jesus' death as a "guilt offering" that would satisfy God's requirement and remove the guilt of sin from the people. His death was divinely ordained and its result was that it provided sinners' peace with God, and salvation (Eph. 2:14-15; Col. 1:20).

In verse 12, Isaiah describes the death of the servant as victorious in that, He conquered the devil and death. This is the whole idea of victory in resurrection. He paid the penalty of our sins and declared hope for our salvation. He became victorious not only in His resurrection but also as a substitute and sin intercessor (v. 12c). It was due to God's love for sinners that Jesus died as the ultimate sacrifice for our sins. God destined Jesus to be a sacrifice for human's sin. God made Him sin, though He knew no sin. Christ's death was out of God's perfect will, but not Pilate's or His persecutors. Bruce Demarest coherently concludes his discussion of Isa. 53 by saying:

> The coming Servant, Messiah, lifts up and takes up himself man's sickness and bears the weight of his worrisome sorrows. Nothing could more graphically portray the vicarious sacrificial of work of Christ who bore the penalty for man's sin so that man may receive God's righteousness and justified before Him. In addition, Dan. 9:24 provides

a comprehensive description of the work of "the anointed One." some 490 years after the decree to rebuild Jerusalem the Messiah will appear "to finish transgression, to put an end to sin, to atone for wickedness (lepper awon), to bring in everlasting righteousness.138

Reflecting on the salvation theme of Isa. 53, the term "all" is repeated twice which means that Christ's death was for all without limitation. Sin and iniquities are universal to all, and therefore Christ's saving work was provided to all, that is whoever will accept it by faith. In verse four, Isaiah adds that, "He (Christ) took up our infirmities and carried our sorrows." The term "our" is repeated twice which indicate the plurals and collectiveness as well as inclusiveness. Verse 5 states that, "He was pierced for our transgression; He was crushed for our iniquities." This also shows that all are the object of Christ's suffering and with the Old Testament view of common solidarity; none of the people are excluded. The death was for all but the condition is for those who will accept it as a free gift.

With the same concept of the universal death of Christ for the salvation of all, John expresses God's love by saying that, "for God so loved the world that He gave... whoever believe in Him will not perish...."139 Still alluding to Isa. 53, John asserts that Jesus died for the world, which means people (Jn.3:16). John the Baptist proclaimed that the Lamb of God will take the sins for all (Jn. 1:29). The Samaritan woman affirmed that, "we know that this man really is the Savior of the world."140 Jon also talks about Jesus as, "the bread of God... who comes down from heaven and gives life to the world."141 Supporting the scriptural view that Jesus died for all, Bruce Demarest asserts:

---

138 Ibid., 173.

139 John 3:16-17 (New International Version).

140 John 4:42 (New International Version).

141 John 6:33 (New International Version).

The atonement's universal provision removes every barrier between a holy God and sinners, unleashed in the world a power for good that restrains evil, guarantees the future resurrection of all people from the dead (Jn. 5:28-29), provides an additional just basis for the condemnation of unbelievers, and offers motivation for the proclamation of the Good News to every creature... Christ's atoning work on the cross is unsurpassable and unrepeatable for it is final, "Christ died once and for all.[142]

Hebrew Concepts of Salvation

In the Old Testament, the Hebrew concept of salvation (*Yasha*) is a multifaceted one; in one case it signifies freedom or deliverance (Heb. *nasal, gaal*) from the bondage or physical restrictions (Ex. 3). Hebrew terms like *hayah, padah* and *kopher* also refer to the salvation of human beings. *Hayah* was used to signify "to be alive," "to perceive," "to keep alive" or "to give full and prosperous life," to someone (1Sam. 10:24). The meaning of this verse is that it is God who saves (Gen. 45:7; 50:20).[143] *Yasha, yeshua* and *yesha* mean "to bring into a spacious environment," "free to develop without hindrance" which was the work of God (Ezek. 34:22; Hos. 1:7; 13:10-14, 43:11).[144] *Padah* basically means "to acquire by giving something in exchange," that is, redemption of life by the surrender of another life to die in its stead (Ex. 13:13; Deut. 7:8).[145] *Kopher* means "ransom" price which was normally paid by a person for his life so as to be free (Ex. 21:28ff, 30:12, Job 36:18, Isa. 43:1- 4).

Padah and *kopher* are only applied to God in His redeeming

---

[142] Bruce Damarest, 191-92, 195.

[143] E. M. B. Green, *The Meaning of Salvation* (London: Hodder & Stoughton, 1965), 13.

[144] Ibid., 19.

[145] Ibid., 31.

activity.[146] To experience this sort of salvation, people have to be liberated from their physical. Besides salvation as deliverance, the other terms that are used in the Old Testament are peace (shalom) and reconciliation (*kaphar*) which are relational, particularly to God.

Deliverance

In Hebrew, the term *padah* or *yasha* means "rescue" "ransom" or to "release a person detained in bondage." It is salvation through deliverance. When the verb *padah* is used figuratively, it describes the deliverance of God's people from bondage to sin or physical bondage, and it is only God who effects it. The Psalmist noted: "He Himself will redeem Israel from all their sins" (Ps. 130:8; 34:22). The noun *pedut* describes the redemption or deliverance which God effects through the atoning sacrifices that is, "He provides redemption (*pedut*) for His people" (Ps. 111:9; 130:7).[147]

However, deliverance was often physical liberation of the people from any danger or social chaos. When there was deliverance, peace, harmony, and reconciliation among the people and God, that situation was termed as salvation of God. Deliverance was carried out by God's human agents (Judg. 2:18, 6:22, 1Sam. 14:45, 23:2). For physical deliverance to occur through a human agent, most of the time there was a sequence of events such as in Deut. 26:6-11 (Israel's historic creed).[148]

- Need: "But the Egyptians oppressed us." (v. 6)

- Call out of need: "Then we cried to God." (v. 7a)

---

[146] Ibid., 32-32.

[147] Bruce Demarest, *The Cross and Salvation* (Wheaton: Crossway Books, 1997), 176-77.

[148] Claus Westermann, *Elements of Old Testament Theology* (Atlanta: John Knox Press, 1982), 46.

- Hearing: "And God heard us and saw our affliction." (v. 7b)

- Saving: "And God brought us out of Egypt." (v. 8)

- Response of the saved people: "And now I bring the first fruit." (v. 10):

- "You shall bow down and rejoice." (v. 11)

In some other cases, God was delivering people without using human mediators (Ps. 20:6, 34:1ff, Isa. 61:10, Zech. 3:4). Deliverance was sometimes individual (Ps. 86:1-2) or corporate (Neh. 9:27, Ex. 14:14, 1Sam. 12:2, 14:45) and its main purpose was to portray the love of God in saving His people from social trouble as well as reconciling them back to Himself (Ps. 6:4-5; Ps. 69:1-2; Isa. 38:20; 43:11-12; 48:6).[149]

To experience deliverance either from enemies, drought, diseases, etc, repentance of sins, faith, obedience and righteousness were required (Gen. 15:6; Numb. 14:11, 20:17; 2Kings 17:14, Jonah 3:5; Hos. 5:13-6:3; Isa. 31:1, Ps. 33:16-20). God was the sole source of deliverance as well as object of faith (Numb. 14:11, 20:12, Ps. 3:16; Jonah 2:9; 3:5). The result of deliverance, which was a form of salvation was victory (1Sam 14:45, vindication (Ps. 54:1; 72:4; 76:9), satisfaction and complete well being of the people (Ps. 18:19).[150] It was the righteous who were assured of God as their rock and their salvation.

Whenever the people of Israel turned from righteousness to wickedness, they would not experience deliverance, and therefore there was no salvation. Their salvation included forgiveness of their sins on condition of repentance. The people's blessings, victory over their enemies, restoration, etc. were related and

[149] Charles L Ryrie, *Basic Theology* (USA: Victory Books, 1994), 279.
[150] E. M. B. Green, 28.

connected to their spiritual and moral condition, that is, God's favor was upon them when they sought Him with a repentant heart (Ps. 34:6). Salvation as deliverance was more physical and was facilitated by people's inner attitude and behaviors toward God.[151]

In God's act of deliverance, His aim was to continue relating to His people so that they would experience blessings as part of salvation. A good example of deliverance is how God delivered the children of Israel from Egypt, so they could relate with Him by worshiping Him. In the act of deliverance, God revealed to them that His ultimate purpose was for Israel to be His, and for Him to be their God (Gen. 21:27; 1 Sam. 18:3; Ex. 19:4). To be God's people meant to obey Him and to avoid all that He prohibited them from doing (Ex. 19:5-8).[152]

In case of deliverance, the intention was for God's people to continue in relationship with God and with one another. This was after being delivered from all sorts of problems like slavery, drought, famine, diseases, pestilence, enemies, and exile. They could experience the complete salvation of God. In the book of Deut. 28:1-14, the Israelites settlement in the land of Canaan consisted of deliverance from all that might hinder God's blessings. Hence, salvation brought peace, harmony and acceptance in the land.[153] When they cried to God from captivity, God would rescue them from any problem. Salvation was therefore an experience which included physical deliverance from social problems (Gen. 18:16-33).[154]

---

[151] H. D. McDonald, *Living Doctrines of the New Testament* (Grand Rapids: Zondervan Publishing House, 1972), 87.

[152] Robert H. Culpepper, *Interpreting the Atonement* (Wake Forest: Eerdmans Publ. Company, 1966), 20.

[153] Lewis Sperry Chafer, *Systematic Theology V. III: Soteriology* (Texas: Dallas Seminary Press, 1948), 3.

[154] C. Ryder Smith, *The Bible Doctrine of Salvation: A Study of the Atonement* (London: The Epworth Press, 1946), 20-22.

Peace (Shalom)

Shalom (translated to mean peace) is another Hebrew concept of salvation. In the Old Testament, the term *shalom* is not a concept with a single clearly defined meaning, but it is a rich, multifaceted and complex word. *Shalom* has been used 312 times in the Old Testament of which 28 times are in the book of Isaiah and 21 times are in Psalms. The most significant usage signifies totality or completeness of life, which is facilitated by people's obedience to God, and their practice of righteousness. For peace to be experienced or rekindled, *shalom* offerings were offered to God, and therefore this type of *shalom* is used 20 times in the book of Leviticus.[155] Although *shalom* has several dimensions of usage, the most significant one was used as one of the elements of complete salvation. The actual root of *Shalom* is "to be whole, sound and safe."[156] The fundamental idea is totality and anything that contributes to this wholeness makes for "shalom." The *International Bible Encyclopedia* describes *shalom as*:

> Shalom has a concept of peace which is harmonious life. It is a word which is primarily for interpersonal or social relations where it comes close to meaning "justice." Shalom has a Semitic range of meaning which stresses totality or completeness of life. The whole idea of totality includes fulfilment, completion, maturity, security, well-being, welfare, friendship, health, community, harmony, tranquillity, agreement, success, and prosperity.... Harmony between God and His creatures Isa.27:5) and among the creatures themselves (1Sam. 16:4ff; Job 5:23) is at the heart of the Old Testament. This totality of life is experienced when there is no war and therefore, shalom is linked

---

[155] Robert Young, *Young's Analytical Concordance to the Bible* (Nashville: Thomas Nelson Publishers, 1982), 736-737.

[156] Douglas J. Harris, *The biblical Concept of Peace: Shalom* (Grand Rapids: Baker Book House, 1970), 14.

with the absence of war (Ecc.3:8; Ps. 120:7; Judg.1:13; 1King 2:5, 4:24). [157]

It is also observed in many Old Testament Semitic languages, particularly in the Akkadian tribe that "shalom" means to be whole and complete. In one form or another, the notion of wholeness, health and completeness inform all the variants of this word. [158]

In its holistic meaning, "shalom" should mean wholeness, completeness and peace not only of human beings but also of their properties like animals, crops, farms and even their entire land. If this totality of human life was not experienced, a designated priest could offer sacrifices so as to evoke God for shalom. "Shalom" would bring with it harmonious fellowship between God and people. Since total "shalom" was for both people and their properties, the Israelites would specifically and consistently pray and ask God to give them "shalom" of their land, animals and for their king. For a king, they would pray and voice the hope that was in his reign and ask if a complete peace will prevail so that they may enjoy their well-being, a well-ordered life, a harmonious life that unites material property, a national greatness and social justice.[159] All these elements of life contributed to the concept of salvation of the people and their properties. This type of "Shalom salvation" was experienced either individually or in a community.

It is well noted that in the Old Testament, "shalom" of the people was not only external but also internal; people would experience continuous peace with God and with one another, harmony with Him and with other members of the community. There was equilibrium of their life. When people were experiencing

[157] *T he International Standard Bible Encyclopedia K-P* (Grand Rapids: Eerdmans Publishing Company, 1986), 732.
[158] *The Anchor Bible Dictionary V. 5 O-SH* (New York: Doubleday, 1992), 206.
[159] Robert Davidson, *The Old Testament* (Philadelphia: J. B. Lippincott company, 1964), 107.

the totality of physical life, they were at the same time experiencing inner peace which they called salvation of God. With this idea of totality of life and well-being among the people, Erland Walter describes *shalom* as:

> The Word *shalom* has to do with totality of things and the relationship of all things within that totality ... with the harmony of all things, human and otherwise in God's creation, the harmony of relationships, the coming together in gentleness of that which shares participation in the creation of Yahweh..... It has to do with well-being... not only of no-physical ... it includes physical property, material property and all that we are. *Shalom* has to do with the well-being and prosperity of the most fully-blossomed possibility for all that we are. [160]

From Walter's definition of *shalom*, it has to do with community or cooperation in the society whereby individuals experience totality of life, which is made up of many life aspects. All that the person is or has should experience shalom in totality.

In all Hebrew aspects of *shalom*, God was said to be the ultimate source. He was known as its ground and without Him, there was no shalom at all. In their prayers, the Israelites would declare that God was the source of *shalom* (Numb. 6:24-26). God made shalom in His heaven and could give or promise it to people (Job 25:2; Ps. 35:27; 147:14). As the source of *shalom*, God would pronounce or speak it to His people if they had followed His divine instructions (Ps. 85:8ff). In his prayer, Hezekiah attributed the source of shalom to God (Isa. 38:17, 19) and the psalmist (Ps. 4:8, 28:11) also acknowledged that the key source of "shalom" was God. Proverb 16:7 recognizes that shalom comes from God. One would not expect consistency of *shalom* and yet continue walking

---

[160] Erland Walter, *Brethern Life and Tought*, "Shalom and Wholeness," 147.

in the stubbornness, disbelieving, rebelling, or mistrusting of God. God conditionally gave *shalom* to the people but they were expected to obey and fulfill His commands.

In a more specific concept of shalom, when all the spiritual and physical elements were in existence among the people, the whole environment was understood as "salvation." When people were experiencing prosperity but on the other hand they were suffering from diseases, there was no "shalom salvation" because the health and well-being of the people was not complete.

The Israelites understood the personality and the nature of God as redemptive, and therefore He was "shalom salvation" Himself. Their concept of God was that He was a liberator and could redeem human beings from all problems. He was understood as a redeemer right from the Exodus event and even in the wilderness. As God instructed them to sacrifice and offer things to Him, it was to facilitate their salvation. Salvation was a result of consistent peace from God. When they failed to do His will, they were captured and taken to captivity, hence breaking their "Shalom salvation." *A*s salvation, *Shalom* meant victory in the struggles with evil people and even with other nations. With the Hebrew concept of shalom, Douglas Harris differentiates peace as an element of salvation and salvation itself by saying:

> The difference between peace (shalom) and salvation is that peace is rather the lasting state of harmony and happiness in salvation and salvation is the momentary acquisition ... the whole state of life. This difference also implies that salvation in a more particular sense denotes victory over one's enemies; but in reality it compresses all acquisition of happiness ... like victory in the court of justice, rain and fertility are included in salvation.[161]

---

[161] Douglas J. Harris, *The biblical Concept of Peace* (Grand Rapids: Baker Book House, 1970), 22-23.

Among the Hebrew people therefore, salvation would mean a complete wholeness of life where peace is included. The opposite of "shalom salvation" was trouble, that is no peace but sorrow. After being cured from any disease, a person could claim that he or she had regained his or her salvation (Ps. 6:38). A sick person would ask God for forgiveness so as to regain his or her salvation (Ps. 51:14). Peace was therefore one of the content of salvation in the Hebrew Old Testament thought form.

As one element of salvation, *Shalom* had also an eschatological aspect: it focused on what God would do to His people either in the near future or far future. People were always waiting to see what God had for them in their future, and therefore they would eagerly wait upon Him. The future shalom is the major emphasis of the Old Testament prophets, particularly in that which is traditionally called Messianic passages. Most of these passages clearly speak of a future age of *shalom* which will not only positively affect human beings but also animals and the whole creation in general ((Isa. 9; 11:6-9). As the created order, the earth will be restored to its fertility; harmony and cooperative relationship between Adam and the earth will be reinstated (Joel 4:18).[162] The Old Testament passages like Isa. 7, 9:6-7, 11:1-4, 53, 54 understand *shalom* as future salvation which will be brought or established by a Messianic figure. These verses affirm that the Messianic figure will not only declare divine *shalom* to the people but also to the created order. In his apocalyptic perspective of *shalom*, the prophet Isaiah sees a total transformation of nature and its participation in shalom (Isa. 11:6ff. Describing the result of eschatological *shalom*-salvation, the prophet Zechariah says that:

> On that day there will be no light, no cold or frost. It will be unique day, without daytime or nighttime - a day known to the Lord. When evening comes, there will be light.

---

[162] *Dialogue V. 26* (Spring 1987), Jerry Folk, "Salvation as Shalom," 105.

On that day, living water will flow out from Jerusalem, half to the eastern sea and half to the western sea, in summer and in winter. The Lord will be the king over the whole earth.[163]

In Zechariah's text above, the future salvation will be characterized by peace, physical enjoyment and God's kingship. Zechariah's perspective is that the ultimate shalom will be culminated by the rule of God on the earth; and the whole well-being of human beings will be realized. This idea of *shalom* reflects on future salvation where life will totally be transformed by the Lordship of Christ.

With the same eschatological aspect of *shalom*-salvation, Amos (9:11-15) also implies that there will be God's blessings in that future time. It will be a time of great prosperity (Ps. 72:3; Isa. 66:12-14, Jer. 33:9). A total transformation of nature is also envisioned in that age (Hos. 2:18-23; Lev. 26:3-14; Ezek. 34:25-31). Messiah will be with His people as their king (Isa. 7:14).

Reconciliation

Reconciliation, which in Hebrew is *kaphar*, is another Old Testament's aspect of salvation, where a sinner and God come together in harmony. This term is used to mean "to obtain forgiveness and "to reconcile" (Lev. 6:30, 8:15, 16:20; Ezek. 45:15, 17, 20; Dan. 9:24)."[164] Another usage of reconcile is *chata* which means "reconciliation" (2Chron. 29:24), and the other usage is *ratsah* which is found in 1Sam. 29:4, meaning the "act of reconciling or reconcile." Specifically, these two terms mean "to make oneself pleasing or to obtain favor."[165]

Reconciliation is also "bringing again into unity, harmony

---

[163] Zechariah 14:6-9 (New International Version).
[164] John F. Walvoord, *Jesus Christ our Lord* (Chicago: Moody Press, 1995), 178.
[165] Ibid., 178.

or agreement that which has been alienated."[166] In the Hebrew context, there was no reconciliation without an offender, a mediator and a person who is offended. Reconciliation was done to unite the two parties, restoring their relationship. Once this is done, the two parties would start experiencing their expected salvation benefits. As perceived in the Old Testament, *Unger's Bible Dictionary* defines reconciliation: "Reconciliation is the restoration to friendship and fellowship after estrangement. Reconciliation contains the idea of an atonement or covering for sin (Lev. 6:30, 16:20; Ezek. 45:20)."[167]

Reconciliation between people and God was commonly effected through sacrifices (Lev. 17:11; Deut. 12:23; 1 Sam. 23:17; Ps. 72:14). Sacrifices offered some means for a sinner to approach God. Before God would forgive sins, people were supposed to demonstrate their genuine repentance and surrender before Him. An animal was to stand between a sinner and God, as a mediator for a sinner's salvation. After those sacrifices, through the voice of a priest, God would announce peace and harmony to the forgiven sinner or sinners and there afterthere was reconciliation.

Briefly stated, each of the three Hebrew concepts of salvation are relational; for them to be experienced, a person or people were to be obedient to God. Salvation was the result of people's acts of righteousness before God. People were always to stand for righteousness. As portrayed by these Hebrew terms, salvation relational, physical and eschatological. The following diagram illustrates the interrelationship of these terms:

---

[166] *Zondervan Pictorial Encyclopedia of the Bible V. 5*, Merril C. Tenney, (Grand Rapids: Zondervan Publishing House, 1975), 44.
[167] *Unger's Bible Dictionary* (Chicago: Moody Press, 1973), 914.

Figure 14. Hebrew Concept of Salvation

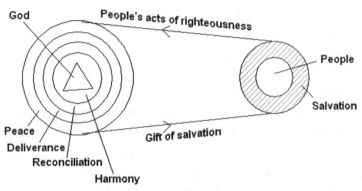

To summarize this section, the Hebrew concept of salvation was and is more relational: it had to do with a good relationship between people and God, and with their fellow neighbors. Salvation was and is complete life which is composed of peace, deliverance, harmony, reconciliation, acceptance and favor. All these components were actualized by God but facilitated by people. In the Old Testament, God is seen acting for the people's salvation and the people facilitating it through sacrifices.

Christian Concepts of Salvation

The Christian way of salvation is explained in the New Testament text. The New Testament uses the term "salvation" signifying preservation from the present or incoming danger. The most outstanding danger is present or future spiritual and physical death which is eternal separation from God (Matt. 9:22; Acts 27:20, 31; Rom. 5:9; Heb. 7:25).

In the New Testament, salvation is something which is less physical and environmental like in the Old Testament. It is a life relationship with God which is spiritual and demonstrated by all believers. It is not only present but also expressed as future which emphasizes entering in the kingdom of God (Matt. 18:11-13, Lk. 5:17). In the epistle to Romans, Paul states that, "For the wages of sin is death, but the gift of God is eternal life in (through) Christ Jesus our Lord."[168] This verse expresses the idea that before God all humans are sinners that is, there is no fellowship between a holy God and them. Due to their sin, human beings need to do something so that they can be reconciled back to God. Humans have no harmony, peace, acceptance or reconciliation with God because their sins have already alienated them from Him. Their sins have made impossible a relationship with the righteous God and with one another. "For all have sinned and fall short of the glory of God.... If we claim we have not sinned, we make Him (God) a liar and His word has no place in our lives."[169]

The New Testament vividly affirms that all human beings are born as sinners and they need redemption from that situation (Rom. 5:12). Out of His love, God had a final solution for sinners (Jn. 3:16). Christ's death was to reconcile all sinners with God so that they may continuously enjoy His fellowship, harmony and peace (Matt. 1:21, Heb. 2:3). The following verses show how human beings desperately needed salvation which caused Jesus to die for us.

Who gave Himself for our sins, to rescue us from the present evil according to the will of our God and Father."[170] And from Jesus Christ, who is the faithful witness, the first born from the dead, and the ruler of the kings of the earth. To Him, who loves us and has freed us from sins by His blood."[171] [He] gave Himself for us to redeem us from all wickedness and to purify for Himself a people that are His very own, eager to do what is good.[172]

[168] Rom. 6:23 (New International Version).
[169] Rom. 6:23, 1John 1:10 (New International Version).
[170] Galatians 1:4 (New International Version).
[171] Revelation 1:5 (New International Version).
[172] Titus 2:14 (New International Version).

These three verses show that there was no hope for the humans to restore their relationship with God until Christ died on the cross to effect reconciliation between them and God. The death of Christ was God's final offering for sinners, it was a comprehensive and absolute work that was done for sinners' salvation. It was on the cross that Jesus dealt with sin conclusively.[173]

Salvation in the Gospels

The gospels are the records of Christ's life, teachings, death, resurrection, appearances and ascension. His teachings about the kingdom of God and salvation were based in the Old Testament, which He declared that He had come to fulfill (Isa. 7:1-19), 9:1-7), 11:1ff). His presentation of salvation messages was on the kingdom themes (Lk. 8:10-12; Mk. 10:15, Lk. 22:30). To indicate how serious human sins were and why they needed salvation, Jesus would use some parables and relevant day-to-day stories (Matt. 7:24-29, 11:25-30, 13:1-23, 18:10-14, for an example - the lost sheep, the rich man (19:16-30), the sending of the twelve (Lk. 9:1-9) and the prodigal son, the lost coin (Lk. 15:1-31).

The gospel of Matthew starts with the genealogy that tells us that Jesus is the one whom God had planned to send on earth so as to redeem sinners from their sins (Matt. 1:1-25). In this narrative, Matthew tells us the birth story of Jesus and stresses that the child who will be born to Mary will be called Jesus[174] "because he will save his people from their sins" (Matt. 1:21b). Matthew also sites an Immanuel passage from Isaiah 7:14 and says that, "will give birth to a Son, and will call him Immanuel which means, "God

---

[173] Harry Rimmer, *The Purpose of Calvary* (Grand Rapids: Eerdmans Publishing Company, 1939), 51.

[174] "Jesus"- in Greek is "*Iesous*" which corresponds to the Hebrew "*Ye hoshua*," meaning "The Lord will Save!"

with us."[175] Matthew shows that salvation was necessary and will come from God Himself.[176] As he continues with his narratives, Matthew indicates that Jesus the God-Man came to men, which means that it was God who initiated the relationship and not human beings. Through Christ, salvation brought to us a peaceful relationship with God the Father.

Both Matthew and Luke present Jesus' preaching about the kingdom of God which was both immediate and future (Matt. 4:18-22; Lk. 3:1-6). The whole kingdom concept was about God's immediate and future salvation for those who accept His Son Jesus Christ. To enter into God's kingdom, Jesus called people to repent of their sins (Matt. 18:3). Conversion was the main requirement of human beings that Jesus wanted so as to enter into God's salvation (Matt. 13:15; Mk. 4:12). Concerning how Jesus was calling people for conversion, Leon Morris notes that:

> Conversion is not a meritorious action which ought to be suitable reward. Conversion, as the New Testament understands it, means a wholehearted turning away from sin. It means ceasing to rely on one's strong right arm. It means a coming to rely entirely on the mercy of God. Apart from that mercy, conversion would be aimless, futile, and meaningless. Conversion roots salvation squarely in the action of God and it takes its meaning from the action of God.[177]

Repentance of sins and conversion were in Jesus' message because His emphasis was that after a sinner repents and confess his sins, he will be reconciled back to God and start enjoying an ultimate fellowship and communion with Him (Mk. 1:4ff). Failure

---

[175] Matthew 1:23 (New International Version).
[176] Leon Morris, *The Cross in the New Testament* (Grand Rapids: Eerdmans Publishing Company 1965), 16.
[177] Ibid., 17.

to take this direction reinforces ones reprobation in a more strong sense, that is, God's severe judgement (Matt. 11:20-24).

The Gospel of Matthew and Mark show that human sins merit punishment and the only solution is repentance. Repentance causes God to rekindle His divine love toward a sinner. God is concerned with human sin because it is serious in consequence (Matt. 3:12). The serious consequence of sin is God's eternal judgement to sinners. Unless they repent and accept God's free salvation, they "will be burned up with unquenchable fire" which also means that they will be baptized with fire. This implies that sinners are under God's wrath (Matt. 3:7-9). To receive God's salvation therefore, Jesus invited people to repent (Matt. 3:1ff, 4:17, Mk. 6:12).[178]

Was the death of Christ in God's will? This is a very important question to ask especially in this section where we are establishing the basis of salvation. The gospel of Matthew and Mark trace the death of Jesus right in the absolute will of God and His economy (Matt.26:24, 54-56; Mk. 14:21, 27, 49). His death was intended to fulfill what God had already designed and spoken through His prophets (Mk.. 14:27). For sinners' salvation, Christ's death was out of God's divine will that, He "must"[179] suffer so as to bring human beings back to God (Matt. 16:21, Mk. 8:31). Without Christ's death, there is no forgiveness of sins (Matt. 26:28). His death brought forgiveness of sin for many (Matt. 20:28; Mk. 10:45).

Besides Matthew and Mark, Luke and John stress the same seriousness of sin in human's lives and how important Christ's death was for people's salvation (Lk. 16:11; Jn. 1:29, 2:19, 3:14, 6:51-53). Both gospels clearly affirm that Jesus was calling sinners to repentance so that they may have eternal life (Lk. 5:32,

---

[178] Ibid., 21

[179] Leon Morris' Notes, 27: "*Must*" (*dei*) - There is God's compelling divine necessity. It is not a possibility. There is no other possibility.

11:13, 13:35, 17:10, 18:19; Jn. 3:16). The main theme of these two gospels is the salvation of sinners which was effected by God through the death of His Son Jesus Christ.

Salvation in Acts

In the book of Acts, the early apostles specifically taught the essential need of human beings for salvation. The content of their message was Jesus' life, death, resurrection, appearances and ascension (Acts 2:36, 11:36-43). Their message of ascension did not mean that He retired from His saving work but, He is "still Lord of the universe and active Savior."[180] A good example of His saving work after His ascension is the conversion of Paul (Acts 9). Paul encountered the ascended Lord and Savior and God gave him repentance and the remission of his sins including the stoning of Stephen (Acts 5:31, 7:57-58). Other examples are like Paul and Silas in prison (Acts 16:17) and Paul at Athen and Corinth (Acts 17:30-34; 18:5). Paul himself was commissioned to preach repentance of sins by the risen and ascended Savior, "I am sending you to them, to open their eyes and turn them from darkness to light and from power of Satan to God, so that they may receive forgiveness of sins and a place among those who are sanctified by faith in me."[181] The sinfulness of human beings, God's love for sinners, Christ's death to reconcile sinners with God and with one another, resurrection of Christ, His appearances and His present saving work were the main components of the apostolic preaching.

Salvation in Paul's preaching

After Paul encountered the risen Lord, he had a new life, in full relationship with Christ. Previously he was a blasphemer, persecutor, and injurious (1Tim. 1:13) and after conversion he

---

[180] C. Ryder Smith, 168.
[181] Acts 26:17-18 (New International Version).

became Christ's slave, which means he had a new master (Rom. 1:1). He understood that the cross was the power and hope for his life. He came to know that God's wrath is revealed against all unrighteous people (Rom. 1:18). He recognized that all have sinned and fallen sort of God's glory and they desperately need God's salvation (Rom. 1:20, 3:9, 3:19). He realized that the final result of sin is both physical and spiritual death, which means sinners will be eternally separated from God (Rom. 1:32, 2:5, 3:22, 6:16, 6:21-23; 1Cor. 15:56). Paul clearly came to His senses and understood that people are not only sinners but they are enslaved to sin (Rom. 7:14), "sold under a cruel slave master, sold into a captivity from which they cannot escape"[182] and are under the law of sin (Rom. 7:23).

Besides sin and its consequences, Paul talks of its remedy, which is through accepting God's salvation through Christ (Eph. 6:19). Christ's death is the primary fact on which salvation of all those who accept Christ depends (Rom. 4:25),; 1Cor. 15:3). Paul emphasizes that Christ died for our sins (Gal. 1:4), He died to sin once for all (Rom. 6:10) and He was an offering for our sins ((Rom. 8:4). Christ died for the ungodly (Rom. 5:6) and He died for us (1Thess. 5:10). All of these Pauline verses show that Christ's death is the only solution to solving the human problem. It was the only absolute and necessary thing that would have brought human beings back to God's love and fellowship.

After accepting Christ and being saved from sin, Paul describes the convert as having a new relationship with God. Those who are in Christ have crucified their flesh (Gal. 5:24, 6:14), they are dead to sin (Gal. 6:2), are justified from sin (Gal. 6:6ff), they are dead to sin but alive unto God in Christ (Gal. 6:11), they are not under dominion of sin, nor are they servants of sin (Rom. 6:14, 17, 20) and they are free from sin (Rom. 6:18, 22, 8:2; Eph. 2:1, 5).

---

[182] Leon Morris, 185.

More significantly, Paul describes a person who is saved as living "in Christ" (Gal. 2:20). New life in Christ is a result of accepting Christ's atoning work on the cross (Rom. 5:17). "In Christ" (2Cor. 12:2) is Paul's favorable way of describing the most important fact and reality of a changed person, that is, a person who is already in harmony and peace with God. This is a new life that one enjoys with God and with other believers who are saved.[183]

When Paul talks about "in Christ," he too describes the new world and sphere of life that one enters at his conversion. This new life includes new goals, objectives, values of life, new life expectations and perspectives, new hope, new beliefs, new source of power and new world.[184] His new life in Christ motivated him to boldly say that, "if anyone is in Christ, he is a new creation; the old has gone the new has come."[185] George Land interprets this verse as, "All of the desires and appetites of this unregenerated man have passed away and have been replaced by an entirely new set of desires and appetites."[186] The conversion of Paul did three things to him: first, it impressed on him the unity of the divine action for salvation of all men; second, it taught him the salvation value of the death and resurrection of Christ, third, it gave him a new vision and understanding of salvation.[187]

By Paul accepting Christ, it gave him a relationship with God. Paul describes "a new life" in an analogy of baptism (1Cor. 12:13) which means that after one accepts Christ he or she is

---

[183] F. W. Farrar, *The Early Days of Christianity* (New York: Funk and Wagnails, 1983), 10.

[184] Rudolf Bultmann, *Primitive Christianity: In its Contemporary Setting* (Philadelphia: Fortress Press, 1955), 186.

[185] 2Corinthians 5:17 (New International Version).

[186] George Eldon Land, *Theology of the New Testament* (Land: Lutter worth, 1974), 479.

[187] *EAJET*, O. Obijole, "The influence of the Conversion of St. Paul on His Theology of the Cross," 1987, V. 6, No. 2, 30.

identified with His death and resurrection as well as incorporated in the body of believers (Rom. 2:12-13, 6:3-6; 1Cor. 12:12). One is placed in God's salvation (Rom. 1:16; Gal. 2:20; Eph. 2:8-10), which means that when one saved, it is through God's work. The human responsibility is to put faith in Christ. To Paul, salvation is founded on God's absolute grace through the death of Christ, and salvation and repentance are inseparable.

Salvation Concepts

Like the Old Testament, the New Testament has some distinct concepts that are associated with or that imply life in Christ. Some of these are: reconciliation, adoption, peace, redemption and deliverance.

Reconciliation

The term reconciliation (Gr. *katalasso*) has an idea of changing, thus a person changing from being an enemy to a friend. In relation to God and human, the use of this term shows that it is God who accomplishes the act of reconciliation. He exercises His grace towards a sinner on the ground of Christ's death (2Cor. 5:19). All sinners are in enmity with God (Rom. 5:10) and the above verse vividly indicates that it was God who was reconciling people to Himself (Gr. *Katallasson*). He is behind the process of reconciliation.[188] The whole work of reconciliation is from God, and therefore it does not require human effort.[189]

A sinner is already separated from God because of sin and therefore, God always invites him or her to be reconciled back to Him: "but now he has reconciled you by Christ's physical body through death to present you holy in his sight, without blemish

[188] M. R. Vincent, *Word Studies in the New Testament* (Wilmington: Associated Publishers and Authors, 1972), 824.
[189] G. Campbell Morgan, *The Bible and the Cross* (Grand Rapids: Baker Book House, 1975), 54.

and free from accusation."[190] In his writing to the Romans, Paul expresses the idea of reconciliation: "When we were God's enemies, we were reconciled to him through the death of his Son, how much more, having been reconciled, shall we be saved through his life!" Until there is this change of attitude, human beings are under God's condemnation. The death of His Son is the only solution to this problem, and therefore it is the only way we can be reconciled with God.[191] Paul affirms this by stating that, "God reconciled us (believers) to Himself through Christ ... that God was in Christ reconciling the world to Himself."[192] Reconciliation is like the act of a woman who returns to her husband and is accepted back into his household where she can have full fellowship with her husband and regain peace and harmony with him and her neighbors 1Cor. 7:11).

The basic idea behind reconciliation is making peace after enmity or a quarrel; hence it is to bridge over an enmity.[193] It is the good relationship that follows or is established when an enmity has been overcome. [194] In the above passages, Paul has clearly indicated that the root cause of human enmity with God is sin, which opposes His ways, friendship, fellowship, peace, harmony and communion. It was Christ on the cross who dealt with this acute situation and now we have peace with God through (Gr. *dia*) our Lord Jesus Christ (Rom. 5:1-2; Phil. 5:23). Reflecting on Rom. 5:1-2, John Walvood understands the act of reconciliation as:

> The act of reconciliation in salvation of a believer in Christ is the application of the death of Christ to the individual by the power of the Spirit changing his status from that of condemnation to complete acceptability to God. It reconciles man to God by elevating man to God's level

---

[190] Colosians 1:21-22 (New International Version).

[191] W. E. Vine, *An Expository Dictionary of New Testament Word* (New Jersey: Fleming H. Revell Company 1966), 260 - 61.

[192] 2Corinthians 5:18-20 (New International Version).

[193] Leon Morris, 1965, 250.

[194] Leon Morris, 1978, 133 - 43.

morally and therefore, is far deeper in meaning than reconciliation on the human plane where harmony between parties estranged is often accomplished by compromise.[195]

The act of Christ on the cross is the focal point of God's work of reconciliation. It was out of God's loving nature that He reconciled the world to Himself, not attributing to them their sins (2Cor. 5:19).[196] The result of reconciliation is a person being united back to God and in the body of Christ (1Cor. 12:13) and becoming a new creation in God (2Cor. 5:17-21).

God's redemptive plan was revealed after the fall (Gen. 3:15) and therefore, reconciliation is possible through Jesus Christ. Before reconciliation, the two parties have to do something, that is human sinners have to repent and ask for forgiveness from God and God has to grant forgiveness which is available through nothing else than the finished atonement work of Christ. Both of these two have to come together for reconciliation. Concurring with this idea concept of reconciliation, Peter Forsyth states that:

> Our reconciliation is between person and person. It is not between an order or a process on the one hand and a person on the other. Therefore, a real and deep change of the relation between the two means a change on both sides. That's surely clear if we are dealing with living person. Any reconciliation which only means change of one side is not a real reconciliation at all.[197]

Since God is a personal and eternal being and human sinners are finite beings, reconciliation has to occur between them. Humans must ask for forgiveness from God through repentance of their sins and He responds in forgiving them on the basis of the

---

[195] John F. Walvood, *Jesus Christ Our Lord* (Chicago: Moody Press, 1991), 155 - 56.
[196] J. B. Phillips, *Making Men Whole* (New York: The MacMillan Company, 1953), 41- 42.
[197] Peter Taylor Forsyth, *The Work of Christ* (London: Independent Press LTD. 1958), 75.

sacrificial death of Christ which is already available for all and for whoever needs it (Jn. 3:16). When a person receives forgiveness and is reconciled with God and God is reconciled with the person, the person extends that reconciliation to his neighbors or the community. This is to say that reconciliation has two aspects, with God and with one's neighbors (with other people whom one has sinned against) (Matt. 18:15-20, Lk. 15:17-31, Lk. 19:8-9). When this is done by the sinner and God, the person starts experiencing the presence of God's salvation in his new life in relationship with God and others (2Cor. 5:17). These dynamics of reconciliation are illustrated in Fgure 17 below.

Figure 15. Dynamics of Reconciliation

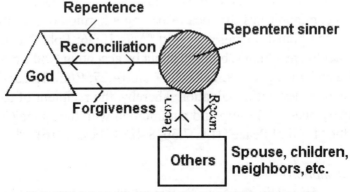

(Luke 19:1-9 Zaccheus, Luke 15:11-32 Prodigal son)

The reconciled person is no longer guilty before God because his sins are forgiven and relationship with God is restored. The person then seeks to reconcile himself with others and acknowledges that, "if anyone says, "I love God," yet hates his brother, he is a liar...whoever love God must love his brother."[198] Reconciliation is two way, and the person who is reconciled with God goes to His neighbors to settle things with them too.

---

[198] 1 John 4:21-22 (New International Version).

142

Adoption

With salvation, the New Testament declares that believers are incorporated in to the family of God (Jn. 1:12-13; Rom. 8:15, Gal. 4:5) through adoption (Gr. Huiothesia). The New Testament root of this term is from huios, - a son, and "thesis," a placing, which holistically signifies the place and condition of a son given to one whom it does not naturally belong.[199]

Peace

The way the New Testament uses the term eirene is some times means "save" (1John, Acts 7:26) and when it is translated "peace," it signifies a harmonious relationship between people (Matt. 10:34; Rom. 14:19), between nations (Lk. 14:32; Acts 12:20, Rev. 6:4), friends (Acts 15:33), freedom from molestation (Lk. 11:21; 19:42; Acts 9:31) and peace as rest (Acts 16:36). It also communicates the idea of having a harmonious relationship between human beings and God (Acts 10:36; Eph. 2:17).[200] It is contentment which is brought about by accepting God's provision, care and guidance (Lk. 1:79, 2:29; Jn. 14:27; Rom. 1:7, 3:17, 8:6). It is one element of salvation whereby, the recipient of salvation experiences fellowship and communion with the triune God who is the "Lord of Peace" (Lk. 7:50, 8:48; 1Thess. 3:16). [201]

Redemption

Basically, the New Testament uses this term for the idea of buying out or buying back (Gr. *agorazo*). It is an act of deliverance (Gal. 3:13, 4:5; Rev. 5:9, 14:3-4).[202] The idea of "buying or purchase" applies to Christians who have been redeemed or bought through the death of Christ (1Cor. 6:20, 7:23; 2Pet. 2:1; Rev. 5:9, 14:3-4). It also means "to buy from" or "to purchase

---

[199] Vine, 31- 32.
[200] W. E. 169 - 70.
[201] Ibid., 170.
[202] Ibid., 263

back" (Gal. 3:13, 4:4).[203] With this idea of "purchasing back," Paul says that, "Christ redeemed (*ezagorazo*) us from the curse of the law by becoming a curse for us ... it is written: cursed is everyone who is hanged on the tree."[204] The Pauline perspective of the term is that believers in Christ were purchased back to Him. They were in sin and are now back to God, where they can fully fellowship and enjoy Him. They are now at peace and harmony with God. God has pardoned their guilt and has accepted them in Christ. It is also to say that God has completely accepted sinners who have believed in Him (Eph. 1:7).[205]

Biblical Way to Salvation

With the gospels and many other New Testament writers, Paul vividly affirms that the gospel is the means to salvation. In 1Cor. 15:1-5, Paul summarizes the gospel and calls it "the gospel by which we are all saved and reconciled to God." This means that the Gospel is the means to salvation. Since the gospel is the means to salvation which is Christ's life, death and His resurrection, Christ is the only Way to Salvation (John 16:6).

Gospel as the Means to Salvation

In 1 Cor. 15:1-5, Paul refers the gospel message that he received from Christ as "the Good News of salvation" for all human beings who are saved by Christ, who is the gospel. The meaning of salvation is the Good News that Jesus incarnated Himself, He came on earth with a human body, died for sinners and resurrected and therefore, sinners have salvation if they repent and have future hope to be with Him in heaven. If the verses 1-5 are paraphrased, they can read as follows:

---

[203]Ibid., 30
[204]Galatians 3:13 (New International Version).
[205]W. E. Vine, *The First and Last* (London: Pickering and Inglis, n.d), 73.

I want to bring back to your memory my brothers and sisters, the message of Good News of your faith that I enthusiastically preached to you at the beginning. This message I carefully and vividly delivered to you (having myself received it from Christ and from the apostles who were before me). This message is the most important, the core of truth. It is this very message that you in turn received from me and relevantly appropriated to yourselves. It is this message which allows you to have standing before God; it is your foundation for faith. It is the message which is the means through (Gr. dia) which you were and are being saved. However, you must keep carefully in mind its content and firmly hold to it but not wavering. This is necessary; otherwise you are pulling out the foundation stone of your faith when you deny the resurrection. I therefore would carefully want to restate this message which I myself received, transmitted it to you such that you were saved and you might do the same for others.

The initial word of v. 3b is "Christ" who is the subject or the person of the message. Specifically, Christ means "Savior." The word Christ implies the incarnation of Christ, the process of liberation which His role involved, and the sinless life which He lived.[206] The verse declares that He died at a specific place and time. Jesus in the gospels vividly mentioned His mission which was to die for sinners (Matt. 16:21; Jn. 10:15-18). The reason why Christ died was, "for our sins (*Gk. huper ton hamartion hemon*) which indicates the meaning of His death. He not only died but, He died for (Gk. *huper*) His people's sins.[207] His sacrificial act was done "in behalf of" mankind.[208]

---

[206] Donald H. Launstein, "The Theological Concept of the Gospel According to St. Paul' (Dissertation, Grace Theological Seminary, 1969), 2.

[207] F. F. Bruce, *1 and 2 Corinthians: New Century Bible* (Greenwood: The Attic Press, 1971), 138.

[208] F. Godet, *Commentary on the First Epistle to the Corinthians 2 v.* (Grand

The preposition *huper* implies "in our place" (Isa. 53) and "because of" human's sin, which indicates the reason why Jesus died. "In our place" signifies that it was an atoning death that Christ died.[209] The epistle to the Hebrews describes the meaning of Christ's death in terms of His priestly function (Heb. 5:1-3, 7:27, 9:7, 10:2). By using the plural form "our" (*ton hamartion*), Paul is reflecting on Isa. 53 where it says, "for our transgressions."[210] The root of this act of sin (*hamartion*) is founded in a perverted and rebellious will that is humans stand in a rebellious attitude against God.[211] The final phrase is repeated in v. 4 in conjunction with Christ's resurrection. "According to the Scriptures" is a phrase that is still an allusion to Isa. 53. His death was in God's will and before it happened it was already prophesied.

The second clause (v. 4a) is introduced by *hoti* this is, *kai hoti etaphe*, "he was buried." Burial here implies the fact that Christ died and His death was officially proved (Isa. 53:9; Matt. 27:58-60; Mk. 15:44-46; Lk. 23:52-53; Jn. 19:38-41). All these verses record the reality of Christ's death which was officially witnessed and sealed by Pilate.

In v. 4b, we see a third *hoti* which deals with resurrection on the third day (*kai hot egegertai te hemera te trite*). The reference to Jesus' death (*kata tas graphas*) is repeated and alluded to in Psa. 16:10; Isa. 53:10-11; Hosea 6:2; Jonah 1:17 and Acts 2:25-32. This clause indicates past action which means resurrection of Christ was a fact, that it was verified. As it is clearly recorded in the four gospels, Jesus was raised to life and many witnessed and saw Him

---

Rapids: Zondervan Publishing Company, 1957), 331.

[209] Leon Morris, *The First Epistle of Paul to the Corinthians: Tyndale Bible Commentaries, New Testament Series, v. 7*

[210] W. E. Vine, *First Corinthians: Local Church Problems* (Grand Rapids: Zondervan: 1961), 203.

[211] George E. Ladd, *A Theology of the New Testament* (Grand Rapids: Eerdmans, 1974), 412-13.

((Matt. 28:5-20; Mk. 16:6-20; Lk. 24:6-53; Jn. 20:1-31).[212]

The other *hoti* in v. 5a talks about Christ's appearances, which provide more evidence for His resurrection.[213] In the same way that Christ's burial is mentioned as proof of His death, the appearances of Christ are given as evidence for His resurrection. If Christ therefore, did not die for our sins, there could be no remission of sins. There would be no way human beings could go back to God (Jn. 1:29; Rom. 3:25, 5:9, Eph. 1:7; Col. 1:20; Heb. 9:12, 9:22; Rev. 1:5, 5:9). His death procured our salvation, which is life with God, enjoying fellowship with Him, His communion with us, harmony, peace, acceptance and being reconciled with Him and with one another. The message of salvation is therefore, that Jesus Christ died to do away with human sins that whoever will accept Him will not eternally be separated from God but will spend eternity with Him. The other fact of the gospel is that, He not only died, but he was buried, resurrected, appeared to many, ascended into heaven where He is continuing in His saving work, and He will return to establish the Millennial Kingdom where all believers in Him will live and reign with the Triune God (Rev. 19:11-16, 20:1-15; 21; 22).

Christ as the only Way to Salvation

Summarizing, God in Christ is the source of human salvation. The Old Testament sacrifices and offerings were types of the coming Savior, Jesus Christ. Christ is the only way to God and through His death, whoever repents of sin and confesses before God is accepted, and reconciled back to Him. The way to God is exclusive in that, besides the death of Christ there is no other way to Him. God has exclusively provided the only absolute Way to His salvation.

---

[212] Ibid., 413.
[213] Leon Morris, V. 7, 205.

Right from the Old Testament, God has declared that there is only one way to reconcile human beings back to Himself, "I, even I, am the Lord, and apart from me there is no Savior."[214] Along with this verse, in the gospels, in Acts, and also in Pauline epistles, there is also an exclusive message:

I (Jesus) am the way, the truth, and the life. No one comes to the Father except through me" (Jn. 16:6). At Sanhedrin, Peter affirmed that, "Neither is there salvation in any other, for there is no other Name under heaven given among men by whom we must be saved" (Acts 4:12). John the apostle solemnly expressed only two options (3:36), "He who believes in the Son has everlasting life; and he who does not believe the Son shall not see life, but the wrath of God abodes on him.[215]

These statements discount any other way to salvation except through Jesus Christ. "Salvation is not cosmic such that, all non-Christian religions of the world can share in it."[216] Christ is the only Way, and beside Him there is no salvation at all.

God has provided Jesus as the only Savior; and only His death and blood can wash away human sins. Christ was the only one who was sinless, and therefore He was the qualified only one to die and purchase our salvation. Since the other actors in "salvation" among the Bantu people were sinners, how could they have provided salvation for other sinners? Christ is the only one who had no sin. He was born without sin and was free from sin in all aspects of His life. He is God's Son and possesses God's holy attributes. He is the only one who could die on our behalf (Isa. 53:6). His death provided the only absolute Way. Through His death and resurrection; salvation is achievable. With this biblical

---

[214] Isaiah 43:11 (New International Version).

[215] Stanley A. Ellisen, *"Are the Lost without Christ Really Lost*?" Conservative Baptist Pamphlet, 1983.

[216] "Class notes," Presbyterian Theological Seminary (Seoul - Korea), Fall 1994.

conviction that Jesus Christ is the only unique and qualified Savior of the sinful world, Norman Douty notes that:

> Accordingly, Christ is termed the Savior of the world (Jn. 4:42; 1 Jn. 4:14), that is potentially so. The Father sent Him in the world that the world should be saved through Him (Jn. 3:17). While here, He was the light of the world (Jn. 8:12; 9:5), and expressed a desire that the world should know His love for and obedience to the Father (Jn. 14:31); that it might believe and know that the Father had sent Him (Jn. 17:21, 23).... God gave Christ that anyone in the world might not perish but have everlasting life (Jn. 3:16). This was the Lamb of God who took away the sin of the world (Jn. 1:29) by becoming a propitiation for our sins; but not our only but also for the whole world.[217]

It is Christ that believers are joined with by His death. Through His death and resurrection, He paid for our sin, which was credited to Him, and He forgave us. How then can the world have another savior? Christ is the absolute Savior; He obeyed unto death, so as to redeem the sinful world (Phil. 2:1ff).

The Bible declares emphatically that Jesus Christ is the only Way to salvation, the only Savior of the world, and that the world needs no other savior at all. Stanley Ellisen affirms conclusively:

> [Christ's] offer of salvation is universal, inviting all to come freely.... The Bible declares that His provision of propitiation, ransom, and reconciliation was made for the entire world (1 Jn. 2:2; 1 Tim. 2:6; 2 Cor. 5:19). Paul argued that, "God has included them all in unbelief that He might have mercy on all." Therefore, His mercy is extended to all.[218]

---

[217] Norman F. Douty, *Union with Christ* (Swengel: Reiner Publication, 1973), 94.
[218] Stanley A. Ellisen, 3.

Chapter 5

THEOLOGICAL MEANING OF SALVATION

Both the Old and New Testaments clearly teach that a divine motive of salvation is God's love for sinners and His ultimate desire to restore fellowship with them. Out of His very nature, the holy and loving Father has given for His estranged creatures His final and ultimate sacrificial gift, the life, death and resurrection of Jesus Christ.

This chapter adopts narrative evangelism as a way of presenting the meaning of the theological doctrine of salvation, respecting the Holy Scriptures as understood by many evangelical churches, tracing the meaning of salvation from Bible history. Salvation encloses the concepts of atonement, conversion, forgiveness, deliverance and new life in Christ. The theological meaning of salvation is union with Christ, and the believers experience includes a profound sense of assurance that one is eternally saved.

Salvation as History

Zwingli, the Protestant reformer, summarized the doctrine of salvation:

> Salvation is by faith alone. One is only free from sin when his mind trusts itself unwaveringly to the death

of Christ and finds rest there, that faith is born only when a person begins to despair of himself and to see that it is perfected when a person wholly cast himself off and prostrates himself before the mercy of God alone, but in such fashion as to have entire trust in it because of Christ who was given for us.[219]

In Zwingli's expression, we can deduce a few things such as: salvation is life with God through Christ, it is by faith, one has to recognize his or her sinful condition and desire to be delivered, one has to trust God for deliverance, that this life is perfected only by God through trusting Him and salvation is through Christ who died for us. The basis for salvation is God's grace and love towards a sinner. In the study of salvation, there is the love and the grace of God, the sinner and his or her sin and the solution of sin that was provided by Christ on the cross. In his salvation sermon, John Wesley (1703-1791) described salvation as:

> The salvation which is here spoken of is not what is frequently understood by that word, the going to heaven, eternal happiness. It is not the soul's going to paradise, termed by our Lord, "Abraham's bosom." It is not a blessing which lies on the other side of death, or (as we usually speak) in the other world. The very word of the text itself put this beyond all question. "You are saved." It is not something at a distance: it is a present thing, a blessing which, though the free mercy of God, you are now in possession of. Nay, the word may be rendered, and that with equal propriety, "you have been saved." So that the salvation which is here spoken of might be extended to the entire work of God, from the first dawning of grace in the soul till it is consummated in glory.[220]

---

[219] Kenneth Latourette, *A History of Christianity, Vol. II._*(Harper and Row, 1975), 749.
[220] *Tabor Heights United Methodist Trinity Sunday Worship Bulletin,* "Sermons of

Besides church historians' view of salvation, the Bible has its clear historical record of salvation. From the New Testament point of view, the gospel writers, apostles in Acts and the apostle Paul view the death of Christ not as a tragic accident of history but as a fulfillment of God's plan in history, thus it was according to the Old Testament Scriptures (Gk. *kata tas graphas*) (John 19:24 alludes to Ps. 22:18, Lk. 22:37 alludes to Isa. 53:1-12, Mk. 15:27 alludes to Isa. 53:12 and Ps. 22:1, and 1Cor.15:3-5 alludes to Isa. 53). All these passages see the death of Jesus as historically ordained so that sinners may be reconciled with God and with one another.

In His writing, the apostle Paul insists that the death of Jesus which provided salvation was an absolute necessity, without which there is no solution for the sinner, no matter what his social or religious privileges might be. It is God who historically destined Jesus to be a sacrificed for our sin (Rom. 3:25). It is God who made Him to be sin who knew no sin, in order that we in Him might be clothed with the righteousness of God (2Cor. 5:21). The crucifixion of Christ is the tangible proof of the measure of God's love for sinners (Rom. 5:8). It is the expression "par excellence" of the extraordinary wisdom of God (1 Cor. 1:24). It is "according to the Scriptures" (not according to the order of Pilate and Jews) that Jesus died (1 Cor. 15:3).

The gospels too, (and Jesus Himself) understand the death to be in accordance with the will of God, and not simply the incidental end-result of the conflict with the Pharisees and their religious system of the day. Even less was it due to the treachery of His disciple Judas or the weakness of the Roman governor. His death was the fulfillment of what was historically prophesied in the Scriptures, (He had to suffer) (Luke 24:25-27, 46). This necessity, expressed in Greek by the particle *dei* (through) rings again and again as Jesus foretold His approaching death. Fully realizing what awaited Him in Jerusalem, Jesus sets His face to go there (Luke

John Wesley," June 15, 2003.

9:51), and when one of His disciples tried to dissuade Him from going the way of the cross, Jesus replied with exceptionally strong language (Mark 8:33). Jesus seemed almost preoccupied in the gospels with the necessity of His death (Mark8: 31, 9:31, 10:33). The fourth gospel is entirely in agreement "No one takes my life from me, but I lay it down of my own accord. I have authority to lay it down and the authority to take it up again. This command I received from my Father."[221] Jesus had come to do the will of His Father, and in the garden of Gethsemane He deliberately aligned Himself with that will, namely to drink the cup of suffering and death which the Father had prepared for Him. Indeed it was for this only reason that He had come on earth.

It is therefore, on the necessity and basis of God's grace and love that our salvation was historically and divinely ordained. Grace here means "love in God which is free and unpurchased, coming out of its own accord to bless undeserved." [222] The grace of God is His unmerited favor. It is favor that none can deserve or buy. Grace in Hebrew is "hen" and in Greek is *Charis* which also means affordable joy, pleasure, delight, acceptance, good will and favor.[223] The complete meaning of this is that the salvation of human beings historically originated from the free will and loving favor of God. God saves people because of His love but not on the basis of their goodness. In his understanding of salvation history, Tokunboh Adeyemo describes it as the grace of God rooted in Christ. To him salvation is a personal and a singular dimension toward reconciliation with God and with mankind. He affirms this by stating that:

> Salvation is holistic: body, mind, soul and spirit. It is both vertical and horizontal. The one who is reconciled

---

[221] John 10:18 (New International Version).
[222] H. Orton Willey & Paul T. Culbertson, *Introduction to Christian Theology* (Kansa City: Beacon Hill Press of Kansas, 1994), 261.
[223] McDanald, 78-84.

with God is sent to his world, to his neighbor and to his community to live out a righteous, holy and just life in the power of the Holy Spirit. All of these is by God's grace, total unmerited, un- earnable and undeserved. Christ has finished it, all that man does is not man trying to reach God; but God reaching down and out to man. It is full and free.[224]

The history of God's grace for salvation can be viewed in two aspects: common and special. The common grace is God's kindness towards all human beings in spite of their sin. Common grace does not deal with salvation, but it is God's goodness to all sinful people. It restores to each person the ability to respond favorably to God (Rom. 2:4). The special grace of God draws people to Christ (Jn. 6:44), renews their hearts and sets them free from sin. Willey and Culbertson talk about special grace as:

> It is the grace that goes before, preparing the soul for its entrance into the initial state of salvation. It is the preparatory grace of the Holy Spirit exercised toward man helpless in sin. As respects the guilt, it may be considered mercy; as it respects the impotent, it is enabling power. It is that manifestation of the divine influence which precedes the full regeneration. [225]

It was historically on the ground of God's grace that Christ came so that through His death, He would restore peace between God and sinners, provide wholeness, as well and provide sinners with unmerited restoration and favor with God. Through this special grace, there are some benefits which go with salvation such as, sinners are declared not guilty before God, they are given abundant life and the gift of righteousness (Rom. 5:17), they have eternal life, comfort and hope (2Thess. 2:16).

---

[224] Tokunboh Adeyemo. *"Concept of Salvation", East Africa Journal for Evangelical Theology* (EAJET) 2:1, 1983.
[225] Willy & Culbertson, 261.

If salvation started in the mind of God and thereafter was actualized through Christ, then, what is it? Salvation can be defined as physical and spiritual. In the physical sense which historically dominates the Old Testament, salvation is being taken from danger to safety (Dan. 6:20; Phil. 1:19), from disease to health (Jam. 5:15) and from death to life (Jam. 5:20). In the spiritual aspect which mostly dominates the New Testament, it refers to deliverance of human beings from their sinful condition to a life and love relationship with God and to other people.[226] The spiritual aspect of salvation recognizes that sin has separated humans from God's fellowship, harmony and peace, and has caused people to be corrupt to one another. As summed up in 2Cor. 1:10, "who delivered us (past) from such a great peril, and does deliver (present) in whom we trust that he will (future) yet deliver us," this spiritual aspect of salvation has three dimensions. In its past aspect, it is when a person believes in God's work through Jesus Christ, confesses his or her sin to Him is declared righteous before the holy God. At the present, a believer in Christ is saved and also being saved from power of sin. In its future aspect, a believer will be saved from sin, have eternal life with God in heaven (Rom. 13:11; 1Pet. 1:9).[227]

Trying to define salvation from Romans where Paul says that, "I am not ashamed of the gospel because it is the power of God for the salvation of everyone who believes,"[228] Thomas Simmons states that:

> The Hebrew words for salvation imply the ideas of deliverance, safety, preservation, healing and soundness. Salvation is the great inclusive word of the gospel, gathering itself all the redemptive acts and processes: as justification, redemption, grace, propitiation, forgiveness, sanctification and glorification. Salvation therefore, in its broad sense, has to do with both the soul and the body, with the present life

---

[226] Earl D. Radmacher, *Salvation* (Nashville: Word Publishing, 2000), 5.

[227] Ibid., 6.

[228] Romans 1:16 (New International Version).

as well as with the future life. It has reference, not only to the remission of sin's penalty and removal of its guilt, but also to the conquering of the power of sin and to the final removal of the presence of sin from the body. [229]

Simply, salvation is life in Christ which was historically offered by God and presently achieved as a result of trusting and accepting Christ as Savior and Lord of one's life. It does not only involve our spiritual deliverance from sin but also our physical deliverance from social problems (sometimes) like diseases. Salvation is a process as well as an event, in that it has past, present and future. It is the work of God in us: we are conformed into the image of His Son (Rom. 8:29). The one who is saved (has received salvation) should seek to continue being in Christ in the present, continue reflecting His righteousness, continue obeying Him, continue being transformed into the image of Christ, implicitly desire to please Him and finally be with Him in heaven.

Considering the general historical meaning of salvation from the two Testaments, Charles Chafer describes it as:

> The word communicates the thought of deliverance, safety, preservation, soundness, restoration and healing; but though so wide a range of human experience is expressed by the word salvation, its specific, major use is to denote a work of God in behalf of man ... to be saved is to be rescued from a lost estate, while on the other hand, to be saved is to be brought into a saved state, vitally renewed, renewed, and made meet to be a partaker of the inheritance of the saints in light. It may warn the wicked to flee from the wrath to come, or it may woo them by the contemplation of those benefits which God's infinite grace provides.[230]

---

[229] Thomas Paul Simmons, *A Systematic Study if Bible Doctrine: A logical Arrangement and a Diligent Treatment of the Teaching of God's Holy Word* (Russell:, n.p., 1955), 329.

[230] Lewis Sperry Chafer, *Systematic Theology*, 5.

Salvation is deliverance from sin, which has permeated the whole person that is his thoughts, attitudes and actions. Human beings are holistically sinful. There is not even one aspect of human beings that is righteous and therefore, salvation is that deliverance and meditorial work of Christ that saves human beings from guilt and the penalty of sin.[231] If salvation is being saved and rescued from sin, the only way of this rescue is through the act of atonement which was done once for all by Jesus Christ, the High Priest.

Salvation as Atonement

Since salvation was provided by Jesus Christ through His death on the cross, it was therefore a good example of an Old Testament act of atonement. One might ask this question: Was the atonement of Christ necessary for the salvation of sinners? In order to answer this question, we should first trace what Jesus said about His death in such statements as:

> My Father, if it is possible let this cup pass from me; nevertheless, not my will but your will be done (Matt. 2:39). The Son of man must suffer ... and be rejected and killed and afterward, He will be raised again (Mark 8:31, Luke 9:22). As Moses lifted up the serpent in the wilderness, even the Son of Man must be lifted up (John 3:14). Without the shedding of blood, there is no remission of sin (Heb.9: 1). [232]

Adding to the above verses, John the gospel writer in 1:29, 3:16; 1 John 2:2 indicates that the atoning death of Christ made it possible for the holy God to forgive sin. This happened when Jesus died on the cross for all human beings so that God would be just and at the same time be the justifier of whoever believes in Him (Rom. 3:26). This also affirms that the death of Jesus was

---

[231] A. W. Pink, *The Doctrine of Salvation* (Grand Rapids: Baker Book House, 1975), 9.

[232] *Bible* (New International Version).

essential for the forgiveness of human sin. Thiessen concurs with this by noting that:

> The Son of man must be lifted up if man is to be saved (Jn. 12:24). God cannot pardon sin merely on the ground of the sinner's repentance. He can pardon only when the penalty is first paid.... Christ paid the sinner's penalty (Rom. 3:25ff). Paul sought to prove to the Thessalonians the necessity of Christ's death (Acts 17:3). From God's stand point, the death of Christ is an absolute necessity if man is to be saved.[233]

Since it was necessary for Christ to atone for our sins, we will not have to die for them. "God could not and would not be holy and just if He let Christ pay the price for our sins on the cross and then made us pay for them."[234] In their confession of faith, churches in the United States of America agree with the Bible's affirmation that Christ's death was necessary to redeem all mankind by saying:

> We confess that in the execution of Jesus Christ, the sin of the human race reached its depth. The only innocent One was condemned and put to death, not by the sinfulness of one nation, but by the sinfulness for all of us. We believe in the death of Jesus on the cross God achieved and demonstrated once for all the costly forgiveness of our sins. Jesus Christ is the reconciler between God and the world. He acted on behalf of sinners as one of us, accepting God's condemnation of our sinfulness.[235]

The above affirmation indicates that when Christ died on the cross, He by the grace of God tasted death for every human (Heb.2:9). He removed the sting of death from us (1Cor. 15:55).

---

[233] Thiessen, 231.

[234] Homer Duncan (Ed), *Heart to Heart Talking with Mormons* (Texas: Missionary Crusader, 1972), 97.

[235] Lukas Vischer, *Reformed Witness Today* (Seoul: PTS, 1982), 282.

His death destroyed Satan's work and the power of death. Through His atoning death, He delivered them who through fear of death were subject to bondage (Heb. 2:14-15). In God's giving His Son to die for sinners, He demonstrated and proved His love for them (Jn. 3:16). Through Christ's atoning death, God can give salvation as a free gift to all who believe in Christ and ask for forgiveness of their sins. It was very necessary therefore for Christ to die for all.

In his studies on atonement, Robert Morey contributes toward the necessity of the atonement:

> Once God freely decided out of His sovereign electing love to save sinners, there was but one way of bringing about His desired salvation which would be in harmony with God ... , the law of God, the nature of sin and the need of man ... This one way was by the substitutionary blood of His incarnate Son Jesus Christ.[236]

Morey explicitly has indicated to us that the nature and character of God necessitated Christ's atonement for the human beings and therefore, His death was the only absolute one that was in harmony with God's moral characters. Since justice is one of God's characters, it was necessary for a perfect and proper substitute that did not have sin of His own to bear the full punishment of sin in the place of sinners. It was only God Himself who would offer a perfect and proper substitutionary sacrifice for human sins so that the sinners would be acceptable in His sight.[237]

The Bible clearly says that the Old Testament sacrifices of animals could not absolutely atone for human sin (Heb. 9:26, 10:4); neither could angels (Heb. 2:14), nor could man have done it, because he is a sinner (Ps. 49:7-8). Jesus Christ alone would be the only fitting High Priest because He is holy, innocent, undefiled, separated from sinners and exalted above the heavens (Heb. 7:26).

---

[236] Robert, A. Morey, *Studies in the Atonement* (USA: Crown Publishing Company Inc. 1989), 9.

[237] Ibid., 11.

The sinlessness of the substitute was necessary for, "God made Him who knew no sin to be sin on our behalf that we might become the righteousness of God in Him."[238] The death of Christ was necessary because it was His death alone that would satisfy the demands of God's righteousness (Romans 3:24-26). God's holiness too necessitated Christ's atonement so as to remove human sins and impart God's perfect holiness in them (Exod. 15:10). The separation of human beings from God because of sin required perfect atonement so that they would be reconciled with Him.

By nature, sin provokes God's anger and creates enmity between Him and sinners (Ezek. 18:4, Rom.: 23, Ps. 11:4, 7). It is by nature that sin makes us unreliable and diserving of the death penalty. Our needs that sin created necessitated an atonement that will satisfy them. Since human beings are spiritually dead (Eph. 2), they need regeneration (John. 3:3). Since human beings are by nature defiled by sin (Ezek. 22:11), they need sanctification because they are slaves of sin (John 8:34). It is only through the atonement of Christ that sanctification, reconciliation and justification are attained.

Atonement is seen both in the Old and New Testament originating with God. The Old Testament sacrifices for sin were instituted by God and in the New Testament; God gave His Son to die as an ultimate sacrifice. Animal sacrifices were only a shadow of what Christ would do in the New Testament. God Himself initiated salvation through His Son Jesus; He reconciled humans with Himself (1Cor. 5:19). It was in His ultimate love that God gave us Jesus Christ to redeem us from our sins (John 3:16; Romans 5:8).

Concurring with the above historical necessity of the atonement, Charles Horne adds other reasons:

1.   God's holiness will not allow Him to simply overlook sin;

---

[238] 2Corinthians 5:21 (New International Version).

His justice must be maintained (Ex. 34:6-7; Numb. 14:18; Rom. 3:25-26).

2.   The immutability of the divine law, as reflective of God's very nature, made it necessary for Him to demand satisfaction of the sinner (Deut. 27:26).

3.   The truthfulness of God requires atonement (Numb. 23:19; Rom. 3:4). In the garden, God had declared that death would be the penalty of disobedience (Gen. 3:16-17; Ezek.18:4; Rom. 6:23). The veracity of God demands that this penalty should be executed on either the offender or a substitute.

4.   The inestimable cost of this sacrifice implies the necessity of the atonement. It is scarcely conceivable that God would have done this unnecessarily (Lk. 24:26, Gal. 3:21; Heb. 2:10; 9:23-25).[239]

    Since God is holy, He would have not allowed the existence of sin without punishing it. Because human beings deserved God's punishment, His love for them was so great that, He gave His only Son to die in their place. Before the atonement, a sinner stands guilty before God. He is alienated from Him, under His curse and wrath and is in the bondage of sin. After the atonement, a separated sinner has a new relationship with God and can fully enjoy fellowship with Him. Because of its necessity, the atonement of Christ reconciles us with God for He takes our sins and puts them on Himself, so that we may stand as righteous before God (2Cor. 5:21).[240] The apostle Paul gives us reasons why the atonement was necessary, "God made Him (Christ) who had no sin to be sin (or a sin offering) for us, so that in Him we might become the righteousness of God."[241]

    "Christ died for our sins" (1Cor. 15:3) and "He gave

---

[239] Charles M. Horne, 24-25.

[240] Ibid., 39.

[241] 2Corinthians 5:21 (New International Version).

Himself for us" (Eph. 5:2). "For us" and "for our" sins means that the atonement of Christ was necessary, for it was both sacrificial for us and a substitutionary on our behalf or in place of us. H. McDonald summarizes Christ's atonement:

> It was a sacrifice at its Fullness: "offered Himself."
> It was a sacrifice at its Holiest: "unblemished"(Heb. 7:26).
> It was a sacrifice at its Costliest: "the blood of Christ" (Heb. 9:22). It was a sacrifice at its most Divine: "through the eternal Spirit" (Heb. 7:16). It was a sacrifice at its Fittest: "cleanse our consciences from acts that lead to death, so that we may serve the living God" (Heb. 10"2).[242]

Salvation as Conversion

For salvation to occur in a person's life there must be conversion. Repentance, faith and confession are necessities on the human side if forgiveness from God is to be granted and salvation to be given. When these are in place, conversion is experienced. When the person willingly does these, then he is saved. These human requirements are not solely the cause of God's forgiveness but are to be demonstrated on the human side. The cause of God's forgiveness is His nature, that is, out of His love and mercy, He forgives sinners. However, one has to petition God, through those "conditional" moral acts. These are distinct human responsibilities that God demands, though they don't thwart His nature of forgiveness. Affirming these human acts towards God's forgiveness, especially on repentance Donald Bloesch states:

> Forgiveness is both an attitude and action. God's forgiveness is for all, but the way it is carried out, the way it becomes effective, differs according to the response of the hearer. Yet the response of the hearer by no means

---

[242] H. D. McDonald, *Forgiveness and Atonement* (Grand Rapids: Baker Book House, 1984), 129-31.

creates the divine forgiveness but instead bears witness to it. God's forgiveness does not bear fruit except through man's decision and repentance....[243]

According to God's demands, before He reconciles Himself with a sinner, one must first repent (by faith) of his sin before Him. Repentance comes after acknowledging that one is a sinner and accepting the atonement work of Christ on the cross for his or her sins. God requires a genuine, deep and sincere repentance before He would forgive any sin. Repentance is vital act for salvation just as faith is. "Except you repent, you shall all perish."[244] "Then God has granted gentiles repentance to life."[245] Affirming that the theme of all gospels as the call to repentance, Padilla says:

> The gospel is always proclaimed in opposition to an organized lie - the great lie that man realized himself by pretending to be God, in autonomy from God; that his life consists in the things he possesses; that he lives for himself alone and is the owner of his destiny.... The gospel involves a call to repent from this lie. The relation between the gospel and repentance is such that preaching the gospel is equivalent to preaching "repentance and forgiveness of sin" (Lk. 24:47) or to testifying "of repentance to God and of faith in our Lord Jesus Christ" (Acts 20:21). Without this call to repentance there is no gospel ... repentance involves. but a change of attitude, a restructuring of one's scale of values, a reorientation of the whole of one's personality. It is not simply giving up habits condemned by a moralistic ethic but rather laying down the weapons of rebellion against God in order to return to Him. [246]

---

[243] Donald G. Bloesch, *Essentials of Evangelical Theology Vol. 1* (San Francisco: Harper and Row, 1978), 164.

[244] Luke 13:3 (New International Version).

[245] Acts 11:18 (New International Version).

[246] Padilla, 19.

Repentance and faith go together and are followed by confession. One cannot truly repent without faith, and there is no saving faith without repentance. For a sinner to experience conversion, repentance and faith go together, and we cannot separate one from the other. Wayn Grudem describes their relationship as follows:

> Scripture puts repentance and faith together as different aspects of the one act of coming to Christ for salvation. It is not that a person first turns from sin and next trusts in Christ, or first trust in Christ and then turn from sin, but rather that both occur at the same time. When we turn to Christ for salvation from our sins, we are simultaneously turning away from the sins that we are asking Christ to save us from. If that were not true, our turning to Christ for salvation from sin could hardly be a genuine turning to Him or trusting in Him.[247]

Lewis Chafer too describes the relation of these two as:

> The problem, then, is to regard repentance and faith as different elements, not as two different aspects of one element. Repentance should not be thought as a separate step toward salvation.... Repentance is essential for salvation and that none could be saved apart from repentance, but it is included in believing by faith and could not be separated from it....[248]

In an understandable sense, we should therefore regard repentance and faith as two different aspects and conditions that go together in the converted sinner to accomplish one act of achieving salvation. If the gospel of salvation calls a sinner to lay down all the weapons of his rebellion against God so that he can freely go back to Him by repentance, faith and confession, what then is the meaning of each of these three aspects?

---

[247] Wayn Grudem, *Systematic Theology*, 713.
[248] Lewis Sperry Chafer, *Salvation: God's Marvelous work of Grace* (Grand Rapids: Kregel Publiction, 1991), 373 - 76.

Repentance

Repentance is an act that is clearly explained both in the Old and New Testaments. In the Old Testament, the prophets were sent by God to ask people to repent otherwise they may face His wrath. Repentance was also the message of Jesus, John the Baptist, the gospel writers, the apostle Paul and other New Testament writers.

Repentance in the OT

In the Old Testament, the term "repent" (Hebrew - *naham*) is found in such verses like Numb. 23:19, "God is not a man that He should lie, neither the son of man that he should repent." "The Strength of Israel will not lie nor repent ... "(1Sam. 15:29). These and other verses use the term "repent" to mean a "change of mind." Repentance is a realization of the sinfulness of sin.[249] A person forms a new decision in view of his or her sinful condition and has deep sorrow over those sins which he or she knows will lead him or her to destruction. The person deeply seeks to forsake and rectify the situation. All these steps are done by the help of the Holy Spirit who usually convinces a sinner of his sins. In an illustrative way, Payne describes repentance as, "true repentance involves a man's admission of his sins, his feelings of sorrow, and his decision to turn from a life of sin to a life that is dedicated to God."[250]

Going back to the actual Old Testament definition of *naham* which is translated as repentance, Payne describes it as, "to be sorry, to console oneself and to have compassion. It also means to be sorry, to grieve, to grieve of ill done that is, a change of mind about something."[251] Craig Nelson also views Repentance in the Old Testament and says that *naham*,

---

[249] Pink, 47.
[250] J. B. Payne, *The Theology of the Older Testament* (Grand Rapids: Zondervan Publishing House, 1962), 297.
[251] Ibid., 636.

Is commonly translated "repent," but more properly means "to be sorry for" something or for having done something. This regret frequently involves a change of mind regarding the future as well as the past, and this, rather than the feeling by which it is prompted, is often the import of the word. But, however the element of a change of purpose may represent in the use of the verb, the primary sense of "to be sorry for" is always present.[252]

If the verb *naham* stands as a regular verb, with the normal Hebrew translation, the writer translates it to mean, "He was sorry, He repented, He grieved or He turned." The reason for this way of translating *naham* is because the Hebrew regular verbs have no present tense and they (verbs) are translated with past tense. For example if Hebrew *L (prefix)* is fixed to *naham* which is *lanaham*, it means "to repent" or "to grieve."[253] Whatever way *naham* is translated, it conveys a change of attitude. In the same usage of *naham* for repentance, Nelson feels that *naham* has dual usage especially in the LXX (Greek translation of the OT - Septuagint) such that:

"*Metanoein*" means a change of heart either generally or in respect of a specific sin, whereas "metamelesthai" means to experience remorse. "Metanoein" implies that one has later arrived at a different feeling about it. But it is easy for the two ideas to come together and even marge, since a change of view often carries with it an uncomfortable feeling.[254]

In the Old Testament, *naham* (repent or I repented) involves the whole person that is, his will, intellect and emotions. By intellect, the person has to exactly know and acknowledge that he is a sinner and that he should turn from his sins. Self-realization

---

[252] Craig W. Nelson, Microfilm.
[253] Hebrew I "Class Lecture," North Park Theological Seminary, Fall 2001.
[254] Crag W. Nelson, Microfilm.

and recognition especially of the danger of sin should be there. A sinner has to recognize that he is under God's wrath because of the sinful state he is in.

In Ps. 51:3a, David recognized that he was a sinner for he knew his transgressions, *ki pesaay ani eda* (for or because I know my transgressions). This shows that before repentance, there is knowledge of what one is changing his mind from or turning from. It means knowing that one is a sinner, and that the sin will cause grief, and seeing the need to take the step of turning away from it and turn elsewhere. By the Hebrew term, *ani eda,*[255] it stresses the fact that David himself (ani - I) "knew" (*yadah* - know, knew) that he had sinned against God. He recognized the nature of his sin which he had committed and therefore, through the help of Nathan, he turned away from it to God with confession. David knew and was very conscious how dangerous it would be to cover or conceal that sin. In the emotional aspect of repentance, it is when a sinner takes a step of hating that sin, grieving over it and deciding to turn from it to God. Knowledge of sin comes first, and grieving over sin comes second.[256]

From knowledge and grief over sin, then the will has to be involved. A sinner has to genuinely and deeply make a choice of turning from sin towards God (Jer. 25:5). Jeremiah urged the people of Israel who were in captivity to, "turn now, each of you, from your evil ways and your evil practices."[257] Through an act of the will the person turns from sin and its practices. After turning away from it, Hosea says that, "come, let us return to Yahweh... He will heal us (*venasubah el Adonah*)."[258] In turning from sins, the person has to turn or return to God. When this turn is complete, then the person can confess and ask for forgiveness from God and

---

[255] Hebrew Bible, 1958.

[256] Craig W. Nelson, Microfilm.

[257] Jeremiah 25:5 (New International Version).

[258] Hosea 6:1 (New International Version).

experience conversion. By summing the turns in repentance, King Solomon prayed for the Israelites as:

> If they have a change of heart in the land where they are held captive, and repent and plead with you in the land of their conquerors and say, we have sinned, we have done wrong, we have acted wickedly; and if they turn back to you with all their heart and soul in the land of their enemies who took them captive, and pray to you toward the land you gave their fathers, toward the city you have chosen and the temple I have built for your Name; ... hear their prayers.... And forgive your people, they have sinned against you; forgive all the offenses they have committed against you and cause their conquerors to show them mercy.[259]

Repentance in NT

Describing the New Testament meaning of repentance, Radmacher state that "the verb "repentance" (Gk. *metanoia*) ...*metanoeo* is composed of *meta* (after) and *noea* (to think or perceive); thus its basic meaning is "to perceive afterward." The common meaning of the noun *metanoia*, then is a "change of mind."[260]

Most of the New Testament passages that talk about repentance are in reference to sin. People are either called to repent of their sins so that they may approach God or are commanded to repent or face punishment (2Cor. 12:21; Rev. 9:20-21). By repenting of their sins, people are called to change their attitudes toward sin (hate or abandon sin), rectify their spiritual and moral attitude before God so that He may rekindle His relationship with them.[261] In his understanding of the New Testament usage of the term "repentance," R. Moyer defines it as:

---

[259] 1Kings 8:47-50 (New International Version).
[260] Radmacher, 131.
[261] Ibid., 131.

Repentance clearly means to change the mind. In salvation contexts, repentance either implies faith or is associated with faith. Therefore, when used in a Soteriological context, repentance means to change one's mind about whatever is keeping one from trusting Christ and trust Him as the only means of salvation... Once an individual has changed his or her mind about whatever is keeping him from trusting Christ and trust Him for salvation, both faith and repentance have taken place.[262]

According to R. Moyer's perception of repentance, it is to change one's mind from sin and turn toward God. With a view of turning, John Murray describes repentance as: "Repentance unto life is a saving grace, whereby a sinner out of a true sense of his sin and apprehension of the mercy of God in Christ doth with grief and hatred of his sin, turn from it unto God, with full purpose and endeavor after new obedience."[263] Best traces the term repentance from the New Testament and interchangeably uses it with the term "conversion." He describes repentance as,

Repentance is the act of man, by the power of the indwelling Spirit, in repenting and believing, " turn thou to me, and I shall be turned; for thou art the Lord my God. Surely after that, I was turned, I repented and after that I was structured... (Jer. 31:18-19). In repentance, a person has an experience of turning to God. Repentance . . . is always an awareness of what is taking place; therefore, it is experimental. Repentance is the act of turning to Jesus after the heart is opened. In repentance, the power is not of us but in us by God's sovereign choice.[264]

---

[262] R Larry Moyer, *Free and Clear: Understanding and Communicating God's offer of Eternal life* (Grand Rapids: Kregel Publication, 1997), 92.

[263] John Murray, *Redemption Accomplished and Applied* (Grand Rapids: Eerdmans Publishing Company, 1987), 113.

[264] W. E. Best, *Regeneration and Conversion* (Houston: South Belt Grace Church, 1975), 33 - 34.

According to Best's definition of repentance, he sees it as an inner work of the Holy Spirit in a person who makes a definite choice of turning from sins to God. When a person accepts the conviction, he or she makes genuine turn from sin to Jesus' substitutionary death, by faith trust that it is the only way to salvation and to be reconciled with God. With the same view of repentance that is, turning from sin to Jesus, H. McDonald contributes as follows:

> It is a turning from our sins, and turning to our God.... Repentance as taught by Jesus is a radical revolution in one's view of God and in one's relation to Him; it is a total change of attitude in regard to Him. It is an inward decision to turn from sin to God; thus it is a life-shaking and soul-shattering revolt. It is an altering of one's view of God which carries with it a heartfelt sorrow for and confession of wrong done. The result is a decisive turning to God and His righteousness.[265]

With the above view of repentance, it is a genuine act of a sinner whereby, he or she turns away from sin, from an evil life, turns to Christ and seeks to follow Him faithfully as His authentic disciple. It is turning from sin which is always in opposition to Christ's work on the cross. It is decisively making a deep heartfelt turn (in his knowledge, feelings, attitudes, consciences, volition of the will and emotions) to Jesus, and by faith accepting Him as a personal Savior and Lord of his life.

As the writer has already noted, the New Testament Greek word for repentance *metanoeo* has a relevant meaning with Hebrew verb *naham*. Using *metanoeo*, which is sorrow over sin, one cannot change his or her mind and still keep on enjoying sin, otherwise the person, has to completely abandon it. Both *metanoeo* and *naham* express the action of complete change of a sinner's mind, will and is expressed by deep and painful emotions that lead

---

[265] H. D. McDonald, *Forgiveness and Atonement*, 101 - 102.

to confession.[266] As the person turns from sin to God, there must be "deep moral thoughtfulness on the past, on sin, and on God. Thus there is a double turning ... from sin to God."[267]

Since *metanoeo* is a complete turn from sin to God, it should never be confused with the change of life that comes as a result of that drastic step, for "repentance" itself is an act which one does. It is experiential and dramatic turn. Life change occurs after "repentance." Concerning this repentance which later brings forth fruits, Calvin states that, "repentance has its seat in the heart and soul but afterwards yields its fruit in a change of life, in good work."[268] Strong affirms that, "repentance in each and all its aspects is wholly an inward act, not to be confounded with the change of life which precedes from it."[269]

Beside the meaning and description of repentance for conversion in the New Testament, there are distinct persons that legitimately preached about it. People like John the Baptist, Jesus Christ, Peter, Paul and other disciples would call people to repent from their evils, and turn to God through Jesus Christ.

John Baptist's view of Repentance

Concerning John the Baptist who used to call people for repentance, "Repent (Greek- metanoeite) for the kingdom of God is near ...," he was challenging people to change their attitude against God that had delayed the coming of the Savior. He wanted them to turn from their continuous rebellion and rejection of God and be restored to relationship with Him. For the people to see and

---

[266] Ralph H. Isensee, "The Meaning and Significance of Metanoeo and Metanoia" (B.Div. Thesis, 1951), 12 - 13.

267 Ibid., 14.

[268] John Calvin, *Commentary: Harmony of the Gospels* (Grand Rapids: Eerdmans Publishing Company, 1949).

[269] Augustus H. Strong, *Systematic Theology* (Philadelphia: The Judson Press, 1912), 834.

enter into God's salvation, John demanded their complete change of character, attitude that would lead to renunciation of all that was evil before God. He demanded a complete turn from evil or sin to God's expectations.[270] Ralph Isensee notes that:

> *Metanoeo* was used by John the Baptist in the Old Testament sense of the turning to God of His people from the spiritual idolatry and typical adultery in which the faithless of the Jews were involved. This would, naturally, include personal amendment in individuals.... Undergoing such a change would prepare the people to receive Christ and exercise faith in Him.[271]

Jesus' view of Repentance

In His preaching and teaching, Jesus's ultimate goal was for the people to change their attitude toward sin and turn to God through trusting in His death for salvation. After the resurrection, Jesus also affirmed to His disciples that the ultimate goal of His life, death and resurrection was for them to preach repentance and forgiveness of sin, reconciling all people to God (Lk. 24:47). The whole idea of preaching about repentance was for all people of all nations to change their minds and attitudes from sin and receive Christ as their Messiah. It was a repentance that would lead a sinner to see himself being a sinner, guilty of sin, see the fact that he deserves punishment from God and therefore, turn to God and ask for forgiveness. In Luke 13:5, Jesus also expressed the immediate need of repentance, without which sinners would face God's judgment.

When Jesus commissioned His twelve disciples, their message was that of repentance followed by other miraculous signs like driving out demons, healing etc. (Lk. 6:8-12). As they were sent, the disciple preached the message of repentance by which they

---

[270] Ralph H. Isensee, 25
[271] Ibid., 25, 27.

called people to change their attitude toward sin and turn to God through accepting His Son Jesus Christ as their Savior (Lk. 6:12).

Peter's view of repentance

In many of his sermons, Peter would call people to repent of their sins so that they would inherit the kingdom of God (Acts 2:28, 3:19, 5:31, 8:22). Peter was calling people to change their minds that is, from their sinful ways and turn to Christ. He called people to accept the Christ whom they despised and killed. They were called to embrace Him as their Lord and Savior. Since people had turned to their sinful ways, by calling them to repent he was calling them to have a complete reversal of their mind concerning Jesus, that is with a repentant heart, turn to Him. At Pentecost (Acts 2:38), Peter preached to those who had come for the feast, and at the end of his sermon people asked, "Brothers, what shall we do?" Peter replied, "repent and be baptized ... in the name of Jesus Christ for the forgiveness of your sin...."[272]

With the term "repent," Peter called them to immediately have an inner change. He did not call them to have a gradual change of mind from sin to Christ, but they were to immediately do it and demonstrate it through baptism. By repentance, Peter meant that they were to change their sinful attitude and turn to Christ. The rite of baptism was an outside testimony or declaration of their true turning to Christ. It was to identify them with the gospel that is, Christ's death, burial and resurrection and also to identify them with the body of believers. After repentance, baptism was an outward sign that they had completely changed their attitude from sin to Christ and had accepted Him as their Lord and Savior.[273]

In Acts chapter three, Peter uses *metanoesate* (repent) in a dual sense, "repent (turn from sin) and turn to God so that

---

[272] Acts 2: 37-38 (New International Version).
[273] Ralph H. Isensee, 44.

your sins may be wiped out...."[274] This statement shows that Peter was calling people to turn from their sins and to turn to Christ so that through His ransom death their sins might be forgiven. He affirms that it is only through repentance that the remission of sin is granted. His emphasis is that sinners should not keep on procrastinating about in their sinful situation but, they should take a quick and immediate turn from sin and turn to God through Christ so that He might restore their relationship with God.

Paul's view of repentance

In Acts 13:24 and 19:4, Paul talks about the repentance that John the Baptist preached about. It was a repentance of complete departure from their sin. By mentioning John the Baptist, it was a way of concurring with what he was preaching about. Paul views repentance as a complete human change for salvation (Acts 17:30) thus, repentance to him was for eternal life. "Paul views repentance as enveloping man's complete response to the offer of salvation."[275] His message was for the people to "repent" and turn to Jesus Christ by faith (Acts 20:21). Repentance to him must go hand in hand with faith. Commenting on Paul's message of repentance, Isensee says, "One must see sin and its consequences and have knowledge of a degree of the way that sin is viewed by God. If one's mind and heart is not changed concerning these things, he will never feel the need of having faith in Christ."[276]

The repentance message of Paul was therefore like that of John the Baptist, whose aim was for the people to turn from their sins to Christ. He indeed emphasized the substitutionary work of Christ for salvation, so that whoever believed and accepted Him would be saved. As Paul preached it, repenting of sin is the only way that salvation is acquired from God. It is therefore necessary to help a sinner to consider doing it speedily because:

---

[274] Acts 3:19 (New International Version).

[275] Ralph H., 52.

[276] Ibid., 54.

It is inexpressibly dangerous, then, to delay it even for a moment. To delay repentance is infinitely perilous; for the present moment may be your last. Your continuance in sin is a re-acting of all your former crimes, with new aggravations. It strengthens the corruption of your nature, hardens your heart, and so renders repentance the more difficult. It provokes the Lord to deny you grace to repent. Every sin alienates you more from God, and removes you a step further from Him. The final result will be total separation from God. How lamentable is the condition of that sinner who delays true repentance.[277]

Considering the definitions and expressions that we have learned from the two Testaments, we can convincingly conclude that the meaning of repentance is genuine and voluntary act of a sinner, changing his personality from sin to God. By personality the writer means change of mind (intellect, emotions, attitudes, conscience) volition of the will and morals from sin to God through accepting His Son Jesus Christ. By a person changing his mind, this is a way of accepting one's helplessness for his salvation, recognizing how sinful he is before God and because of his unworthiness, he or she willingly seeks God through Christ. The person also willingly seeks to change his or her actions and attitudes before God and other people. In his book, *The Great Doctrines of the Bible*, Evan concurs with the writer's conclusive analysis of the above definition and expression of repentance by saying that, "repentance should be out of the whole person, it should touch the intellect, emotions and will."[278] Repentance should include a spirit of grief (Lk. 18:13) and a broken spirit (Ps. 51:17), for example, Peter wept bitterly for denying Christ (Lk. 22:62) of which was a sign of repentance. Padilla also extensively adds to this by saying:

---

[277] Ibid., 54.

[278] William Evans, *The Great Doctrine s of the Bible* (Chicago: Moody Press, 1968), 140 - 41.

Where there is no concrete obedience there is no repentance, and without repentance there is no salvation (Mk. 1:4; Lk. 13:3; Matt. 21:32, Acts 2:38, 5:32). Salvation is man's return to God, but it is at the same time also man's return to his neighbor. In the presence of Jesus Christ, Zacchaeus the publican renounces the materialism that has enslaved him and accepts responsibility for his neighbors. Behold ... half of my goods I give to the poor" (Lk. 19:8). This renunciation and commitment Jesus calls salvation: "Today salvation has come to this house" (Lk. 19:9).[279]

The following diagram is an integration of Evan's view of repentance with the writer's idea of the same.

Finally, a question might be asked: is repentance commanded by the Holy Scriptures? Passages like Lk. 15:7-10; Acts 2:38, 3:19, 17:30, 26:30; Rom. 2:4 and 2Pet. 3:9 shows that repentance is commanded by the Holy Scriptures and therefore, it is a prerequisite for salvation which means, "it is a condition for salvation that should be done by all sinners."[280]

Figure 16. Holistic Human repentance

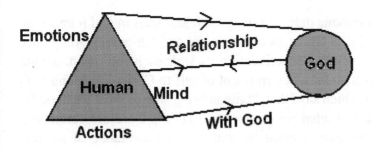

---

[279] Padilla, 20.

[280] Steven Waterhouse, *What Must I do to be Saved?* (Amarillo: Westcliff Press, 1995), 25-29.

Faith

    For genuine conversion to take place, a repentant sinner must have faith. The Holy Scriptures declare that human beings are saved by faith. What then is the meaning of "faith?" The Hebrew word for "faith" is *aman* and it generally means to trust, to have confidence, to believe and to have reliance.[281] The Greek word *pistuo* or *pistio* means either faith or to believe and is generally translated "commit" or such in - Jn. 2:24, Lk. 6:11, Rom. 3:2 and 1Cor. 9:17. Other translations like New International Version translate it as "entrust." When *aman* and *pistuo* are translated they mean "to commit," "to entrust," that is, to have confidence, to commit something to someone because he or she is trusted.[282] John Wesley understood faith as:

> Taking the word in a more particular sense, faith is a divine evidence and conviction, not only that "God was in Christ, reconciling the world unto himself," but also that Christ loved me, and gave Himself for me. It is by this faith that we receive Christ that receives Him in all His offices, as our prophet, priest, and king. It is by this He is made of God unto us wisdom, and righteousness, and sanctification, and redemption.[283]

    Simmons defines saving faith as, "trust in and reliance on the Lord Jesus Christ as one's Savior and sin-bearer. And, since salvation includes sanctification as well as justification, saving faith brings about a commitment of self to Christ."[284] Along with Heb. 11:1 which says that, "faith is being sure of what we hope for and certain of what we do not see," faith is therefore confidence in what we have trusted in, that is, our repentance of sin and

---

[281] Hebrew II, "Class Discussion," 2001.

[282] Steven Waterman, 15.

[283] *Tabor Heights United Methodist Trinity Sunday Worship Bulletin*, "Sermons of John Wesley," June 15, 2003.

[284] Thomas Paul Simmons, *A Systematic Study of Bible Doctrines* (Russell: n.p, 1955), 300.

forgiveness have been granted to us by God. Strong describes faith as, "Faith is a bond between persons, of trust and confidence; it is based on the character and power of whom we trust, not our faith but His fidelity, is a guarantee that our faith is rational."[285] In relation to salvation, Evans too describes faith as:

> Faith is the consent of the will to the assent of the understanding. Faith always has in it the idea of action - movement towards its object. It is the soul leaping forth to embrace and appropriate the Christ in whom it believes. It first says: "My Lord and my God," and then falls down and worships.[286]

Concerning the above description of faith, we should understand it as our knowledge of Christ whom we have never physically seen, but yet we still believe in Him. It is through our inner knowledge that we believe in Christ's incarnation, death, burial, resurrection, appearances, ascension and His definite promises of His return to culminate our salvation in heaven (Rev. 19:11, 21; 22).

For faith to be actualized in believers' lives, believe and confession of sins must be there (Rom. 10:9-10). By faith, a sinner must believe that Jesus Christ died for his or her sins according to the Holy Scriptures, that He was raised on the third day according to the Bible, and He also appeared to many, after His resurrection (1Cor. 15:1-5). By faith, a sinner must believe that Jesus is the Christ, the Son of God (John 20:30-31). One has to acknowledge Him as Lord, and Savior. "Faith believes all that God says as being absolutely true, even though circumstances seem to be against its fulfillment."[287] Commenting on the fact that one has by faith to believe, Zane Hodges states:

> To believe that Jesus is the Christ... in John's sense of

---

[285] Hopkins Strong, *Augustus Systematic Theology V. 1* (New Jersey: Fleming H. Company, 1970), 839.
[286] William Evans, 146.
[287] Ibid., 146.

that term ... is to believe saving faith. It is to believe the very truth that Martha of Bethany believed. To put it as simple as possible, Jesus was asking Martha whether she believed that He fully guaranteed the eternal destiny of every believer... Martha affirmed she did by affirming her conviction about who He was. Thus, by believing the amazing facts about the person of Christ, Martha trusted Him. She was placing her eternal destiny in His hands.... Everything depended on the truth of what she believed.[288]

From the above idea of faith, Hodges views saving faith from the standpoint of what the person should do to be saved. A person should believe in Christ so as to be saved and as Jesus explained to Martha (Jn. 11:25-26), one has to acknowledge the facts so as to be saved. Jesus gave her the facts: "I am the resurrection and the life. He who believes in Me will live, even though he dies; and whoever lives and believes in Me will never die...."[289]

When a person believes in Christ and His work on the cross, repents of his sin, it is by faith that he puts trust in Him and is forgiven by God. It is by faith that one trusts that Christ's death has carried away his or her sins. H. McDonald describes faith as:

Faith is the way in which forgiveness is realized. It accepts the gift of God's holy pardon. It is the only harbor of the soul; it leads man to God, to Christ, and to His rest. Faith is the medium, the vehicle, the channel whereby the forgiveness of God in Christ becomes ours. Faith is the one thing needful; the one thing a man must do is to believe. And the very least faith makes God's pardon ours because it makes Christ ours. For realization of that forgiveness the only way we can contribute is the faith that secures it. This is the one call, the one demand, made upon man.[290]

---

[288] Zane C, Hodges, *Absolutely Free* (Dallas: Redencion Viva, 1989), 39.

[289] *Bible*, (New International Version).

[290] H. D. McDonald, *Forgiveness and Atonement*, 103, 105.

After one's sin is pardoned, it is by faith that he or she believes that Christ has forgiven him or her. After accepting Christ, faith grows in a believer as he continues living in Christ. "The form of faith does not vary. From beginning to end, from embryo to maturity, faith is trust in Christ and His sin-bearing love."[291]

The Bible puts it clearly that faith is a gift from God to those who repent and willingly seek to have continuous a love relationship with Him (Rom. 12:3). Faith is a gift of God's grace through His Son Jesus Christ (Heb. 12:2) and is also executed by the Holy Spirit to those who repent of their sins. It is the responsibility of sinners to take a step of responding to God's love so that they can be given faith which will help them to return back to Him. Faith therefore, cannot be separated with repentance for salvation. Summing up the whole idea of faith for our salvation, William Evans states as:

> The whole of our salvation - past, present and future, is dependent upon faith. Our acceptance of Christ (Jn. 1:12), our justification (Rom. 5:1), our adoption (Gal. 3:26), our sanctification (acts 26:18), our keeping (1Pet. 1:5), indeed our whole salvation from Christ, start to finish, is dependent upon faith.[292]

Talking about faith that saves does not mean admitting that God exists or that Jesus is truly the Son of God and Savior of the world. Non-believers and the demons believe that (Lk. 4:34). Saving faith is a personal trust in Jesus Christ who died and resurrected to provide salvation to whoever will accept Him (John 3:16; Gal. 2:16). Faith embraces the knowledge of the Scriptures about who Christ is and what He did on the cross. Saving faith is that act of believing in the gospel of salvation and trusting in the atoning death of Christ. It is through hearing the gospel either when it is preached, testified about or from the Word of God that one comes to know that Jesus Christ is the Savior. By faith,

---

[291] Ibid., 106.
[292] William Evans, 149.

one consistently entrust himself or herself to the gospel.[293] In his contribution on the meaning of faith, John MacArther states:

> Faith, like grace, is not static. Saving faith is more than just understanding the facts and mentally acquiescing. It is inseparable from repentance, surrender, and a supernatural eagerness to obey. The biblical concept of saving faith includes all these elements. None of them can be classified exclusively as a human work, any more than believing itself is solely a human effort.[294]

With this definition of faith, saving faith is therefore, inseparable from repentance which is actually turning from sins to God, surrendering and confessing to God and eagerness to following Christ. Thus, when one does all these, the person is converted to Christ.

Like repentance, faith involves the whole personality that is, intellect, emotions and volition of the will. Through intellect, the person has to know and understand the gospel. One does not follow Christ without knowing who He is. Faith is not hallucination or delusion of the mind but it has an aspect of knowledge and understanding who to trust or to entrust oneself to. It is through God's word that the intellectual aspect of faith is established in a person. Through the Scriptures one comes to know Christ and encounter His deeds. Through the facts and evidences from the Bible, a sinner comes to believe the gospel and put his faith in Christ (Rom. 10:14). Through that faith "the person accepts Christ and proclaims Him crucified for His or her sins."[295] It is the same faith that one believes that Jesus Christ is the Son of God and by believing, the person surrenders his or her life to Christ and receives eternal life in His Name (Jn. 20:31b).

---

[293] Charles Ryrie, *Basic Theology* (Chicago: Moody Press, 1999), 377.

[294] John MacArthur, *The Gospel According to Jesus* (Grand Rapids: Zondervan 1988), 31.

[295] *Tabor Height's Bulletin,* "Statement of Faith: United Methodist Church of Canada and the Korean Methodist Church," Portland OR., October 2002.

The other aspect of faith is emotion which is the "capacity of inner conviction and trust that certain thing is true."[296] When a person is convinced that Christ is the Savior, that He died for his sins, that He was buried, that He resurrected (1 Cor. 15:3-5), he has agreed with the Scriptures and therefore, he sees the need and value of receiving salvation. By the emotion only that leads the person to feel sorry for his sins, saving faith is not complete without making a decision to follow the Lord and therefore, the third aspect of faith is that of human will.

Will is that capacity in human beings that helps them to make free choices or decisions. In the repentant sinner, it helps the person to decide to embrace Jesus Christ as his Savior and Lord. It is at this time that the person shifts from all self-deceptions and puts his trust in Christ alone, thus believing and accepting Him as his Savior (Acts 20:21; Rom. 10:9).[297]

For the person to receive Christ the three aspects of faith should be active. It is the work of the Holy Spirit to convict the person not only of his or her sin but also, what Christ did for that sin. Besides the human side of faith, there is therefore the divine side of convicting a sinner of his sin, and guiding him to embrace Christ. In a believer, faith should not only be at the time of salvation but also in all of his life. A believer cannot survive in this world of sin without ongoing faith.

Confession

Along with repentance and faith, a sinner should confess his or her sin before God so that he or she can be forgiven. "The confession of sin is a necessary condition of receiving the forgiveness of God."[298] Along with this condition, the writer describes confession as acknowledgment of the new turn from sin to God which results in conversion. It is an declaration that

---

[296] "Christ and Salvation Discussions," Moffat College of Bible, Nov. 1997.

[297] Ibid., Nov. 1997.

[298] John R. W. Stott, *Confess your Sins: The Way of Reconciliation* (Philadelphia: The Westminster Press, 1964), 11.

one has already changed his or her attitudes from sin to follow God. It is dramatizing the act of repentance whereby, the positive turn to God is expressed. A sinner willingly expresses how he is convinced that he is a sinner, how sorry he is over those sins and has decided to turn away from that state of being to God. On the other hand, among the believers, confession of sin should be practiced by all believers so as to keep mutual understanding, harmony and fellowship with one another.

However, the term confession comes from the Greek word *homologeo* which means "saying the same things" (*homos* - same, *lego* - to speak). It also means to assent, to declare, to confess, admit (Jn. 1:20; Acts 24:14, Heb. 11:13). It is admitting that one is guilty of what he is accused of, and this comes as a result of inner conviction. It is willingly speaking of what one has done, without being forced to do so.[299] It is a declaration which comes after the attitude of repentance. It is an expression first to God (Rom. 10:9-11) and also to people Rom. 10:14-15). In the case of repentance and confession to the people, it is public (Lk. 19 - Zacchaeus).

Confession is always a detailed admission of one's sin, that is consistent rebellion against and rejection of God and expressing how one is guilty about it. It is a true and deep act of pouring one's heart to God recognizing and admitting that one is a sinner and needs His forgiveness. It is a way of declaring that one has not been fellowshipping and communing with God and now the person is deeply willing to restore that relationship.[300] After a sinner confesses his or her sins to God, then God places that person in His family and gives him or her eternal forgiveness.[301] Thus, the person is converted to Christ.

---

[299] W. E. Vine, *Expository Dictionary of New Testament Words* (Old Tappan: Fleming H. Revell Company, 1966), 224.

[300] John MacArthur, *Confession of Sin* (Chicago: Moody Press, 1986), 54-55.

[301] David K. Duffy, "A Study of Confession of Sin in Relation to the Context of 1 John" (Capital Bible Seminary, Th.M. thesis, 1980), Microfilm.

Confession in the OT

In the Old Testament, the concept of confession is basically understood in the perspective of a court or council of law; a person was taken to confess before designated people. Confession in Hebrew is *yadah* which means acknowledgment of sin to a court of law or to God.[302]

The Old Testament understands the term *yadah* on two levels. When an individual is confessing sin before God, or when a nation is confessing before God. An example of an individual confession is like the one of king David who declared ". . .then I acknowledged my sin to you and did not cover up my iniquity. I said, I will confess my transgressions to the Lord, and you forgave the guilt of my sins."[303] An example of national confession is like the one of Ezra, Nehemiah and Daniel who, with the people of Israel, confessed their sins to God.

In Psalms 32:1-2, David confessed his sins before God and described how a forgiven sinner is blessed. In verse 3-4, He describes how he suffered in anguish before he confessed his sin to God. After David confessed, he found God's forgiveness and was happy in his restored fellowship with Him. He recognized how sin thwarts human fellowship with God, and that is why he confessed it. In v. 5a he says, *adiaka* (I confess to you) which means, acknowledging and verbalizing it to God. In v. 5b *va aoni lo kossiti* (my iniquities I have not covered" or "I have not covered my iniquities." This is to say that David did not cover it up but, he voiced it out to God in open.[304] He specifically acknowledged his sin and confessed it to God. He really knew that he was the offending person and therefore, he needed God's forgiveness and restoration. Confession was the only way that he could obtain forgiveness. Considering people's need of confessing their sin to God, G. Barrett states that:

---

[302] Ibid. Microfilm.

[303] Psalm 32:5 (New International Version).

[304] Ibid. Microfilm.

We do need it, to disclose to ourselves the full reality of our own sin; for just as silence conceals the sin it refuses to acknowledge, so confession to God drags the sin, as it were, into the light... confession is never rendered without cost; it means pain and humiliation and it is sure sign and proof of the genuine sorrow for sin.[305]

It is only through confession of sin that harmony and peace with God are restored. Since repentance and faith go together before confession, these two (inner attitudes) have to be expressed to God. Repentance and faith are inner convictions that drive the whole person from sin toward God; confession is a verbal proclamation. God knows and looks for the thoughts and attitudes of people but people need to express them to Him.

Following what David did in his confession, first, a sinner should acknowledge his sin and guilt. The second step is to acknowledge it before God. David would have covered his sin but he acknowledged it to himself and to God and asked for forgiveness. In v. 5, David used the word *odiaka* which means, "Acknowledged to you" from the root *yadah* (I know, I knew, I declared, I declare or I declared). Thus, *ha tati odiaka* means that, David acknowledged or declared his sins or iniquities to God.[306] The whole idea is that David knew that he was a sinner and was guilty and therefore, he needed God's forgiveness.

Confession in the NT

In the epistle to John, we find a statement, "if we confess our sins He is faithful and just to forgive...."[307] For God to forgive our sins, this statement declares that confession of sin is vital. Generally, the New Testament explains confession of sins in two

---

[305] G. S. Barrett, *A Devotional Commentary: The First Epistle General to St. John* (London: The Religious Track Society, n.d.), 59.

[306] Hebrew II "Class Lectures," North Park Theological Seminary, Fall 2001.

[307] 1 John 1:9 (New International Version).

ways: at the time of turning from sin to God for salvation and, in the life of Christians, confession of sin one to another. They have mutual fellowship and harmony, and are able to maintain their deep relationship with God and with one another. Charles Ryrie affirms:

> Brethren maintain fellowship with Christ and with one another by meeting a certain condition. That condition is "walk in the light" (1 Jon. 1:7), or walking in obedience to a standard which is God Himself, who is light.... When sin is committed and the standard is not met, fellowship is broken and confession is necessary (1 John 1:9). Thus, fellowship depends on our responding to the standard, which is God Himself, and realizing our imperfect state by confession of known sin. The life of fellowship is a life of no unconfessed sins which is also a life of progressive growth, for confession involves repentance and forsaking of sin.[308]

Confessing to God requires the person to acknowledge that being born in sin, living in sin that his sinful state is leading to eternal separation from God. The person should acknowledge that salvation is only acquired through faith in the death of Jesus Christ. It is only Jesus who wipes away sin. He should "recognize the work of Christ in place of a sinner in his true position before God."[309] It is only when "one recognizes the sinfulness of sin and the need for a Savior that he will be moved to exercise faith, leading to eternal life.... Confession is a necessary evidence of eternal life and salvation."[310]

Salvation as Forgiveness

God's "forgiveness" is a term that cannot be omitted in the process of salvation, that is, God's restoring relationship with

---

[308] Charles C. Ryrie, *biblical Theology of the New Testament* (Chicago: Moody Press, 1959), 341.

[309] David K. Duffy, Microfilm.

[310] Ibid.,

sinners. It is only through Christ that God forgives and through His forgiveness repentant sinners can relate back to Him and to one another. Paul uses the concept of God's forgiveness and chooses the word *charizomai* which generally means, "to bestow or to give." He uses this word to signify that God through His grace has already forgiven our sins (Col. 2:13) for Christ's sake (Eph. 4:32).[311]

As we have already observed, due to the fall of human beings, the Bible is dominated by the word "forgiveness" which reflects who God is and His character. Together with His love, mercy, grace and compassion, there is His forgiveness (Exod. 34:6-7; Neh. 9:16-17; Micah 7:18-20; Ps. 86:5). God's forgiveness through Christ's work on the cross is also emphasized in Lk. 1:1ff; Acts 10:43; Eph. 1:7; Jn. 5:14, 8:11, Lk. 7:36-50).[312] There is no other way a sinner can go back or be reconciled back to God except through His divine forgiveness. Besides expressing *charizomai*, as the divine forgiveness of God, it is also used to express the notion of "letting go, dismissing in peace, and releasing" (Mk. 1:34; Matt. 13:34; Rom. 1:27).

As we discussed the dimensions of reconciliation, forgiveness is not the same as reconciliation or restoration for a fellowship but, it leads to reconciliation. Forgiveness comes before reconciliation because one has to realize he or she is a sinner before God and therefore, must ask God for forgiveness. When one is forgiven, he or she is reconciled with God and with the community (example: the case of Zacchaeus in Luke 19:1ff). Agreeing that forgiveness precedes reconciliation, Vincent Taylor states:

> Forgiveness can only be described as an action directed to the removal or annulment of some obstacle or barrier to reconciliation. This obstacle or to speak more

[311] McDonald, 56.

[312] Ralph R. Martin, "Reconciliation and Forgiveness in the Letter to the Collosians." *Reconciliation and Hope: New Testament Essays on Atonement and Eschatology* (Grand Rapids: Eerdmans Publishing Company, 1974), 113.

precisely, the object of forgiveness, is variously described as "sins," "trespasses," and the "thought of the heart" (Acts 8:22). Everywhere it implies that, if this object is removed, covered, or in some ways adequately dealt with, the forgiveness is accomplished. Forgiveness therefore, cannot be identified with reconciliation; it is that which makes reconciliation possible.[313]

The Bible is clear that God forgives a sinner after he admits that he has sinned against Him, repents and accepts Christ and His ransom death on the cross. God's forgiveness is available to those who accept that they are at a distance from Him. When they repent of their rebellion against Him, they are forgiven and reconciled to Him.

Forgiveness is God's greatest act of love and grace: He pardons a sinner in keeping with the atonement of Christ. Forgiveness is a miracle, because a sinner does not deserve it, but rather deserves punishment. Instead, on the basis of God's nature and Christ's death, He provides forgiveness. Forgiveness is indeed a miracle, because instead of the sinner being put to death, Christ died on his behalf. Expressing this miraculous forgiveness that a sinner receives from God, H. McDonald states:

But this means that forgiveness can only take place as a real and divine act. The sense of acceptance, the certainty of forgiveness, can only legitimately refer to a divine act of revelation, to an explicit communication of this divine secret. Such an act would be the most inconceivable revelation possible something now that it could never be imagined. Further, this forgiveness would have to be imparted in such a way that the holiness of God, the inviolability of the law and logical demands of the penal order would still be maintained. Thus, the perfect revelation of forgiveness

---

[313] Vincent Taylor, *Forgiveness and Reconciliation* (London: Macmillan and Company LTD, 1956), 3.

can only be such as brings out with intense emphasis that it cannot and must not be taken for granted. This means that it must be of such a kind that it will express the reality of guilt, the reality of the divine wrath, and yet, at the same time, the overwhelming reality of forgiving love.[314]

Reflecting on the above quotation, we can in awe realize that God's forgiveness is both a paradox and a miracle. A sinner must be punished but not forgiven, and if forgiveness is granted, someone must have paid. Since the forgiveness is granted on the basis of another person's work (Christ), it is a miracle for a sinner to receive it. It is a paradox because it comes from God's holy nature. God stands for a sinner, judges him and on the basis of His Son, his sins are forgiven. God also stands as a father and a redeemer, and therefore He grants forgiveness to a sinner in those capacities.

"God's forgiveness and mercy do not come as light from the sun, or water from the sea, by a necessary consequence of their natures, whether they will or not...,"[315] and therefore, though love, mercy and forgiveness are in the nature of God and are extended to sinners, there are some conditions that sinners must fulfill because God's forgiveness requires them. Sinners must recognize their sins, repent and ask God for forgiveness. God's forgiveness is not under a certain law that whether He likes it or not He naturally will forgive because of Christ, but sinners have to repent of their sins, accept Christ as their savior, and by faith allow Him to be the Lord of their lives. Before God forgives sinners, these are the only human moral responsibilities that He requires from them. H. McDonald contributes an understanding of God's forgiveness by saying:

God's forgiveness is not a sort of kindly general amnesty which covers all. From man's side it is there for "whosoever will," while from God's side it is for whom He wills.... to say that we are saved by God's grace, which is

[314] H. D. McDonald, *Forgiveness and Atonement*, 19.
[315] John Owen, *The Forgiveness of Sin* (Grand Rapids: Baker Books, 1977), 92.

free to all, does not mean that all are forgiven.[316]

Since forgiveness is a merciful and loving act of God to a repentant sinner, it should not be seen as a way God credits him with righteousness which was originally his. As we have mentioned, it is God's mysterious act toward a sinner that He imputes to Christ, and when a sinner repents and trusts Christ's sacrifice for that sin, he or she is forgiven. H. McDonald also contributes:

> Forgiveness ... is not the crediting to him (a sinner) of an innocence that was never his, nor restoring of an innocence which was once his. God forgives the sinner and thereby opens to him the free actions of His grace. A forgiven sinner is not regarded by God as one who has never sinned before, for that is as impossible as any other contradictory thing. He is regarded as a sinner towards whom God's attitude is no longer determined by his sin.[317]

When a sinner is forgiven, God in His own divine will and loving act counts him or her as being righteous, but not through the sinner's own works (Rom. 4:4-5, 4:13, 5:17, 9:30). Through the atonement of Christ, a repentant sinner stands as a forgiven person to whom God has changed His attitude, that is, from being an enemy to a loving Savior and Friend (Rom. 5:11). It is therefore:

> In the remission of sins, man truly discovers God. Without such an experience of forgiveness, a man's ideas of God may be sound enough, but they are merely affirmations of a borrowed creed and a secondhand religion. Such affirmations, true though they may be for the mind, will be without that warmth of soul and inward energizing power which make faith real, personal and creative....[318]

A sinner receives absolute forgiveness from God. God does

---

[316] H. D. *McDonald Forgiveness and Atonement*, 55.

[317] Ibid., 69.

[318] Ibid., 97.

not forgive him or her bit-by-bit, step-by-step or by installments but, He forgives once and forever. Unlike the way humans classify sins as greater or lesser, God does not quantitatively count whether it has been a greater or lesser sin but, He sees that "all have sinned and have fallen sort of His glory,"[319] that is, a person is a sinner, a transgressor, deserves death but, he needs His grace of forgiveness. He forgives and remembers their sins no more, thus "for I will forgive their wickedness and will remember their sins no more."[320] It is God's forgiveness that is total, clear, complete and forever, and God does not keep on reminding the person of the sinful state that he or she used to live in (Lk. 15:11-32).

Salvation as Deliverance

"Sin is an act, a state or condition one is in. It signifies a deviation from the way or end appointed by God".[321] Sin is deification (making oneself a god) of self and dethronement of God. Sin is a rejection of God and a violation of what He commands (Numb. 15:31, Eph. 4:18, 1Jn. 3:4). Sin is to refuse to do what is right before God and other human beings (Jam. 4:17, Ps. 14:3; Rom. 14:23). Sin originated from Adam and Eve (Gen. 3:1-23) when they willingly disobeyed God. It began in the "self-separation of the will of man from the will of God."[322]

Since sin is disobedience to God and is universal in human beings, it has some results. It has separated people from God and it has broken their relationship with Him and with one another. Sinners are separated from God in their hearts, minds and even their bodies, that is, they are totally distanced from Him (Gen. 1:26; Isa. 29:13; Col. 1:21). Sin twists people's thinking so that they cannot reason as God reasons (Isa. 55:8-9; Gen. 6:5; Rom.

---

[319] Rom. 3:23, 6:23 (New International Version).
[320] Heb. 8:12 (New International Version).
[321] Willey and Culbertson, 160.
[322] Ibid., 164.

1:21). Sin has marred human reason and therefore there is no communication and fellowship between the unrepentant and God. Sin has made humans very powerless, that is, powerless to do what God wants them to do, nor do they seek to fulfill His will (Rom. 7:18, 5:6, 8:7-8). Sin causes humans to be separate from God, for they know that they are guilty, and are ashamed of their sins. Sin destroys relationships between people (James 4:1; Prov. 18:19) and finally "the wages of sin is death" which means eternal separation from God and from one another (Rom. 6:23).[323]

Due to sin, the salvation that takes people back to God is provided through the death of Christ. Without forgiveness of sin there is no salvation. It was out of sinfulness that God's love compelled Jesus to atone for it so as to redeem humans to Himself. The real need of humans is therefore, deliverance from sin.

Deliverance from the Love of Sin

When we receive Christ, God saves us from pleasure or love of sin by imparting to us a nature that hates sin. He puts in us a capacity for loving holiness, for He is holy. This comes as a result of accepting Christ as Savior and Lord (Jn. 3:5-6) and it is actualized in us through the power of the Holy Spirit. It is the foundation of salvation, whereby a sinner is declared righteous and seeks to sin no more (2Cor. 5:17; Rom. 6:1-2, 12:1-2; 1Pet. 3:15, 1Cor. 8:6, Jn.13:13-14). Christ becomes the master of our new life, and were free from dealings with Satan (Eph. 6:11, Jam. 4:7). This is the time the Holy Spirit fills us, and we no longer desire to be in sin (Gal. 5:22-23; 2Tim. 1:7). Instead of loving sin, we continuously love God and live in Him through Christ (2Cor. 5:17).[324]

God delivers us from the love of sin by putting His holy awe in our hearts (Prov. 8:13) and therefore, we hate evil. He saves us from the love of sin by communicating to us about His

---

[323] *Introducing People to Jesus Series*, 7-8.
[324] Ibid., 15.

love for us (Rom. 5:5) and when His love embraces us, love of sin is dethroned. The Holy Spirit causes us to hate sin (Gal. 3:14; Rom 5:5, 2Cor. 1:21-22) for He owns us.[325] How can a believer determine whether the new holy nature has been imparted?

The basic way is to observe how the new nature in the person opposes sin. First, sin is recognized, and therefore a believer will never intentionally attempt to commit it, whether it seems to be sweet or not. Second, when we are delivered from the love of sin, sin becomes bitter and painful to us. We will never like to engage ourselves in a bitter life and therefore, we will ever try to escape from sin.[326]

Deliverance from the Penalty of Sin

In salvation, we are saved from the penalty of sin when we accept Christ, accept we are sinners, repent of our sins and allow Christ to enter in our lives as our Master. By so doing, we are saved from the penalty of sin, its guilt, its wages and being punished for sin (Lk. 7:50). In writing to the Ephesian Christians, Paul says, "By grace you are saved through faith,"[327] which means that Christ has already delivered us from the penalty of sin which is present and also to come (1Thess. 1:10). This penalty is removed from believers through the meditorial work of Christ because "He was wounded for our sins and bruised for our iniquities."[328] This goes with our repentance and faith in Christ, which also implie, having godly sorrow for sin and accepting God's pardon. From there on, "there is no condemnation to those who are in Christ" (Rom. 8:1). Now, all believers in Christ stand pardoned and forgiven before Christ, because the guilt of their sins was transferred to Him. As God sees us through Christ, we are acceptable before Him.[329]

---

[325] Pink, 111 - 12.

[326] Ibid., 113.

[327] Ephesians 2:8 (New International Version).

[328] Isaiah 53:5 (New International Version).

[329] Charles M. Horne, *Salvation* (Chicago: Moody Press, 1971), 13.

Deliverance from the Power of Sin

Though all believers are saved, their nature of flesh, which is corrupt, is still in them. As Paul wrote to the believers at Rome, ". . . do not let sin reign in your mortal body so that you obey its evil desires. Do not offer the parts of your body to sin, as instruments of wickedness...."[330] This means that sin is not eradicated from a believer's life, and therefore one has to wrestle with it. Writing to the Corinthian saints, Paul also admonished " let us purify ourselves from everything that contaminates body and spirit...."[331] A believer still has corrupt sinful nature which wrestles with the holy one but he or she is dead to sin.

Knowing this, the thing is not to allow our sinful nature to overpower us (Rom. 13:14) but to separate ourselves from sin. We should let our light shine before people (Matt. 5:16) and continuously seek and desire to grow in Christ's knowledge (2Pet. 3:8). The Holy Spirit also helps us to flee from sin.[332] Feeding on God's word will also enable us to flee from sin, for we will be always in touch with Christ. The Word of God, too, will deliver and cleanse us from sin (2Pet. 1:4; Jn. 17:17).

Salvation as New Life

After a sinner repents and puts faith in Jesus Christ for salvation, we have noted that God forgives his or her sins and remembers them no more. There is reconciliation between God and the repentant sinner, which brings with it mutual fellowship, harmony and peace. Along with reconciliation, there are some spiritual changes that take place in a person, and some occur in the future. Since God is the source of our salvation through Christ, the drastic spiritual changes in a believer's life are entirely His. Some of these changes are discussed here below.

---

[330] Rom. 6:12-13a (New International Version).
[331] 2 Cor. 7:1 (New International Version).
[332] Pink, 127.

He makes us spiritually alive

Through the message of the gospel, the Holy Spirit convinces people of their sin, but they willingly seek Him, repent and turn to Christ for forgiveness of their sins. When the message calls sinners to repent, sinners have to take a step of moving from the kingdom of darkness to the kingdom of light. The first thing that happens is that one is born again or from above (Jn. 3:3) which means that the person is regenerated. Born from above is sometimes called "the renewal of the Holy Spirit (Titus 3:5) which result is being a new creation" (2Cor. 5:17).[333] Being made spiritually alive is also called "made alive or being quickened" (Eph. 2:5; Jn. 6:63, Rom. 8:1-10). God made us alive with Christ even when we were dead in transgressions; it is by grace that believers have been saved.

Making believers spiritually alive is the work of the Holy Spirit (Jn. 2:3-6); they are born of God (from above). It is a mysterious work of the Spirit in a believer's life (Jn. 3:8). Regarding regeneration in John 3, Wayn Grudem interprets it as, "a secret act of God in which He imparts new spiritual life to us."[334] Berkhof also defines the work of regeneration by stating that, " it is that act of God by which the principle of the new life is implanted in man and the governing disposition of the soul is made holy."[335] W. Best describes the quickening of a believer's spirit as:

> It is immediate act of God in imparting principle of life.... Regeneration is creative act of God and no secondary causes are connected to it. Since regeneration is the act of the sovereign God, it is never presented as a duty of the sinner. The demands of the gospel upon sinner are limited to

---

[333] Charles Horne, 53.

[334] Wayn Grudem, *Systematic Theology: An Introduction to biblical Doctrine* (Leicester: InterVasity Press, 1994), 699.

[335] Berkhof, *Systematic Theology* (Grand Rapids: Eerdmans Publishing House, 1979), 469.

the terms of repentance and faith. Regeneration is a single act of God and is never repeated. The position of a believer in Christ, by virtue of regeneration can be neither increased nor decreased by anything in the recipient. Regeneration is not in itself an experience; it is not a matter of consciousness to its recipient. A person knows nothing about the beginning of its existence.... Regeneration is a once for all cleansing. In Regeneration, we have God's power, the power of indwelling Spirit. Regeneration gives sight to the spiritually blind. In regeneration, God gives understanding to the mind that has no understanding of spiritual things. It takes place in the sphere of the subconsciousness of man that is, outside of the sphere of conscious attention.[336]

Since quickening of one's spirt is the work of God through the power of the Holy Spirit, a believer cannot trace when God did it in his life but, by faith, it is at the time of accepting Christ and His work at the cross (Jn. 3:3-10). One cannot fully explain the experience. As Jesus affirmed to Nicodemus, it is like how a child who is born cannot really explain the beginning of his existence at conception. As the recipients of regeneration, we cannot really explain or know it through our own observation.

When the Bantu people performed cultural "regeneration" (Kikuyu - *gucokia mwana ihu-ini*), it was visible, ritually performed, experiential, and was an initiation. This is not so with spiritual act of regeneration and, that is why Nicodemus could not comprehend it intellectually. It is a mysterious work of God (Jn. 3:6-8) in the begetting of a new life in Christ. Being spiritually alive does not change the recipient's physical features, but only his or her spirit, which now starts knowing and understanding the spiritual things and requirements of God. W. E. Best concurs with this by noting that, "Regeneration of the soul does not change the chemistry of the body. It does not cancel the primeval sentence

---

[336] W. E. Best, *Regeneration and Conversion* (Houston: South Belt Grace Church, 1975), 33-34, 82-85.

of physical death. The body of the Christian is subject to death because it is a mortal body."[337]

Referring back to John 3, where Nicodemus was told by Christ that "you must be born from above," this is the idea of regeneration which is done by God in a believer. When "born again" is translated from Greek it is, *hagiazo,* which means "holiness or "be holy." The criteria for being declared holy is repenting and accepting Christ. The nature of being declared holy (regenerated) is supernatural, for it is done by God through the power of the Holy Spirit. The subject of regeneration is the believing person who has accepted Christ.

There are reasons why the Holy Spirit quickens our spirits: We may be in a position to see and enter the kingdom of God (Jn. 3:3), to have a living hope (1Pet. 1:3), to avoid sin (1John 3:9, 5:18) and to love other brothers and sisters in Christ (1Jn. 3:9, 5:18). Some observable evidences in a spiritually quickened life are: the person is very conscious of new life in Christ, the person is always led by the Holy Spirit and he or she produces the fruit of the Holy Spirit (Gal. 5:16-18, 5:22-23).

He Declares Us Not Guilty

As we have already learned, that once a person receives Christ as savior, his spirit is awakened to Christ and he becomes a new creation. At the same time, God declares the person not guilty of sins, that is, God justifies that person such that he appears legally righteous before the holy God. The person appears before God as if he has never sinned before. Since his sin is imputed into Christ who is his or her sin bearer, God does not see that person as a sinner before Him. John Wesley affirmed this by saying that:

Justification is another word for pardon. It is the forgiveness of all our sins, and (what it necessarily implied therein) our acceptance with God. The price whereby this has been procured for us is the blood and righteousness of

---

[337] Ibid., 87.

Christ. Or (to express it a little more clearly) all that Christ has done and suffered to us, till He poured out His soul for the transgressors. The immediate effects of justification are, the peace of God, a peace that passes all understanding, and a rejoicing in hope of the glory of God....[338]

Declaring a person not guilty is therefore an act of God that declares a person righteous, which does not mean he actually is, but standing before God the person is declared righteous. Describing the meaning of "declaring not guilty," Earl Radmacher says that,

> The Hebrew word *shedeg* refers to the standard God maintains in the word, the norm by which everyone must be judged. "Righteousness"then, is conformity to God's standard, and "justification" is God's declaring that a person is in right standing with God.[339]

In the above quotation, Radmacher indicates that God does not make somebody righteous but He declares righteous. On this term (justification), William Evans contributes as:

> To justify does not mean to make one righteous. Neither the Hebrew nor Greek word will bear such meaning. To justify means to set forth as righteous; to declare righteous in a legal sense; to put a person in a right relation. It does not deal, at least not directly, with character or conduct; it is a question of relationship. No real righteousness on the part of the person justified is to be asserted, but that person is declared to be righteous and is treated as such. Justification is the judicial act of God whereby those who put faith in Christ are declared righteous in His eyes, and free from guilt and punishment.[340]

Summarizing Evans' definition of "not guilty," it has to do with forgiveness of sin, and at the same time removing guilt

---

[338] *Tabor Heights United Methodist Trinity Sunday Worship Bulletin*, June 15, 2003.

[339] Radmacher, 136.

[340] William Evans, 157.

and punishment for the person who believes in Christ. Because of Christ's death on the cross, before the righteous and holy God, the person stands as if he has never sinned before, that is, not guilty (Acts 13:38-39, Rom. 8:1, 8:33-34). The righteousness that the person is seen with is Christ's and therefore, the person already is restored to God's favor and harmony.

To understand the term "justify" in an Old Testament perspective, the term justification was a judicial act of announcing that the person was not guilty, but it does not make the person guilty free. For example, Moses told the Israelites that, "When men have a dispute, they are to take it to court and the judges will decide the case, acquitting the innocent and condemning the guilty."[341] In the court case, it was not the judge's function to make people innocent, but his work was to judge justly and thereafter declare who was wicked or righteous. If the judge did the opposite that is, declaring a wicked person righteous and the righteous person wicked, that was against God's standard (Prov. 17:15).

With the above view in mind, on the side of a sinner, God in His righteous judgement and grace declares a wicked person righteous before Him. By the person being declared not guilty, this does not mean that he or she is not guilty at all but it is God who sees the person in a different eye than before. He sees the person as righteous but not a sinner any more."[342] Affirming believers' righteousness before God, Thomas Simmons notes:

> While the sin of Adam is imputed to us because it is ours, the righteousness of Christ is imputed to us simply because of our union with Him, not at all because of our personal righteousness. In the one case, character is taken into account; in the other, it is not. In sin, our demerits are included; in justification our merits are excluded.[343]

---

[341] Deut. 25:1 (New International Version).
[342] John Murray, 119-20.
[343] Thomas Paul Simmons, 307.

Being declared not guilty is not the believer's state of being but it is his or her standing before the holy God. This declaration has nothing to do with our good action before God, but it has to do with our response to the call of repentance. It has to do with our spiritual relationship with God. In Deut.25:1, it was only the innocent person who was declared "not guilty" and a wicked was declared "guilty" but in the case of justification, through the sinner's new relationship with Christ, God declares him or her righteous before Him. The source of this act is God, the ground is Christ and the subject is the repented sinner. The result of being declared not guilty is that a sinner who is rebellious, wicked, who deserves to be severely punished, is declared innocent before the righteous judge (Rom. 3:20-26, 4:1-5, 5:1). Earl Radmacher has put it thus:

> When a person is persuaded of the genuineness of the offer of salvation and believes in Christ, at that moment he is clothed in the righteousness provided by Christ, so that His righteousness becomes his very own - God legally pronounces him justified. God subtracts the penalty of sin and adds the standing of righteousness. The believer then has an official standing as a member of the "royal family," clothed in the robe of Christ righteousness.[344]

When a repentant sinner is declared righteous before God, there are some benefits that go with that act. A sinner is restored back to the favor and peace with God. He moves from God's wrath to salvation, is reconciled to God and his neighbors, is now an heir of God and has full access to the household of God (Gal. 4:4-5).[345]

He Places us as His Children

In the relation between a believer with God, Paul uses the term adoption five times in his letters (Rom. 8:15, 8:23, 9::4; Gal. 4:5; Eph. 1:5). The Greek term *huiothesia* which is translated

---

[344] Earl D. Radmacher, 138.
[345] Ibid., 310.

"adoption" means "placing as a son"[346] and this is granted to a person who has accepted Christ as his Savior and Lord. It is a relational term that expresses a relationship of a child that once did not belong to a father and now does. The term refers to an intimate relationship between a believer and God (Rom. 18:5). Willey and Culbertson define adoption as, "Adoption is the declaratory act of God, by which upon being justified by faith in Jesus Christ, we are received into the privileges of sonship."[347]

When a sinner accepts Christ and his sins are forgiven, he is declared not guilty, he is declared righteous, and he is placed in a position of being the real son or heir of God. Before accepting Christ, a sinner has no relationship with God. But at the time of repentance, he or she is accepted into the family of God and is able to have all the rights and privileges that attend calling God "Abba Father" (Rom. 8:15). In Roman context, William Evans describes adoption as:

> Adoption means the placing of a son.... It means the taking by one man of the son of another to be his son, so that, that son has the same position and all the advantages of a son by birth.... It takes place the moment one believes in Jesus Christ" (Jn. 3:2, Gal. 3:26).[348]

Herry Thiessen also describes the Biblical view of adoption as:

> Adoption is the act of God of taking people who were not His children and pronouncing them to be His. It is the transfer of the people who had intimate relationship with Him to having a cohesive relationship with Him because of their acceptance and belief in Jesus Christ. At first the person was a slave but due to faith in the Savior Jesus Christ, he is no longer a slave but a son.[349]

---

[346] Ibid., 139.

[347] Willey and Culbertson, 291.

[348] William Evans, 162.

[349] Herry Thiessen, *Introductory Lectures in Systematic Theology* (Grand Rapids: Eerdmans Publishing Company, 1949), 371.

Being placed in the family of God means, we are made sons of the almighty God (Jn. 1:12). We are moved from the place of being slaves to sin and placed in the sonship relationship with God. It is through God's grace and our acceptance that facilitate this new relationship with Him.

The fact of our being God's children points to some vital considerations. First, we are delivered from doubts of our future destiny. We do not wait until we will be in heaven to be His children (Gal. 4:4-5; Rom. 8:17). As sons and daughters of God, we are obligated to live righteously, so that as we continue in relationship with God, we call Him our "Abba Father." We are assured of peace and harmony with God. Our salvation is assured. In God's family there is no distinctions, neither racial nor social, neither male nor female, neither rich nor poor, we are one in Him (Gal. 3:20). As His sons and daughters, God provides our needs, He cares for us, protects us from falling away from Him and He helps us to be more like our brother Jesus Christ.[350]

Along with all these blessings, we are also heirs of the Father. Though we are heirs of the Father at present, our complete inheritance is to be completed in heaven when Christ comes (Rev. 21:1-4). Besides these blessing that we have, William Evans lists some practical evidences that help us to know that we are God's sons:

- We are led by the Holy Spirit (Rom. 8:4; Gal. 5:18).
- We have a childlike confidence in God (Gal. 4:5-6).
- We have liberty of access to God (Eph. 3:12).
- We have love for the brethren (1Jn. 2:9-11, 5:1).
- We are obedient to God (Jn. 5:1-3).[351]

He Sets Us Apart for Himself

After confession of sin we are set apart as useful, holy people. This is the time that God can use us in any way He would

---

[350] William Evans, 163.

[351] Ibid., 163.

like. Being set apart or being sanctified has to do with our character and conduct. It exhibits the fruit of that relationship with God - it is a life separated from a sinful world and dedicated unto God.[352]

By God setting us apart, it helps us to not be engaged in evil, but to live in total commitment to His service (2Chron. 29:5, 15-18). Being set apart helps believers to abstain from sins, and to continue in fellowship with the holy God. "It is God's will that you should be sanctified: that you should avoid sexual immorality; that each of you should learn to control his body...."[353] When the word sanctification is transliterated from Greek language, it is *Hagiazo* and in Hebrew, *qadash,* which means to "be holy," "harrow" or "set apart." Tracing the meaning of *hagiazo* (set apart) from the Greek Lexicon, Thomas Simmons says that:

> *Hagiazo* has a meaning of to render or acknowledge to be venerable, to hallow, to separate from things profane and dedicated to God, to consecrate; to purify, either externally - whether ceremonially (1Tim. 4:5; Heb. 9:13) or by expiation (Heb. 10:10, 13:12), or internally. The meaning of *hagiasmos* and *hagios* follow from the meaning of *hagiazo*, according to their proper use.[354]

According to the above quotation, sanctification seems not only to be an act of God to a repentant sinner but also a process of spiritual growth. Through God's grace and empowerment, a believer is separated from self and inward sinfulness and by the in filling of the Holy Spirit, set apart to holiness and God's service. It is a time that a believer consecrates himself or herself to fulfill the holy purposes for which God has set him apart.

Setting a believer apart is the work of God. We are internally renewed, causing us to die to sin and be conformed into the image of Christ. It is a continuous operation of the Holy Spirit

---

[352] Ibid., 163.

[353] 1Thess. 4:1- 4b (New International Version).

[354] Thomas Paul Simmons, 313.

whereby, He helps us to be holy before God and in our relationship with Him. He strengthens our holy stand before God and helps us to remain in obedience to Him. It is therefore, a position (our stand), and is progressive. This means that a pardoned sinner is continuously associated with God so long as he continues living in peace and harmony with Him.

As we have already highlighted, sanctification is both instant and progressive and the results are that believers have power to endure many afflictions in this world, they have victory over sin, the Holy Spirit indwells in them and He has given them spiritual gifts so that they may utilize them in the service of God(1Cor. 12, 14, 15). Being consecrated into a new life in Christ, we are able to resist sin (1Jn. 2:15; 1Pet. 1:14), we appreciate God's discipline (Heb. 12:5-13), and when we do what displeases God, we should always confess so as to be forgiven (1Jn. 1:9; Eph. 1:7). John Wesley conclusively understood sanctification of a believer as:

> In sanctification, there is a real as well as relative change. We are inwardly renewed by the power of God. We feel the love of God shed abroad in our hearts by the Holy Spirit which is given unto us, producing love to all mankind, and more especially to the children of God, expelling the love of the world, the love of pleasure, of ease, of honor, of money, together with pride, anger, self-will, and every other evil temper ..., changing the earthly, sensual, devilish mind, into the mind which was in Christ Jesus.[355]

He Assures our Salvation

Besides many existing theories that talk of security of believers, how should we assure believers that their salvation is secure or certain in Christ? A believer has an internal sense of security of his salvation. It is the work of Christ to sustain every

---

[355] *Tabor Heights United Methodist Trinity Sunday Worship Bulletin*, June 15, 2003.

believer in Him. This is indicated in His prayer, promises and even His work on the cross (Jn. 17:6-19). The work of the Holy Spirit who indwells believers' lives is also active and will complete the work of salvation that He started in the believer's life. Can a believer become a prodigal such that, he gets away from the presence and fellowship of God? This is a very important question to ask because the prodigal son willingly decided to run way from his father's home and wandered around with bad guys. Since there was no one who could satisfy his life, he decided to go back to his father where he used to enjoy companionship, fellowship, harmony and communion with the father. Did his father exclude him from being his son because he had been a prodigal?

The gospel of John vividly records that salvation of a believer is secured by God on God's hands (Jn. 6:39 - 40, 10:27-30, 17:11, 1 Jn. 3:9, 5:18; Phil. 1:6). Though a repentant sinner has to carefully live in the household of God, it is God's responsibility to preserve him, but not by his own effort. These verses assure us that even in our weaknesses and sin (natural), God's grace, power, and love will keep us.[356]

The directive will of God is that not one of the believers to perish (2 Pet. 3:9) but, believers have their own responsibility of persevering to the end. Believers have their own will to stay in God's fellowship and peace or to be prodigals. Very good examples of believers' choices are portrayed by the fall of Adam, the Israelites apostasy, Judas' betrayal of Jesus, etc. One can choose therefore to stay in the presence of God or to wander around in the realm of sin as a prodigal.

In John 10:27-30, Christ made certain that those who are for Him will be given eternal life and will never perish. He affirms that no one will ever snatch them from Him. The verbs that are used here in the verse are continuous in action (hear, know, follow).[357]

---

[356] Charles Horne, 91-93.
[357] Earl D. Radmacher, 192-93.

Does this mean that God has unconditionally guaranteed eternal salvation to believers? John 10:27 gives us the idea that believers have to listen and follow. What if they don't listen and follow? It seems there is a problem here and this means believers have to consistently listen, follow and obey Christ. Listening and following are there for believers so that they may continue having salvation from God.

Concerning our human responsibility for our salvation, the Holy Scriptures give us warnings such as:

- Matt. 13:22ff - not to be like thorny soil which does not produce any fruit.
- Matt. 24:12ff- that the love of some will grow cold.
- Lk. 17:32ff - Lot's wife is an example of looking back.
- Jn. 15:6ff - a person who does not remain in Christ will be cut off.
- Not to be like the Israelites, who many times forsook God and were taken into captivity.

These and many other verses show that there are some believers who might not be listening and following Christ, hence, they will not remain in relationship with Him. Our responsibility is to remain in Him and not to be distracted from our relationship with Him.

Our salvation is eternally secured but not unconditionally because the condition is to abide in Christ (Jn. 15:6, Rom. 11:17-21). These verses, too, teach us that the eternal life that we possess is not an independent gift to us but it is ours as we remain in Christ (1Jn. 5:11-12). "This does not mean that God casts us off when we sin, nor does He disowns us, but His love, grace and forgiveness set us free, not to sin, but to serve and love Him without fear in the present and future."[358]

Summarizing what God does to a believer who has accepted the death of His Son Jesus Christ, Galen Currah perceives that he (believer) enters into salvation, which has three dimensions, "past, present and future. Believers' salvation has aspects such as: Material, physical, spiritual, social, behavioral and moral.[359] Salvation may be "Past" (Eph. 2:8) "Present" (Rom. 6:11) or "Future" (Phil. 3:20) and Be Positional (I have been saved), Experiential (I am being saved), or Awaited (I will be saved). The following table illustrates these dimensions and aspects.

Table3. Several Aspects of Salvation

Material	Riches in Christ	Supplies all I need - Phil. 4:19	Eternal rewards 1 Cor. 4:5
Physical	Belong to Christ	Some Physical healing – James 5	Resurrection Eph. 3:21
Spiritual	"In Christ"	Communion - God through Christ by Holy Spirit	See face to face 1 Cor. 13:12
Mental	Come to know	Grow in knowledge - Col. 1:9	know fully 1 Cor. 13:12
Social	Community - Acts 2:47	Household (family of God) - Heb. 3:6	Reunited-body Heb. 12:23
Behavioral	Baptized - Acts 2:36	Obedient to Jesus Christ - Matt. 28:19	Power 2 Cor. 5:5

---

[358] Charles Horne, 94-95.

[359] Galen Currah, "Discussion on Dimensions of Salvation," Western Seminary, Oct. 18, 2002.

Moral	Forgiven	Way of escape - 1 Cor. 10:13	Sinless
Demoni-cal	Delivered	Victory especially in war-fare - Eph. 6	Judge angels 1 Cor. 6:3
Legal	Justified - Rom. 5:1	Affirmed - Rom. 3:24	Exonerated Rom. 8:30
Rela-tional	Adopted - Gal. 4:5-6	Provided for - Matt. 6:33	Received Home Jn. 14:1ff
Emo-tional	Assurance - 1 Thess. 1:4-6	Joy through the Holy Spirit - Gal. 5:22	Eternal bliss 1 Pet. 1:8

Salvation as Union with Christ

The Biblical teaching of a believer being in Christ is an objective aspect of the application of our salvation. In another words, a believer is identified with Christ or incorporated into Christ (Jn. 15:5; Gal. 2:20; Col. 1:27). The reason for Christ being in the believer is because He is the Savior who is inside us but not outside us. Biblical writers like Paul and John have used phrases: "In Christ," "in Christ Jesus" to imply the positional and progressive union or situation which the believer is after accepting Christ.[360] The union between a believer and Christ has two phases such that, "in Christ" is on the believer's side and "in us" is Christ's side.

---

[360] Bruce Demarest, 313.

In Christ

The New Testament describes the whole life of a believer to be "in Christ" or "life in Christ." "In Christ" is a human phase which is an experiential union of a believer with Christ. It is a new unique relationship with Christ where the believer is fully identified with Him. The person is no longer alienated from God nor does he or she alienate God. Bruce Demarest describes this relationship as:

> It is the notion that the believer has died with Christ and is raised to a new life with Him (Rom. 6:3-11). Accordingly, the New Testament portrays the believer in Christ (Jn. 14:20; Rom. 8:1; 2 Cor. 5:17; Eph. 2:13), Christ in the believer (Jn. 14:20; Rom. 8:10), Jesus and the Father in the believer (Jn. 14:23), and the Christian as a partaker of the divine nature (2 Pet. 1:4). Concerning Greek "en Christos" motif, "en" has a local sense; it describes the believer's new situation, sphere, or environment as transferred the domain of sin to the realm of new spiritual life. Union with Christ thus marks the end of the old existence and the beginning of the new.[361]

This mystical union (Eph. 5:32) is a new life and is the work of God through the power of the Holy Spirit (1 Cor. 12:13; 1 Jn. 3:24). This life is not static but dynamic: one lives for and in Christ throughout life. The conditions are repentance, confession of sin, listening to Christ, obeying Him and following Him. Through the power of the Holy Spirit, one is empowered to live a holy life.

The new life of a believer is not only an individual renewal, at the time of salvation, but is a whole way of Christian life. This life is as broad as the universe in that, it starts from the time of

---

[361] Ibid., 323.

conversion, and continues into eternity, when Christ will return in glory to culminate our salvation. With this inclusive spectrum of the union, Lewis Smedes in part states:

> Being in Christ is too inclusive to be restricted to what happens inside my soul... Being in Christ, we are part of a new movement by His grace, a movement rolling on toward the new heaven and new earth where all things are made right and where He is all in all.[362]

Descriptively, Robert Thieme talks of the union with Christ as an effect in the believer's life which is caused by Christ's death and resurrection, that is:

> The substitutionary work of Christ on the cross releases from the power of sin and death, and His resurrection provides a new life "in Christ" (Rom. 6:1-11). That new life is the personal possession and destiny of every believer. It is a union by which the totalities of God's gifts are obtained.[363]

Wayne Grudem describes this experiential relationship as:

> Union with Christ is a phase used to summarize several different relationships between believers and Christ, though which Christians receive every benefit of salvation. These relationships include the fact that we are in Christ, Christ is in us, we are like Christ and we are with Christ.[364]

Union with Christ has its base in Christ Himself. His atoning sacrifice on the cross effected this act (Gal. 2:20). It is received by those who by faith accept His death and resurrection such that, through repentance, His life is imparted in them (Rom. 6:8-10; 2 Cor. 5:14-17).

---

[362] Lewis B. Smedes, *Union with Christ* (Grand Rapids: Eerdmans Publishing Company, 1983), 57, 91.

[363] Robert B. Thieme, "*Union with Christ*" (Portland: Theological Research Exchange Network, 1987), Microfilm.

[364] Wayne Grudem, *Systematic Theology*, 840.

Since union with Christ happens at the time of acknowledging Jesus as Savior, it cannot be traced how it happens but the fact remains, it is there and is progressive such that, the person experiences "Christ in him" and reflects on what He did on the cross for Him and seeks to faithfully live in Him and for Him. Adding to what it means to be "in Christ" or "union with Christ" Robert Thieme says that:

> This union cannot be consummated without in-dispensable work of the Holy Spirit in baptism by which the body of Christ is formed (1 Cor. 12:13). "To drink of one Spirit" is the fulfillment of our Lord's invitation of Jn. 7:37-38. As such it is illustration of faith in Christ at the moment of salvation when the baptism of the Spirit occurs. This occurrence of baptism in the Spirit at salvation is corroborated by Eph. 4:4-5 and Gal. 3:1-5, 4, 26-27. The reception of the Spirit is the beginning of the Christian life (Gal. 3:2-5).[365]

The biblical fact behind the believers' union with Christ is that, Christ is in us, "I have been crucified with Christ; it is no longer I who live, but Christ who lives in me."[366] What distinguishes a believer from other people is that Christ lives in him; he is identified with Christ (Rom. 8:10; Rev. 3:20) who is his present and future hope. This life "in Christ" affects the whole person that is, his mind, decisions, will, attitudes, behaviors, and beliefs, such that, one is able to keep His commandments. By doing the requirements of Christ, this indicates that the person is in Christ and He is in that person through the present of the Holy Spirit (1 Jn. 3:24).[367] Lewis Smedes adds to this by stating that:

> The believer's speech, his thought, his hopes, his

---

[365] Robert Thieme, Microfilm.

[366] Gal. 2:20 (New International Version).

[367] Wayne Grudem, 845.

relationships, his attitudes, and his entire style of life are all set within his existence in Christ.... Our speech is clear and decisive in Christ (1 Cor. 4:17) and we are enriched in Christ (1 Cor. 1:5). We are wise in Christ (1 Cor. 4:10). We are safe in Christ (Rom. 16:10). Our whole pattern of life is changed in Christ. The style, the dynamic, and the perspective are all defined by our status or location in Christ. The new situation is so inclusive of life in all its dimensions that it can be called "new creation". The new creation is already present because the Spirit of the Lord is here and at work in the whole life.[368]

Wayne Grudem also describes the whole Christian life as life with Christ and with the Triune God that is, "personal fellowship with Christ and union with the Father and with the Holy Spirit."[369]

Before His ascension, Christ promised all believers that, "I am with you always, to the very end of the age."[370] After His ascension, He sent the Holy Spirit to be with us which implies His presence in us (Jn. 16:7; 17:11; Acts 1:9-11). This is not only an act of Christ in us but also a process of "Christ in us." It is not a one time experience at salvation, but is a continuous life of a believer. Believers live their whole lives in His presence (2 Cor. 2:10; 2 Tim. 4:1). All believers are deeply aware of Christ's presence in their lives and have no reservation in witnessing. Does this mean that believers live a sinless life? Absolutely not! If we say we have no sin in our lives, we make God a great liar. This is a life of ongoing confession before God, as to remain in His fellowship.[371]

---

[368] Lewis B. Smedes, 57, 91.

[369] Wayne Grudem, 846 -47.

[370] Matt. 28:20 (New International Version).

[371] Subjectively, the writer has been practicing this for many years and many of his friends have been trying to live this sort of life.

In relation to God the Father and the Holy Spirit, the Scriptures explicitly record that this relationship (union) is not only present but also is eternal. Believers are related to God the Father because they are in Him (Jn. 17:21) and the Father is in them (Jn. 14:23). We are also like the Father and we have a unique and intimate fellowship with Him (Matt. 5:44-45; 1 Jn. 1:3). The Holy Spirit too has ownership, for He is in us, that is He lives in us, (Rom. 8:9, 11) and His seal in us shows that we belong to God. Like God the Father and Jesus Christ, we are also in fellowship, harmony and communion with Him. Wayne Grudem describes this distinct and mystical union as:

> Both now and in eternity we (believers) relate to the Father in His distinct role as our heavenly Father, to the Son in His distinct role as our Savior and Lord, and to the Holy Spirit in His distinct role as the Spirit who empowers and continually applies to us all the benefits of our salvation.[372]

The whole life of a believer is immersed in Christ or in the Triune God such that, the believer lives in and for Christ. A believer stands in a status that is no longer his but that belongs to Christ, meaning the person is Christ's man or woman freed from sin. The person lives to the glory of Christ (Eph. 1:12).

Illustrations of the Union. The New Testament, especially the gospel of John, gives many illustrations of the union between a believer and Christ. The illustrations are used to help the believers fully understand their relationship with Christ not only at the time of accepting Him but throughout their life here on earth and into eternity. Some of these were used by Christ Himself and some by the apostles. In John 15:1-17, Jesus referred to Himself as the true vine and believers as His branches. Though He was referring primarily to His disciples, He was referring to all believers. "As

---

[372] Wayne Grudem, *Systematic Theology*, 847.

branches live and bear fruit only in union with the vine, so disciples derive their life and productivity from intimate union with Christ and in fellowship with His word (v.4)."[373] The apostle John also records the words of Jesus as: "I am in my Father, and you are in me, and I am in you."[374] Jesus' union with God and all believers is the union He has with God the Father. Because Christ has a unique relationship with the Father, He also shares that love and union with all believers who remain in Him (Jn. 14:20).

With the analogy of a stone house, Paul uses it to illustrate that the union between believers and Christ is very firm. Neither believers nor Christ can live without the other (Eph. 2:19-22). Paul goes on to say that it is in the believers' lives where the Triune God lives (Eph. 2:22). Because believers are the houses in which the Triune God lives, this means that they are under the control of the Holy Spirit and God always uses them in fulfilling His purpose.

Illustrating the same union with Christ, Paul uses an analogy of the human body whereby, all parts contribute to one body and basically one cannot do without the other. Though believers are many in number, through baptism of the Holy Spirit, they are uniquely united to Christ who is the main body and to one another - the church (Rom. 12:4-5, Eph. 1:22-23). This illustration signifies the union of a believer and Christ and therefore:

> Corporate, describing the church universal, and yet the individual believer is not lost sight of in the community of saints. The words (the body of Christ) themselves imply two things: personal union with Christ and incorporation in the collective Christian fellowship ... "in Christ we who are many form one body and each member belongs to all the others" (Rom. 12:5).[375]

---

[373] Bruce Demarest, 328.

[374] John 14:20; 17:21-23 (New International Version).

[375] Ibid., 329.

Another Paul's illustrations of the union is that of the marriage relationship (Eph. 5:23-32; Rom. 7:2-4). Since a man and woman become one in marriage, it is in the same way believers are united with Christ. Before accepting Christ, the person belonged to the world and when he repents and confessed his sins before God, he or she was forgiven and united in the righteousness of Christ and mysteriously became His part.

Nature of the Union. How Christ makes His home in the believers' lives is beyond our human comprehension, and it is just like being "born again" (Jn. 3) for we cannot explicitly explain how it happens. With the Old Testament view of God dwelling in and among His people in the temple, it is the same way that Jesus indwells all believers' lives (Exod. 25:8; 29:45; Lev. 26:11-14). The dwelling of Christ and God in us is said to be not only now but also it is continuous (Jn. 10:28-30; 14:23).

The union is spiritual, because through the Holy Spirit Christ indwells all believers (Jn. 14:16-17). Paul uses the Old Testament view of the temple where God used to dwell and says to the Corinthian believers that, "your body is the temple of the Holy Spirit, who is in you, whom you have received from God" (1 Cor. 6:19; 3:16-17).[376]

The union is holistic because it involves all dimensions and aspects of the believers' lives. A believer does not own even one aspect of his life, but belongs to Christ. His entire life, mind, behaviors, will, attitudes, all stand on the foundation of Christ who uses them for His glory.

The relationship, moreover, is a comprehensive union. The Christian's entire life and actions are to be exercised in relation to Christ - his life, values, power, and rule. The believer's speech is in Christ (Rom. 9:1), his labors are in Christ (1 Cor. 15:58), his proclamation of the truth is in Christ (2 Cor. 2:17), and his exercise

---

[376] Ibid., 330- 31.

of spiritual authority is in Christ (Philemon 8). This means that the entire Christian life is to be Christ - centered. The whole life, from its fundamental being, to its actions, is surrounded by the reality of Christ.

Outcomes of the Union. Paul records some results that occur when we are "in Christ" as:

> We are buried with Him by baptism into death. We know our old self was crucified with Him... So you also must consider yourselves dead to sin (Rom. 6:4, 6,11). I have been crucified with Christ (Gal. 2:20). If with Christ you died to the elemental spirits of the universe (Col. 2:20) . . . . You have died and, your life is hid with Christ in God (Col. 3:3). But God ... made us alive together with Christ ... and raised us up with Him (Eph. 2:4-6). And you were buried with Him in baptism, in which you were also raised with Him through faith in the working of God (Col. 2:12). If then you have been raised with Christ ... (Col. 3:1ff).[377]

With the above verses, a believer is described as crucified with Christ, having died with Him. This is mysteriously actualized through the union between a believer and Christ. Before this happened, the person (a sinner) had united himself with the devil whom Paul refers to as, "the world." One was bound to sin (Rom. 1) and consigned all things to sin (Gal. 3:22). This means that sin had dominated the whole person, his mind (Rom. 1:21), his will (Rom. 7:15-20) and his body (Rom. 7:24). When the person accepted Christ, the Holy Spirit identified him or her with Christ. The person was united to Christ through His death (Rom. 6:5). Bruce Demarest describes the believer's death with Christ as:

> The Greek adjective *systauroo* (grown together or engrafted) signifies a union that is exceedingly close; it denotes the organic union in virtue of which one being

---

[377] *Bible*, (New International Version).

shares the life, growth, and phases of existence belonging to another. So we died with Him which in Greek aorist indicative of (*synapothnesko*) means to die together. So, also Col. 3:3, "for you died, and your life is now hidden with Christ in God." Regarded as having died with Christ, the believer does not respond to the world and its ways (Col. 2:20).... In identification with Christ, the old sinful nature has been excised, and a radical change of life has occurred.[378]

In Christ, a believer experiences a radical transformation of life. He is under control of the Holy Spirit and therefore, there is no room for self. He or she does not respond to sin because figuratively he is dead to it. Like a dead body that does not respond to any stimuli, a believer should not respond to any sin. He does not respond to sin because he has clothed himself with Christ (Gal. 3:27).

Though a believer has died with Christ, it means "a daily process of self-denial and cross bearing. We perhaps do not live as men who died to sin; but this only demonstrates that we betray our origin."[379] A believer should always seek to freely, willingly and genuinely behave according to the requirements of Christ (Rom. 6:1-2).

Not only does Paul portray a believer as dead with Christ but also as buried with Him. If a believer is engrafted to Christ, this means that because Christ died and was buried, he or she is buried with Him. "Buried with Him" (Gr. passive - *synthapto*) means, to bury together, which is symbolized by water baptism (Rom. 6:4). "The significance of the burial imagery is personal death to sin's domination and complete breach with the old way of life."[380]

---

[378] Bruce Demarest, 334.
[379] Lewis B. Smedes, 96 - 97.
[380] Bruce Demarest, 334.

Through union with Christ, a believer is made alive with Him (Col. 2:13). What does "alive in Christ" mean? This has present and past aspects (Eph. 2:5-6). A believer's resurrection with Christ has already taken place (spiritually when he or she accepted Him) and therefore, he or she has to live a life worthy of resurrection which is a new life in Him (2 Cor. 5:17). Resurrection with Christ also means that a believer:

> Has a new point of orientation, a new goal, and is a new creation. More, it means that we live by a new power (Phil. 3:10) within a new life order. Rose with Christ means that we are "in Christ with all that this implies.... There is no resurrection of Christ for me unless I am included with the living Lord in His new order of life.[381]

Not only is a believer resurrected with Christ but also will be glorified with Him at His second coming, "when Christ, who is your life appears, then you also will appear with Him in glory." This glorification is still to be experienced by all believers, and it includes bodily resurrection, enjoying eternal life with Christ in the new heaven and new earth and eternity. It also includes ruling with Him in the millennial kingdom (1 Thess. 4:17-18; Rom. 6:5b; Rev. 20). However, at present, believers have been given fullness in Christ who is their head and the head of everything that is visible and invisible. The following table describes Niel Anderson's view of believers' fullness in Christ:[382]

---

[381] Lewis B. Medes, 98 - 99.
[382] Ibid, 99

Table 4. Who I Am in Christ

	I am accepted in Christ
John 1:12	I am God' Child
John 15:15	I am Christ's friend
Romans 5:1.............	I have been justified
1 Cor. 6:17..............	I am united with the Lord and one with Him in spirit
1 Cor. 6:20	I have been bought with a price; I belong to God
1 Cor. 12:27	I am a member of Christ's body
Eph. 1:1	I am a saint
Eph. 1:5	I have been adopted as God's Child
Eph. 2:18	I have direct access to God through the Holy Spirit
Col. 1:14	I have been redeemed and forgiven of all my sins
Col. 2:10	I am complete in Christ
	I am Secure in Christ
Rom. 8:1-2	I am free forever from condemnation
Rom. 8:28	I am assured that all things work together for good
Rom. 8:33-34	I am free from any condemnation charges against me
Rom. 8:35	I cannot be separated from the love of God
2 Cor. 1:21	I have been established, anointed and sealed by God
Col. 3:3	I am hidden with Christ in God
Phil. 1:6	I am confident that God will accomplish the good
Phil. 3:20	I am a citizen of heaven
2 Tim. 1:7	I have not been given a spirit of fear but of power
Heb. 4:16	I can find grace and mercy in time of need
1 Jn. 5:18	I am born of God and the evil one cannot touch me
	I am Significant in Christ
Matt. 5:13	I am the salt and the light of the earth
Jn. 15:1-5	I am a branch of the true vine, a channel of His life
Jn. 15:16	I have been chosen and appointed to bear fruits
Acts 1:8	I am a personal witness of Christ
1 Cor. 3:16	I am God' temple
2 Cor. 5:17-20	I am a minister of reconciliation
2 Cor. 6:1	I am God's coworker
Eph. 2: 6	I am seated with Christ in the heavenly realm
Eph. 2:10	I am God's workmanship
Eph. 3:12	I may approach God with freedom and confidence
Phil. 4:13	I can do all things through Christ who strengthens

Metaphors of the Union. In his writing, Paul figuratively describes union with Christ with the metaphor of baptism and circumcision. He sees a believer entering into the union with Christ through a sacramental rite or initiation and to him; it is an initiation or rite done to a believer which has both present and future effects. At present, a believer is in Christ through accepting Him as a Savior and the Spirit identifying him or her with Christ (1 Cor. 12:13). In the future, a believer will also be united and glorified with Him.

1. Baptism. In Gal.3:14-27, Paul indicates that the Holy Spirit is the one who makes believers God's children as well as puts them in Christ. Union in Christ is further described as being "baptized into Christ" (Gal. 3:27). This status is given to all believers through their faith in Christ, which can be compared with an initiation rite (v. 26). Through the rite of baptism, Paul urges believers to cloth themselves "with Christ," which figuratively means spiritual transformation that makes one a believer.[383] Clothing oneself with Christ is a "picture of entering into the relation of union with Christ."[384] This believer's incorporation into Christ is not effected through a believer's effort but by the Spirit Himself (1 Cor. 12:13), and He does this by quickening one's spirit, resulting in spiritual rebirth. Dunn says that, "this is done by the Holy Spirit by baptizing (Gk. - *en pneuma ti* - in Spirit, so as that one enters through spiritual rebirth (Gk. *Nata Pneumati*) (Gal. 4:29)."[385]

Paul wrote to the Corinthian brothers and sisters that, "For we were all baptized by (or with) one Spirit into one body - whether Jews or Greeks, slaves or free - and we were all given the one Spirit to drink."[386] By this statement, Paul uses the Greek *eis*

---

[383] James G. Dunn, *Baptism in the Holy Spirit* (Philadelphia: Westminister Press, 1970), 110.

[384] Robert B. Thieme, Microfilm.

[385] James Dunn, 112.

[386] 1Cor. 12:13 (New International Version).

which is "into" or "with" "soma" (body) that is "into one body" connoting, "the basic sense of motion toward or "into" some goal. In this case, the goal is the one body, and the effect of baptism in the Spirit is incorporation into the body or alternatively union with Christ."[387] This implies that it is through baptism of the Spirit or of the Spirit that effects that union with Christ. Taking John's idea that baptism of the Holy Spirit is a sinner's spiritual rebirth (Jn. 3), union then has its initial point which is at the time of accepting Christ. In Christ therefore, is a result of baptism "into Christ" (*en Pneumati eis soma*). James Dunn adds by stating that:

> The fact is that, for Paul *baptizein* has only two meanings, one literal and the other metaphorical. It describes either the water - rite pure and simple (1 Cor. 1:13-17) or the spiritual transformation which puts the believer "in Christ," and which is the effect of receiving the gift of the Spirit (hence, baptism in Spirit).[388]

In this view of Spirit baptism, it is achieved at the time of repentance and confession of sins to God. It is this time when a person acknowledges that he or she is a sinner and decides to turn from sin to Christ. Upon doing this, one is born again and divine righteousness is imparted to the person (1 Cor. 1:30, 2 Cor. 5:21). The person is identified with Christ in His death, burial, and resurrection, and Christ indwells in him or her through the presence of His Spirit.

When a believer is in Christ through the Spirit, God counts him or her as righteous because Christ who is in him or her is righteous. Through Christ who is in them, they are entitled to all God's blessings (Rom. 4:6, 11). "In Christ" signals to believers that there is total security: God's eternal judgment is no longer upon them.

---

[387] Robert B. Thieme, Microfilm.
[388] James Dunn, 130.

Through baptism of the Holy Spirit, who unites us with Christ, there are also some other significant benefits: "To be related to Christ is to be related to His redemptive action procured for us.... It is not a question of God handing out a blessing to him who believes and is baptized, but of God uniting us with Christ and with Him freely giving us all things."[389] The believer is a new creation because he no longer belongs to the old life but to the new in Christ. He is initiated into the historical work of Christ on the cross. The person now possesses Godly positional benefits such as eternal life (1 Jn. 5:11-12), Christ's righteousness (2 Cor. 5:21), sonship (Gal. 3:26), heirship (Rom. 8:16-17), priesthood (Heb. 10:10-14) and future kingship (2 Tim. 2:11-12). Indeed, Christ made all these benefits available for all believers when He died. His death once for all was sufficient such that, He dethroned the power of sin over all who believe in Him.

2. Circumcision. In Col. 2:11-12, Paul uses "circumcision" as a metaphor signifying that all believers are initiated into Him, and therefore through the circumcision of hearts, they are united with Christ. Paul uses an Old Testament rite which to the Jews was a mark of identification with God, a physical badge that announced that the circumcised person belonged to God and it was also a mark of spirituality of God's people - Israel. Those who were circumcised had several benefits, such as inheritance of the land and properties from the head of the household; they were called after Abraham the partriachs' head ancestor and were people of the Promised Land. Circumcision was a mark of separation from sin, evils of other nations, and consecration to God. The circumcision rite was performed once, and its significance was ongoing.

In the New Testament, circumcision is a spiritual rite which represents a seal of the righteousness of faith (Rom. 4:9-12), or the putting off of the body of flesh, the seat of sin (Col. 2:11). Writing to the Roman Christians (Rom. 6:5-6), Paul calls,

---

[389] Robert B. Thieme, Microfilm.

"The putting off of the body of flesh,"the crucifixion of the old man, a reference to Greek *Sapx* in its ethical usage as man's human (sin) nature, the seat of sin. The equivalency of the terms "flesh" and "old man" is suggested by the use of the Greek root a *Pekduoma*i, "put off," in this verse and in 3:9.[390]

Since the Colossian believers were "circumcised," this metaphor suggests that they were indeed spiritually so and it was effected by the Holy Spirit. Their position was that they were "in Christ." The idea of circumcision expresses that a believer is no longer living in the sinful nature and practices but he or she lives in Christ's righteousness. The sinful nature in the believers' life has been denied its sinful authority because Christ has taken over the life of all believers. The spiritual seal of the Holy Spirit reminds a believer that he belongs to Christ, and therefore no longer to the sinful nature.

3. Resurrection. Not only are the believers dead to sin which is portrayed by baptism and circumcision, but also they are resurrected with Christ (Col. 2:12). Believers are identified with the resurrection of Christ which signifies their new life with Him. In this verse (Col. 2:12), Johnson states that,

Paul's thought goes beyond the rite of water baptism to the reality of believer's death with Christ through the operation of God. The rite of circumcision typifies the reality of death and resurrection with Christ. Death is the negative side and resurrection is the positive.[391]

Since a believer has been resurrected into new life in Christ, he or she can therefore be living and walking in that new life (Rom. 6:4). Through resurrection with Christ, believers have a new

---

[390] Ibid., Microfilm.

[391] Lewis Johnson, "*The complete Sufficiency of Union with Christ.*" *biblical Theca Sacra* 120 (Jan. - March 1963), 16.

orientation which is in Christ. He or she is free from being ruled by the sinful nature and yielding to it.

As a believer continues being united with Christ, he can continuously reject the devil and his temptations. Unity with Christ makes rejecting sin possible, thus one continuously walks in newness of life. Being identified with Christ's death and resurrection grants us a new life that is under His control. Summarizing the whole concept of believers' union with Christ in His death and resurrection, Thieme states that:

> Identification with Christ in His physical death and burial is positional separation from evil. Identification with Christ in His physical death and resurrection is positional victory which breaks the power and authority of the sin nature as the sovereign of the world. Hence, because of our positional sanctification in which the rule of sin nature has been canceled, the command in Romans 6:12 is now given to cancel experientially the rule of that nature by living up to our potential.[392]

Christ in Us

From the human aspect of living in Christ, He also lives in all believers. The apostle Paul tells us that Christ is "in us." This is not only at the time when one accepts Christ but is also the continuous life of a believer and will be perfected and completed when Christ physically comes again.

In Rom. 8:10; 2 Cor. 13:5; Gal. 2:20 and Col. 1:27, clearly affirms that Christ is in the lives of all believers (Gk. *en umin*) "in you." Along with Christ being in the believers' lives, Paul also says that the Holy Spirit too indwells in them. This is the Old Testament idea of God dwelling in the temple, thus Christ, the Holy Spirit and God the Father have their dwelling place in all believers. A good

---

[392] Robert B. Thieme, Microfilm.

illustration is Isa. 6 where theophany (a manifestation of God) was observed in the temple in which God spoke to Isaiah, commissioning him to proclaim about the sinfulness of His people - Israel.

In Col. 1:27, Paul's explains that there is a clear continuity and uniqueness of God's indwelling in believers' lives. As God used to dwell in the Old Testament temple, God dwells in believers' lives. Since believers have given Christ their lives, Paul describes their lives as God's holy of holies, where Christ richly dwells. His indwelling is not only present but is also continuous; He is the hope of glory which will be revealed when He comes back the second time. About Christ's present and future in the believers' lives, Harrison states that:

> The coming into the world and the crucifixion belonged to the first stage of the unfolding of the mystery; the resurrection and the ascension, together with Christ's residence in His saints, constitutes the second stage, which continues in force to this very hour; and the experience of being with Christ in glory will be the third and final stage. The hope of glory is Christ Himself, for His presence in His people gives substance to the promise of being glorified with Him at His coming again (Col. 3:4).[393]

In conclusion, believers should clearly understand that their union with Christ starts at the moment they repent of their sins and trust Christ as their Savior and Lord, and continues until Christ will appear in glory at His second coming. Every believer has positionally received Christ's righteousness, and is placed in union with Him and is indwelt by His Spirit. Because of Christ's substitutionary death, God Himself declares every believer to be righteous in His sight. He deals with our unrighteous deeds through the position that we are in, which is, "in Christ."

---

[393] Everett F. Harrison, *Colossians, Christ All -Sufficient* (Chicago: Moody Press, 1971), 36.

Chapter 6

COMMUNICATING A CONTEXTUAL GOSPEL

This chapter advances a number of contextual methods that ministers can use to teach the gospel of salvation to three classes of individuals, the unchurched, the unbelievers and the believers among the Central Bantu. The dominant teaching method in Bantu cultures require a "narrative evangelism."[394] The unchurched include those who follow cultural religious practices and have never become church members; unbelievers are those who may be church attenders, yet have never trusted Jesus Christ as their Savior and Lord. Believers, then, are those who are saved, but still misunderstand the doctrine of salvation.

A contextual gospel message that should be presented must address many of the salvation themes mentioned by Bantu Christians during field research. This should include gospel tracts for believers to present to unbelievers. Smith explains:

---

[394] This is the writer's understanding how the Bantu people communicate and understand a message. It is narrating the story, reciting the key ideas and images that conceptualize the doctrine of salvation. A good example is the story of Jesus and Nicodemus where Jesus used childbirth to convey what it means to be a legitimate member of God's kingdom (Jn. 3). This method of communicating the gospel corresponds with the Bantu cultural way of communicating a message, for their mind set is not structural but is more contextual. In doing so, a messenger should exactly know the main theme of the story (narrative), where he or she is driving the message and hearers and the expected response.

Contextual words and symbols should be chosen by a communicator so that the hearers will develop the intended meaning. The sender must be aware that many filters always stand between him and the hearer's experiences, contexts, mood, personal needs and physical environment. The message heard should be relevant to the context of the people so that they make sense out of it.[395]

Process of contextualization

Why is there a need for contextualizing the gospel to the Central Bantu people of Kenya? Contextualization is needed because the Scriptures were written thousands of years ago, and the writers lived in a different culture than the Central Bantu people. To understand, and bring the assumptions and unstated premises of the ancient culture to the Bantu people is to contextualize the gospel message. The Central Bantu people therefore, will continue having difficulties in understanding the gospel of salvation until it is presented in a manner relevant to their cultural context. By cultural context, the writer means a gospel that is addressed in their cultural concepts, thought forms, terms, meanings and language. This concern corresponds with the preaching of the apostle Paul, who presented a contextual message to the religious Athenians whose concept of God was contrary to the teaching of the Bible. Paul addressed them as:

Men of Athens! I see that in every way you are very religious. For as I walked around and looked carefully at your objects of worship, I even found an altar with this inscription: TO UNKNOWN GOD. Now that what you worship is something unknown I am going to proclaim to you ... but now God commands all people everywhere to repent...[396]

---

[395] Donald K. Smith, "Class Lectureship," Sept. 1998.
[396] *Acts 17:22-31* (New International Version).

Expressing his deep desire to present the gospel message, Paul wrote to the Corinthians:

> Though I am free and belong to no man, I make myself a slave to everyone, to win as many as possible. To the Jews I became like a Jew, to win the Jews. To those under the law I became like one under the law ... so as to win those under the law. To those under the law I became like one under the law (though I myself am not under the law), so as to win those under the law... to the weak I became weak, to win the weak. I have become all things to all men so that by all possible means I might save some.[397]

According to the above quotation, Paul's intention in teaching the gospel is to present it in a manner that people will understand and embrace it. He sought to win some to Jesus Christ. Unless people understand the gospel in their own cultural context, there is no way they can be saved.

Until gospel workers clearly understand the meaning and the process for contextualizing the gospel, they cannot effectively communicate the gospel of salvation. Considering the process of contextualization as the only main way used for presenting the gospel, Enoch Wan defines this term as:

> Contextualization is an effort of formulating, presenting and practicing the Christian faith in such a way that is relevant to the cultural context of the target group in terms of conceptualization expression and application; yet maintaining theological coherence, biblical integrity and theological consistency. [398]

The main idea is to present the gospel message in a way which is understood in the culture, but remains biblically sound

---

[397] 1Corinthians. 9:19-22 (New International Version).
[398] Enoch Wan, "Jesus Christ for the Chinise: A Contextualized Reflection," CATW, Nov. 2000, 14.

and theologically coherent. It is a functional method under which after presenting the gospel, people can freely express it in their own cultural contexts, language and understanding. In other words, it is bringing together the relationship of the gospel message from the biblical text to the cultural context. Defining contextualization in the audiences' side, Bruce Bradshaw notes that:

> Contextualization is the capacity to respond meaningfully to the gospel within the framework of one's own situation. It is the process by which a local community integrates the gospel with the real life context, blending text and context into that single, God-intended reality called Christian living.... Contextualization ... takes into account the process of secularity, technology and the struggle for human justice.[399]

According to the above description of contextualization, the term means a process of integrating the gospel with people's context so that it will be meaningful and relevant. This also means that when the gospel is contextually presented, there is a hope for them to experience the impact of that message, decide to change their lives and embrace Christ as their only Savior and Lord.

Through the process of contextualizing the Scriptures, we should make sure that people understand the message in their own contexts, so in their response they may be transformed. Acts 17:22, validates this, because when the apostle Paul presented a gospel message at the meeting of Areopagus, many people decided to change their way of life from paganism to Christianity. From the context of the Athenians' view of God, he expressed the Good News of the true God. Paul used the package of their unknown God in the Greek concept (Pantheon) and persuasively welcomed people to know more about the true God. The great concern of contextualization

---

[399] Bruce Bradshaw, *Bridging the Gap: Evangelism, Development and Shalom* (USA: MARC, 1993), 54.

is that the gospel should be communicated relevantly to people's cultural knowledge, concepts language, and values.

In their study of Mission and how the message of the gospel should be presented in any cultural context, Terry, Smith and Anderson define contextualization as:

> Concepts and methods relevant to a historical situation.... Contextualization can be viewed as enabling the message of God's redeeming love in Jesus Christ to become alive as it addresses the vital issues of a social-cultural context and transforms its worldview, values and its goals.[400]

The person who presents the gospel utilizes skill, with a concern that people will embrace the message and as a result, decide to change their sinful lives and follow Christ. Presenting the gospel that way does not mean changing the word of God, but it is the unchanging Word of God presented carefully, meaningfully and relevantly to their changing cultures.

With a view to an incarnational theology of mission, Hwa Yung expresses the process of contextualization as:

> It is the desire to indigenize, to live as Christian and, yet as member of one's own society, and to make the church a place to feel at home. The desire to do this is tied up with the very nature of the Gospel; it is patterned in the incarnation itself. When God became man, Christ took flesh in a particular family, members of a particular nation, with the traditions of customs associated with that nation. All that was not evil He sanctified. Wherever He is taken by men in any time and space he takes that nationality, that society, that culture, and sanctifies all that is capable of sanctification by his presence. No group of Christians has

---

[400] John Mark Terry, Ebbie Smith and Justice Anderson, *Missiology: An Introduction to the Foundations, History, and Strategies of World Missions* (Nashville: Broadman and Holman Publishers, 1998), 318.

therefore any right to impose in the name of Christ upon another group of Christians a set of assumptions about life determined by another time and place.[401]

Following closely Yung's definition of contextualization, if the gospel is presented to the Central Bantu in their cultural contexts, there is a high possibility that they will experience a spiritual shift. They will change their beliefs about salvation, behaviors, understand the basis and the meaning of salvation, and seek to embrace Christ as their Savior and Lord.

A good contextualized gospel message should not seek to devalue or undermine existing cultural values and concepts, but should correct where necessary, modify, purify, strengthen where possible, retain what is biblically sound and, wisely eradicate ideas that are not biblical. What is true or false, ethical or unethical, scriptural or unscriptural, Christian or cultural, should be determined by the relevant way of understanding and presenting the Word of God to the Central Bantu cultures.

In his article, "Critical Contextualization," Hiebert mentions two extremes which will happen if contextualization is not done and sometimes if it is wrongly done:

> If this is not done, one of two consequences will result. There will be either rigid rejection of the old beliefs which introduces foreignness and a "double standard" in the church. Or the result will be an uncritical acceptance of traditional beliefs and practices, which usually leads to syncretism[402]

---

[401] Hwa Young, *Mangoes or Bananas? The Quest for an Authentic Asian Christian Theology* (Coxford: Regnum Book International, 1997), 62.

[402] Paul Hiebert, "Critical Contextualization," *International Bulletin of Mission Research, II, No. 3* (July 1987).

Contextual Message

The message of salvation is effective only when it is contextualized. This process needs to be understood by the Bantu pastors. They should be able to utilize existing concepts like traditional priests, sacrificial system, mediators, sacrifices, ancestors, and many others. Since many unchurched Bantu are still involved in traditional sacrifices like sacrificing goats and sheep in order to evoke peace, reconciliation and harmony with God, the concept of sacrifice can be used to present the gospel to them. When they ask God for peace and harmony it is not only for themselves but also for their properties, such as domestic animals. They also ask for peace during ethnic war, drought, political instability, severe sicknesses, and during untimely death.

Using the sacrificial concept, a gospel messenger should present the person of Christ and His sacrificial death on the cross as the ultimate and finished work, which reconciles all human beings with God. Christ should be presented as a Mediator and a reconciler between humans and God and with the fellow neighbors. Christ should not only be presented as a reconciler between people and God but also between people and their enemies. Peace and reconciliation should be expressed as some of the results stem from Christ's salvation.

There are also other concepts that can be used. For example, blood sacrifices, fear of spirits, fear of life after death and traditional specialists like a priest, a medicine-man and a prophet. Christ can be presented as our ultimate healer, high priest and prophet. The most significant thing in our message is to have a clear agenda of what we want to communicate and accomplish. Charles Kraft agrees with this by saying that, "effective communicators need to have a clear agenda, a clear understanding of what they intend to get across."[403]

---

[403] Charles H. Kraft, *Communication Theory for Christian Witness* (New York:

As the writer noted earlier, the gospel message we present should be totally rooted in Christ's work on the cross for the salvation of alienated sinners, through which He unites them with God and with one another. In the process of contextualization, there should be no other gospel than that (Lk. 19:9-10). The gospel is the finished work of Christ on the cross, and this is what we should present.

When the gospel message centered on the sacrificial death of Christ and His Lordship is relevantly taught, Paul notes that, "the gospel is the power of God unto salvation to everyone who believes."[404] It is also through the gospel message that sinners in their contexts will be reconciled to God and seeks to live out their new life in His Son Jesus Christ. Grundmann talks about the gospel as:

> The power of God in the gospel consists in the fact that it mediates salvation that by the gospel God delivers man from the power of darkness and translates him into the kingdom of His dear Son. It is grounded in the divine act of deliverance accomplished by the preaching of the gospel.[405]

When we present the gospel of salvation, we should explain clearly how people should respond to it. Human responsibility such as repentance, confession, peace and reconciliation with God, which are already Bantu concepts, must be clearly explained. Since the Bantu use peace and reconciliation concepts when they are experiencing a good harvest or diverse wealth, we can therefore use them to talk about how Christ's death reconciles us with God and creates a peaceful relationship with Him.

Orbis Books, 1991), 11.

[404] Rom. 1:16 (New Internatial Version).

[405] *Theological Dictionary of the New Testament 9 Vol.* (Grand Rapids: Eerdmans Publishing Company, 1974), 310.

Contextual methods

Generated from "narrative evangelism method ideas,"[406] the first effective method should be the one that addresses contextually the basic needs of people. Second, we need to use cultural tools for communicating a message, such as parables, participation and stories. Third, we must utilize cultural dynamic equivalences and functional substitutions such as sacrifices, offerings, ancestors and traditional actors such as priests or medicine-men.

Since in chapter four we observed that the Soteriological terms have more abstract ideas and sometimes multiple meanings in the Bantu culture, the current chapter has utilized some of the them to convey key ideas which conceptualize the doctrine of salvation. The following diagram illustrates some of the terms, and how they can be used to convey the doctrine.

Figure 17. Concepts in Cultural Salvation

---

[406] Tom A. Steffen, *Reconnecting God's Story to Ministry: Crosscultural Storytelling at Home and Abroad* (La Habra: Center for Organizational and Ministry Development, 1996), 73-81.

Contextual Messengers

In the Bible, we encounter God reaching out to people with His word, for example, through His message of reconciliation. He communicates using monologue (Exod. 3 - Moses and the the burning bush), dialogue (Adam and Eve) or life involvement (Jn. 1; Phil. 2).[407] God's message to Moses was to go to Egypt and liberate His people from slavery. The Israelites needed physical and emotional liberation from bondage. Out of His love, God would communicate His word to them in their slavery environment. He addressed them from their context (their needs) and showed them where to go (Exodus story).

From the Exodus story, God's way of presenting His message was to pass along what He wanted people to do. As He corresponded with them, He used their language and concepts so that they could understand and respond.[408] His message was always clear and relevant such that, people were able to understand. Since God's aim of communicating a message is also ours, we should therefore emulate His method, that is "Our message should be clear, comprehensive ..., based on the concepts and illustrations with which the audience is familiar. We need to start where people actually are - not where we wish they were."[409]

Another way of addressing the gospel to people's needs is seen in an example of Jesus Christ. In the gospels, Christ chose His twelve disciples (Mark 6:6-7), instructed them, sent them out and later had them report to Him what they did (6:30). Before they started teaching and preaching about the salvation of God, there was first and foremost Christ's input. After their preaching, there was consistent feedback. This also corresponds with Paul's strategy in 2 Tim. 2:2, where Paul instructed Timothy to teach

---

[407] Charles H. Kraft, 1991, 60.

[408] Charles H. Kraft, *Communicating the Gospel God's Way* (Pasadena: William C. Library, 1979), 4 - 5.

[409] *Media and Message Resource: A Resource Book on the Use of Media in Evangelism* (World Evangelistic Fellowship: The Paternoster Press Ltd., 1989), 32.

"reliable" people, and those reliable people were to teach others who were qualified. His way of teaching was first Timothy, then reliable people and finally others.

Depending on individual or group needs and context, the gospels reveal to us that Jesus presented the gospel message differently to each person or group. The way He talked to Nicodemus, to the young rich ruler, was different from the way he passed the message to the Samaritan woman. The key factor in His teaching and preaching was the way He would fit the message to each hearer's need and context. A good example is His message to Nicodemus whom He told that "you must be born again" (Jn. 3). He talked to the Samaritan woman mentioning her context about where the Samaritans worshipped their gods. From the context of the Samaritan woman's need of water, Jesus presented the message of eternal heavenly water. Affirming that Jesus' way of presenting the gospel message was according to people's needs and context, *Media and Message Resource book* state that:

> Jesus healed and fed people, even as he preached. He understood the needs and background of his audience, told stories that they would understand, and adapted his approach to different individuals. With Nicodemus he was capable of holding a relatively philosophical discussion (Jn. 3:1-15), but with a woman at the well he employed a different approach.... Jesus loved the rich young ruler (Lk. 18:18-25) but would not water down his demands in order to win him. Presenting his claims in a deceitfully persuasive manner was not part of his strategy.[410]

Concurring with Jesus' method of gospel presentation, Richard Halverson states that:

> Jesus employed a different approach with each person. He reminded Nicodemus that he "must be born

---

[410] Ibid., 32.

again;" so far as we know Jesus never said these same words to any other person. He spoke quite differently to the Samaritan woman at the well. And with the rich young ruler or the questioning layer he again used entirely different techniques. Jesus dealt with no two seekers alike.... One factor alone remained constant in Jesus' contact with me: His personal presence.[411]

Along with Jesus' method of addressing His message to people's needs, He had a high awareness of their background. When He talked with Nicodemus and stated, "You must be born again" (singular) but not "you" in plural form, He did this because He knew the concept of worship among the Pharisees was collective, but not individual. To Nicodemus, worship of God was collective, but not individual, and that is why he responded in the plural, "we know ..." expressing a group form or opinion.[412] Wareing notes Nicodemus' answer by saying, "Nicodemus' type of religion fails at three points: at the point of individualism; men cannot be saved, at the necessity for regeneration, at the necessity for doctrine of salvation to reclaim men for the effect of sin by a means external to himself."[413]

Considering that Central Bantu culture is collective, like that of the Jews, the gospel must be presented to fit not only the need of the community but also to touch individual needs and background. Some Bantu people think that salvation is having peace with God and their fellow humans, it is being in harmony with God and people, being accepted by God and people and being reconciled with Him. These cultural terms sound biblical but are always used in people's traditional religion. The gospel messengers should carefully seek to relate the gospel message to these terms.

---

[411] Richard C. Halverson, "Methods of Personal Evangelism," *Christianity Today,* Oct. 28, 1966.

[412] Earnest C. Wareing, *The Evangelism of Jesus* (New York: The Abingdon Press, 1918), 13.

[413] Ibid., 13.

Cultural Tools

In presenting the gospel to the Central Bantu people, cultural communication tools (folk media) such as stories, parables and participation can be used. Stories and parables should come from the natural context, such as day to day events,. environment, festivals, and even from animals that they know. These tools are used effectively through audience participation, throughout presentation of the gospel message, and through persuasion. These tools reinforce the gospel message when people hear it in their own understanding. If these communiucation tools are properly used, they can motivate people to make decisions for Christ, trusting Him as their Savior.

Participation

Since the Central Bantu like to participate and interact, it is culturally relevant to use participation folk media to enhance their understanding of the gospel message. A communicator should let people participate by allowing them to ask questions, discuss issues in the message, reason, and dramatize the message and, along with that, persuading them to accept the biblical truth. In audience participation that stimulates discussions and questions, Donald Smith notes:

> Discussion produces greater change in beliefs, preferences, and attitudes than do lectures, documentary presentation or any other passive exposure to information. Questioning to stimulate discussion develops active participation, the key to attitude change... starting discussion is a stimulus to verbalizing beliefs, an excellent way to develop greater consistency between beliefs and behavior.[414]

By using this channel among the Bantu people, communicators should always remember that "communication

---

[414] Ibid., 139.

is involvement;"[415] if we encourage them to participate, it will reinforce their understanding of the message.

Communicators can use participatory folk media sometimes, by introducing case studies. For example "how to introduce a Kikuyu or a Kamba traditional religious person to Christ, how the Africa Inland Missionaries faced difficulties when they were propagating the gospel among the Bantu tribes, " and many others that fit the culture. Bible case studies, such as the story of the prodigal son, the lost coin, the lost sheep and a young farmer are very relevant to discuss. From these case studies, a communicator and the audience can organize a role-play and dramatize the stories. Depending on the theme and aim of the gospel message and the communicator, a role- play may be geared to change people's attitudes, behaviors, knowledge or beliefs, especially the Bantu view of "salvation." In His book, *Creating Understanding*, Donald Smith stresses the effectiveness of role-play: "Role-play is effective in changing attitudes because it involves active participation, it is enjoyable, and it permits individuals to "pretend" that they are changing without having to admit publicly that they ought to change."[416] He also analyzes a good role-play, noting that it is aimed to change or influence attitude, and says that:

> The best kind of role-play (for attitudinal change) stimulates the actors to use imaginations and improvise many of the lines spoken. The actors develop the arguments that are most convincing to the key audience-the players themselves. Giving freedom to imagination and creativity develops a powerful experience for changing attitudes, one that is immensely enjoyable.... Role-playing moves a step beyond discussion by requiring that the role in a situation be acted out, rather than talked about. This

---

[415] Ibid., 23.
[416] Ibid., 140.

increases active participation because it depends mental effort to imagine and portray someone else's attitude and behavior. When role-playing, one is forced to assume attitudes one may dislike or disagree with. Thus one cannot avoid grappling with issues one may prefer to sidestep. At the least, this creates a sympathy for another point of view....the role-play is a powerful tool to bring attitudes and behavior to closer agreement.[417]

When participation channel is used, we should aim to help the Bantu people to embrace the biblical truth in a manner relevant to their cultural thought. At the start, prayer should be made for the people to respond to the Holy Spirit; persuading their hearts to respond to the message positively. Enough time to synthesize the truth of the message should be allowed, and to help them to reasonably and prayerfully accept the gospel message and culturally appropriate it into their lives. By doing so, a decision to change their way of life and accept Jesus Christ as their Lord and Savior will be apparent. This is to say that they will make right decisions because they have already participated in the message and were given time to think and understand the content of the message. This corresponds with what Charles Ryrie stresses about human act and will in decision making for salvation:

> Efficacious grace does not exclude the human act of believing. It is the work of the Holy Spirit which moves men to believe; therefore, it may be said that no man is saved against his will. It is not a work apart from the human will, but it guarantees effective action upon that will without forcing it.[418]

---

[417] Ibid., 140-141

[418] Charles Ryrie, *The Holy Spirit* (Chicago: Moody Press, 1965), 61.

Story Telling

Story telling is another cultural tool that is effective in communicating the gospel message to the Bantu people. The Bantu people like hearing stories, especially those that are culturally familiar. When a preacher or a teacher gives a contextual story, it is observed that people tend to listen and understand the message more than when a story is not used.[419] When narrating a story, it should be from Bantu contexts, one that is easy to follow, short, easy to be understood and true to the theme and aim of the gospel message. The story should also be applicable to the point that one is trying to put across. A good example is: *The hare and the chameleon* (Kikuyu) and, *the monkey and the crocodile* (Meru). Hare represents "quickness" and chameleon represents "slowness," and these two can be used to pass the gospel message along, for example in describing how some people are quick in making decision to follow Christ while others are slow.

Another good example of story telling is when a message is prepared to address the sinful nature of human beings. A messenger should use a contextual story similar to that of the prodigal son. The prodigal son willingly chose to disassociate himself from his father, and went to live by himself. By so doing, he deliberately decided to live in sin and not to follow his father's expectations. After suffering, he reasoned within himself, saw how miserable and sinful he was, willingly repented before God, and went home to his father. His father's love for his son compelled him to receive him back. He incorporated him back into his family fellowship, reconciled the son back to himself and rekindled friendship with him.

With a biblical application, one can say that, sin has separated man from God (Isa. 59:2). Though God loves us, our sins have put us very far from Him and we are under His judgement (Isa. 1:15). From there, one can talk about what sin is, its consequences and its results.

---

[419] Interviews, January 15, 2003.

Parables

Jesus used parables to communicate the gospel message to His hearers. Among the Central Bantu, parables are an effective cultural communication folk media. Parables use customs, tools, and events that are familiar to people. For example, to communicate the gospel, Jesus used Jewish cultural things like, sower, weed, mustard seed, hidden treasure and fishing net (Matt.13). All of these were culturally known by the Jews. Similarly, the audience of this study can effectively use Bantu parables to communicate the gospel message. Depending on the theme of the message, we can use such things as corn fields, a lost cow or sheep, a plough, a wedding festival, builders, fruit trees, snakes, rabbits, foxes, to mention a few.

When using cultural parables, one has to be careful to use those that have no multiple meanings, because in the Bantu culture some are in that category. In the event that one needs to use them, he or she should clearly state what it means. For example, a parable of a lion can sometimes be used to communicate an idea of courage, fearlessness and or power, and sometimes to teach about meanness and carelessness. In a message, a preacher has to give and interpret a parable according to the theme of his or her message. Spiritual application from parables should address people's spiritual need, and challenge them to make a decision to leave their sinful life and follow Christ.

Since most Bantu people are farmers, such parables as the sower, the weeds and a rich farmer (Matt. 13) can be contextualized and communicated to them. For example, in the parable of the sower, instead of a sower, a relevant term is "a planter" because he or she is different from a Jewish sower who would go in a filed and scatter seeds. Instead of "scattering seeds," the suitable word for the Bantu is "planting." The parable should fit the words and the context of the people so that it has meaning.

Dynamic Equivalence

Dynamic equivalence methods ask two vital questions: First, among the Central Bantu people, are there some cultural and religious concepts, ideas, functions, elements, personalities, or features. that can be used to convey the message of salvation? Second, in their concept of salvation, are there some concepts or words that can be found in the Bible?

In the Central Bantu traditional religious beliefs there are cultural dynamics and functions such as sacrifices, offerings, mediators and ancestors. When we use them to communicate the gospel, we should respectively "affirm whatever is true and good in the culture, fulfill whatever is lacking, correct whatever is false, challenge whatever is wrong, and replace whatever is harmful."[420]

Sacrifices

As the writer mentioned earlier, many non-Christian Bantu people are still sacrificing to God and to their ancestors. They do so to evoke peace, harmony and reconciliation from God and from their ancestors. John Mbiti affirms this by saying that:

> In the African tribes, sacrifices and offerings are acts of restoring ontological balance between God and man, the departed and the living. When this balance is upset, people experience misfortunes and sufferings or fear that those will come upon them. Sacrifices and offerings help, at least psychologically to restore this balance.[421]

When a Christian asks why they still offer sacrifices, it is often the case that they believe that if they fail to do so, the equilibrium of their life will be broken. They will not (they believe) continue experiencing good health, peace, prosperity and happiness. Sacrifices are done by pouring the blood of an animal

---

[420] Galen Currah, "Cultural Salvation Discussion," Western Seminary, Oct. 18, 2002.

[421] John Mbiti, *Concept of God in Africa* (London: Heineman, 1970), 179.

on a religious sacred place, through that blood, peace, harmony and reconciliation are said to be restored to the people.

In this context, the sacrificial work of Christ on the cross can be communicated as ultimate and absolute, that is, His death is enough to bring peace, harmony and reconciliation between God and human beings. Some Scriptures that talk about this can be used:

1. The blood of Jesus is our atonement for sin (Rom. 3:25).
2. The blood of Jesus washes and cleans our sins and makes us clean (1Jn. 1:9).
3. The blood of Christ is perfect to cleanse our sins (Heb. 9:14).
4. His blood had no blemish and He shed it for us (1Pet. 1:9; 1Cor. 6:20).
5. Through His blood, He brought forgiveness of sins (Eph. 1:7; Heb. 9:22).
6. His blood reconciles us to God (Heb. 10:19).
7. His blood delivered us from sins (Rev. 1:5).
8. Christ's blood was shed once for all and was perfect for removing sins (Heb. 7:27, 9:26, 9:13-14).

Concerning the above Biblical truth, we can also present it in "parable" form:

In one village there was a rich man who had many cows and goats. Every month he used to sacrifice a goat to God. When offering sacrifices, he would ask God to provide peace, material prosperity and harmony for his family. One day, he went hunting in the forest and as he was resting under a tree, an elephant came, attacked him and the man was killed. Not only was the family devastated by the loss of their loved one but they were frustrated and discouraged for they had no one else who could continue offering sacrifices for them. Tragically, they lived as the most devastated people in the whole village.

Application. The sacrifices of goats and sheep are deemed 'repeatable' unlike Christ's work on the cross, which was enacted once only. Man believes he needs to repeatedly offer sacrifices to appease the gods. The sacrifice that Jesus offered through His death on the cross for sinners was once for all. It is not repeatable like that of man. Misunderstandings can also be cleared up for those who offer sacrifices, but then die, leaving the family with no one to offer sacrifices for their families or clans. Jesus offered His sacrifice once for all, and therefore by accepting His sacrifice, we can be reconciled and always have eternal peace and harmony with God. Christ appeased God once for all, so that whoever will accept Him will not perish but have eternal life (Jn. 3:16).

In offering the above functional truths to the Bantu people, we should emphasize that the work of God in His Son Jesus Christ is not limited to cleansing the guilty from sin, but means also liberation from the power of darkness, a transference to the Messianic kingdom which, in anticipation of the end has been made present in Christ (Col. 1:13). "The Christ who forgives sin is also the Christ who liberates from slavery to the world."[422]

Mediation. No sacrifices or offerings in the Central Bantu culture are offered without a mediator. A mediator is normally a traditional priest called in Kikuyu *muruti igongona*, and in Kikamba, *muthambi* or *mundu wa Ng'ondu*. "A priest undergoes a period of apprenticeship to make himself knowledgeable in religious matters."[423] His work is to offer sacrifices and offerings to God and the ancestors. The belief is that peace, harmony and reconciliation between people and God are to be mediated. A mediator has to offer sacrifices on behalf of the people, to rectify their situation. The above parable can also be used: when the man died, there was no mediator between his family and God, which means the family could no longer approach God.

---

[422] C. Rene Padilla, *Mission Between the Times: Essays on the Kingdom* (Grand Rapids: Eerdmans Publishing Company, 1985), 10

[423] Renison, Githige, *Christian Religious Education* (Nairobi: Longman Kenya Limited, 1988), 158.

Using dynamic equivalences, Christ can also be presented Scripturally as:

1. Christ is the permanent mediator between people and God (1Tim. 2:5; Heb. 8:6, 9:15, 12:24).
2. Christ is the great High Priest who united us with God and with one another (Heb. 2:10-11, 4:14-16).
3. Christ as High Priest sacrificed His own life for us (Rom. 5:10; 2Cor. 5:17-19, Eph. 2:16; Col. 1:20). He is also the sacrifice and the perfect lamb offered for sacrifice.
4. As a High Priest, Christ removed our sins (Heb. 5:1-2).
5. Through Christ's mediation, we can now approach God (Heb. 10:10-21).
6. Christ gave us the Holy Spirit as our guide (Heb. 11:1ff; Jn. 14:15-17).
7. Through His mediation, we have direct communication with God (Jam. 5:13).
8. Christ's meditorial work puts us in an eternal relationship with God the Father (Heb. 9:15).

All those who have confessed their sins before God have been forgiven, and now enjoy a peaceful and harmonious relationship with God. Through Christ's work on the cross all believers are atoned for, and now have a Father-son relationship with God (Jn. 1:12-13). God has made us agents of salvation: by proclaiming the gospel, we help reconcile sinners to God and to other humans (2Cor. 5:18-19; Col. 1:21-22). Jesus is now the ultimate mediator between us and God, and there is no other way we can have peace with God, apart from accepting His meditorial work. He is our High Priest:

> The same Jesus whom God put forward as a propi-tiatory offering by His own blood (Rom. 3:25) is now the Lord of all (Rom. 10:12). Having provided the basis for the forgiveness of sin through the sacrifice of Himself, He has occupied the place that is rightly his as mediator in the government of the world (Heb. 1:4).[424]

---

[424] Ibid., 10.

Social Context

As highlighted in the introduction, the audiences of this project are Moffat College students, whom the writer is teaching the doctrine of salvation and related concepts. They are the first people to be equipped with the knowledge of contextualization. By being so, they will be able to effectively and relevantly teach the gospel in their churches. The second group is the Africa Inland Church's pastors and leaders, whom the Moffat college students will educate in small group settings or in seminars. By using methods that we have already discussed, the students and pastors will also be equipped to teach the true gospel to church leaders, church's small groups, families, neighbors and friends and, to the traditionally religious people.

In recent research (January to March 2003), the writer realized that to communicate the gospel effectively requires a small group setting, of between six to twelve people. In a small group the Bantu people will have more time to ask questions, participate, dialogue, discuss issues in the message, interact with one another, and synthesize the message. This agrees with Donald Smith's communication proposition fourteen which says, "Communication effectiveness normally decreases with increasing size of the audience."[425] Each Gospel worker should seek to communicate to the number of people whose attention he or she can hold.

To communicate effectively, small group church members should meet under a tree, or in a believer's house, to provide a relaxed environment for free interaction, discussion, questions and reflection. Along with the teaching, group members should share meals.[426]

---

[425] Smith, p. 181.

[426] Among the Bantu people, eating food together is a symbol of unity, togetherness, and friendship. It creates relaxed time for people to talk, discuss, ask questions and make decisions on certain issues.

Contextual Evangelism

This section outlines a contextualized evangelistic message that addresses the current salvation beliefs of Central Bantu believers. In keeping with field research results, this section uses salvation themes and concepts such as: "peace," "repentance," "reconciliation" and "do's and don't's." The section too has biblically evaluated those conceps and has utilizes them in the gospel presentation to the Bantu Christians. The writer has also provided a contextual gospel tract for unbelievers, which the gospel workers can use to present the gospel message. For both groups, the writer relates the gospel message from both the Old and New Testaments. A communicator should seek to provide a verse or two on each salvation subject.

Gospel Tract 1

In the field research, many believers expressed different views of salvation. Based on the qualitative research results, the following salvation themes should be utilized when presenting the gospel to them.[427]

Peace

The Bantu Christians talk about peace as one aspect of salvation and peace is biblically expressed as an aspect of salvation. "Peace" is used in the Old Testament and is it referred to as *shalom*. Many times the Old Testament has used the word "shalom" especially in the book of Isaiah and Psalms, signifying a quality of life which people experienced through obedience to God. Failuring to be righteous, peace was not experienced.[428] Corresponding to the Bantu expression of peace, the Old Testament

---

[427] This gospel tract reflect the salvation themes that was gathered from AIC believers during descriptive field research (Jan. - March 2003).

[428] Robert Young, *Young's Analytical Concordance to the Bible* (Nashville: Thomas Nelson Publishers, 1982), 736-37.

also expresses it as, "to be whole, sound and safe from dangers."[429]

In the Old Testament, peace means harmony between God and his creatures (Isa. 27:5) and among the creatures themselves (1 Sam. 16:4ff; Job. 5:23). Peace was experienced when there was no war going on in the country (Ecc. 3:8; Ps. 120:7; Judg. 1:13; 1 Kings 2:5, 4:24).

In many Old Testament aspects of *Shalom*, God was said to be its source (Numb. 6:24-26, Job 25:2; Ps. 35:27; 147:14). God would speak "shalom" to His people Israel when they followed His rules and regulations (Ps. 85:8ff). In Prov. 16:7, Solomon recognized that "shalom" comes from God, and that people need God's peace.

The future "shalom" is the Old Testament emphasis announcing the coming of the Savior. Verses like, Isa. 9:1ff; 11:6-9, Joel 4:18, Isa. 7, 53, 54 talk about the eschatological peace which will be experienced by all believers in eternity. The book of Zechariah 14:6-9 also expresses how Shalom-salvation will affect nature, and how peace will be experienced by God's people. Zechariah's view of "shalom" as salvation points to the future salvation when life will be transformed through the Lordship of the Savior, Jesus Christ. As God's blessings, Amos 9:11-15 too implies that there will be peace in the future.

The New Testament also uses the word peace (Gr. *eirene*) signifying harmonious relationship between people (Matt. 10:34, Rom. 14:19), between nations (Lk. 14:32; Acts 12:20), friends (Acts 15:33) and *eirene* as rest (Acts 16:36). Peace is also expressed as contentment, which is achieved by accepting God's provision (Lk. 1:79; 2:29). It is one element of salvation, in which the recipients experience fellowship with God, who is the Lord of "peace"(Lk. 7:50, 1 Thes. 3:16).[430]

---

[429] Douglas J. Harris, *The biblical Concept of Peace: Shalom* (Grand Rapids: Baker Book House, 1970), 4.

[430] W. E. Vine, *An Expository Dictionary of New Testament Word*, 171.

The notion of peace among the Central Bantu Christians is a good springboard for the gospel: it can be used to communicate the gospel. Their expression of peace is biblical and should be affirmed. The only thing which is missing is how, biblically, it must be acquired. The contextual work behind it is to determine how it can be fulfilled, in a way which makes sense in the believers' cultural context.

If peace is to be experienced, the source is God, but humans have to access it through faith in Christ. Peace must be understood as an element of salvation which is given by God. Future shalom will be established by Christ in His second coming. In the future Christ will establish His millennial kingdom, where there will be no diseases, no deaths, and no tribal wars. All believers will be one nation under His Lordship.

Since Bantu Christians perceive that people achieve shalom-salvation through their good deeds, we should affirm that idea. God is always pleased when people practice righteousness and as a result He gives them peace of mind. Since the Bantu do not emphasize on Christ as the source of peace, we must teach that He is the only of real peace. We should also talk about future peace, which will be experienced in eternity (Rev. 21:1-4). Believers' inner peace, which is given by Christ, should contextually be communicated in a story form. For example:

There was a man called Kimani who was born suffering from a severe headache. As a child, Kimani's parents took him to different hospitals, but he did not get well from the treatments. As he was growing up he never developed friendships with other boys, because many times his pain was so great that he was unable to play with other boys. His parents did not have peace either, because they spent many sleepless nights watching their son. This was so for twenty one years.

One day there was a preaching crusade going on in their village, and the preachers were praying for people who had different diseases. When Kimani's parents heard this, they decided to take him there. When one of the preachers prayed for him, he was instantly healed, and not only was he healed, he accepted Jesus as His Savior, and his parents did too.[431]

Application. Not only did Kimani have physical healing but, he also had inner peace. He went back to school and made many friends. Jesus therefore is the source of our peace, when we accept Him. Inner peace does not mean being no longer subject to death, disease or any other physical problems, but it is a peace that helps us keep trusting and keeping faith in Christ. He is the Prince of peace (Isa. 9:6).

Another contextual "peace" story could be:

There was a man called Njogu who used to drink beer every day and night, and most of the time he would not go home to his family. He would fight people on the streets, and would abuse his children, and due to that he did not have peace with his family or his neighbors. He never thought of buying clothes or food for his family. He thought that drinking was giving him peace in his life. To him, having peace came from drinking beer. One day someone found him absorbed in drinking, and told him how he could find a better life which would be more peaceful and joyful. He accepted Jesus Christ. Gradually Njogu's life was changed, and his family and the people who knew him realized he had joy and peace in his life.[432] God had completely removed the desires of evil, and

---

[431] All stories given in this chapter are basically the writer's un-structural created ones and they reflect Bantu mind set and the way they affirm a message.

[432] Having ministered the Bantu people for many years and teaching their pastors in Bible college for three years. All the stories and parable used in this chapter reflect their cultural and contextual mind set. The writer has created most of the stories and parables to reinforce the understanding of the biblical basis of salvation and theological meaning of the same. These cultural logics of communication gear to capture Bantu attention such that, they can experience shift in their knowledge, attitude, behavior and value about the doctrine of salvation.

replaced them with inner peace, with his family and other people. He also had peace with God, because he had accepted his Son Jesus as his Lord and as the Savior of his life.

Application: It is only in Christ where complete peace and joy are found. We will be filled with love, joy, peace, fearlessness, and hope (Gal. 5:22-23).

Dos and Don'ts

Many Bantu Christians talk about salvation as coming from doing good work, either in the church or elsewhere. Concerning the notion of good works as a means to "salvation," this is what James 2:14-26 speaks about. James emphasizes Christian faith, which should be followed by good works. Otherwise works only might cause nominalism in the church. In verse 20, James says that Christian faith without deeds is useless and dead, but faith must come first. Christian faith is judged by what one does, hence the notion of "do's" and "don't's."

In Matt. 5-8, Jesus' teaching emphasized doing good works. In His ministry, Jesus not only preached about the kingdom of God, but He involved himself in social work like feeding the hungry and healing the sick (Matt. 8:14-17). All of these were good works, and doing so among the Bantu should be affirmed.

Concerning what to eat and what not to eat (do's and don't's), Paul warned believers in Corinth and Colosse that they should not emphasize on the outword appearances (Col. 2:6-16, 1 Cor. 8, Rom. 14:1-12) but should exalt things that are inward. On the other hand, in Mark 7:1-23, Jesus declared all food edible. He also said that a believer is free in all he does, because the Holy Spirit is there to guide him. This notion should be clarified biblically among the Bantu Christians.

Contextually, the notion of do's and don't's for Christians should be affirmed and clarified, because there are behaviors believers should avoid, for example stealing, adultery, cheating, witch-craft, sorcery. The person who refrains from doing all these things should decide in his heart that he must not think of doing any of them. One should decide to turn from all sin to Christ, so as not to continue sinning. Christians' practices of do's and don't's should not be legalistic, but should go along with the Word of God. First, the person should accept Christ as Savior and Lord. Second, through the power of the Holy Spirit and help from other believers, the person is to live a life worthy of God's expectations.

A contextual parable to reinforce this would be:

> There was a man who had a mango tree which he had taken care of since it was small until the time of its bearing fruit. The tree looked very beautiful. When it came to bearing fruits, its mangoes were very bitter and nobody would eat them. The man was very angry, and even though he had taken care of it for such a long time, he decided to uproot it and burn it. If it was bearing good fruit, he would have retained it.

Application. Good works are very important in our Christian life, but are produced by the Spirit in our inner self. If our inner self is not changed by Christ, even if we try we cannot do anything good before God. In order to do good work, we must first accept Jesus as our Savior and Lord, and then He will help us to continue doing good works.

Acceptance

Many believers talk of salvation as being "accepted" by God and the members of one's community because of good behaviors before God and people. Some think they are accepted by God because they were born into Christian families. They think that they are saved.

This concept of salvation is not correct. The gospel of John 1:12 declares that people are accepted as God's people on the basis of accepting the death of His Son Jesus Christ. Those who accept Jesus Christ as their Lord and Savior are mysteriously incorporated into God's family; hence they are accepted as His children (John 1:12-13; Rom. 8:15, Gal. 4:5).

From a contextual teaching of "acceptance," we should use a cultural story similar to that of a prodigal son who decided to go back to his father. Even though he had run away, did all bad things, and had no good relationship with his parents, when he finally willingly repented before God and later to his father, he was accepted back. His acceptance was not by birth or good works, but was because of his realization that he had done wrong and his repentance (Luke 15:17). He was incorporated back into his father's family, ready to share fellowship with other members of the family.

Knowing God

Some Bantu Christians think that knowing God's character and what He does qualifies them to be God's children. If they can express who God is, fulfill His ten commandments, they think they are His children or are already saved.

This idea of knowing about God is biblical but partial, and must be accompanied by knowing what He desires for them and from all human beings. Among the Central Bantu, the concept of knowing God must be corrected. People must be taught a biblical knowledge of God: who He is, that Christ died for us and what He desires from us. John the Baptist rebuked the Pharisees, who claimed to know God but did not do His will (John 3:7-10). No one can know God apart from Christ (John3:18). In a story form, one can contextually illustrate this concept as:

Kagai was a taxi driver, and he knew all the safe and convenient roads that went from his village to Nairobi (in Kenya). Though he had that knowledge, Kagai did not believe or trust that those roads were safe and therefore, he did not drive on them. Though he knew the safe road to Nairobi, he would drive on an unsafe one. After a few months of using unsafe roads, he was carjacked by robbers and killed. The fault was his.

Knowing the road is different from driving or walking on it. It is through walking or driving on that road that the person will be able to know about it, accept it and be safe. Without doing so, one is not qualified to talk about it. Our concerned people here must know that knowing God and trusting Him in their lives through Jesus Christ is different from knowing all about Him and yet not doing His will.

Reconciliation

Though the term reconciliation is used by the Bantu in their culture with different meanings, the word and what it means is biblical and is also a Christian virtue. In the Old Testament, reconciliation means uniting two parties, the offender and the one who is offended (Lev. 6:30, 8:15, Ex. 45:15, 1 Sam. 29:4). There was a mediator who offered sacrifices to rekindle friendship of the two people (Lev. 6:30, 16:20). Reconciliation was done not only between people and other members of the community but also between people and God (Lev. 17:11; Deut. 12:23, Ps. 72:14). This term therefore has vertical and horizontal dimensions.

In the New Testament, the word indicates a change from being an enemy to being a friend (Rom. 5:10; Col. 1:12-22; 2 Cor. 5:18-20). It is through the work of Christ on the cross that sinners are reconciled to God, and therefore have peace with God (Rom. 5:1-2). According to these verses, an offender (sinner) has to ask for forgiveness from God, and through Christ's death he is reconciled to Him. Believers are called into the ministry of reconciliation (2 Cor. 5:11-21; Matt. 18:15-20).

In contextual teaching, reconciliation between people and God and between a person and other fellow humans must be explained and clarified among the Bantu Christians. We should not only emphasize our present view of reconciliation, but should also point to the future when all nations will be reconciled together by Christ into His heavenly kingdom.

A contextual story. There was a boy called Mwaniki who was always angry with his parents. His parents loved him and they could buy everything he needed. Though His parents loved him, he did not like them. He had no reason for disliking them. Many times his father would ask him why he did not like them, but he would not say a word. One day, out of nowhere, Mwaniki was angry and he quickly picked up a knife and cut his father's hand, and then ran away. Out of his father's love for him, he did not report the matter. For five month, he looked for his son, but he was nowhere to be found. As Mwaniki's father was in town looking for his son and buying some food, he saw him siting in the dust. He ran and embraced him and asked him to go back home with him. Mwaniki's mother was happy to see her son back. The father and his son talked about the matter, the son repented and they were reconciled to each other.

Though Mwaniki was the offender and the father was innocent, his father's love drove him to look for him. The son's action had made both of them enemies and they needed to reconcile. The son needed to seek for forgiveness from the father and the father had to seek how to reconcile himself back with his son. The son also had to ask forgiveness from the immediate family and neighbors, who knew what he had done. When Mwaniki came home and asked for forgiveness, out of his father's love for him he was forgiven and they were reconciled. Their relationship was restored.

This is what happenes between believers and God. Before Christians accepted Christ, they had sinned against God. There was enmity between God and themselves, but God was still looking for them. By God giving His Son to die for sinners, He was offering reconciliation. There is only one way that people are reconciled with God, and this is through accepting His Son Jesus Christ (Isa. 53:6; Jn. 14:6, 1 Pet. 2:24).

Since in the Bantu Culture reconciliation is also done not

only with God but also with the offended party, this too should be affirmed. Stories like of Zacchaeus (Lk. 19:1-9) and the prodigal son (Lk. 15:11-32) are relevant not only to teach reconciliation but also forgiveness of sins for sinners' salvation. For example, if one steals somebody's animal, this behavior not only affects the owner but also it affects God. The offender too is affected because he is no longer in friendship with either God or the offended person. In the communal society like that of Bantu culture therefore, reconciliation should contextually involve three people: the offender, and the two offended parties (God and the person whose cow is stolen).

Repentance

According to the field research, the way repentance is used by Bantu people is not biblical, because it is confused with mere confession. It focuses on what the person says to God, but not on changing the sinful attitude. It is human effort, without seeking help from God. It does not provide hope for eternal life with Christ. Unless one "repents," he will end up in hell. However, this notion of confession in the culture is very important because it serves as a good starting point for teaching the biblical view.

In the Hebrew concept of repentance (*naham*), it is a one time act of deeply making a choice to turn from sin (includes all evils) toward God (Jer. 25:5). In the New Testament, repentance is when a person decides to turn away from sin and turn to God (2 Cor. 12:21). By repentance, people are changed in attitude, behavior, knowledge and belief. The effort is people's, but is empowerment by the Holy Spirit. The person who repents changes his or her mind towards sin, and places faith in Christ, who enables him or her not to continue sinning (Matt. 3:2; Lk. 13:5, 24:47). The New Testament also views repentance not only to prepare people for the present relationship with God but also for their future eternal life with Him. Repentance is a turning from sin to God (Acts 2:37-38; 3:19) and it is once for all time, though one has to stay repentant. Repentance is commanded by the Bible, for it is prerequisite for salvation, which means it is a condition for all sinners (Lk. 15:7-10; Acts 2:38, 17:30; Rom. 2:4 and 2 Pet. 3:9).

Contextually, the idea of repentance must be affirmed but also corrected. Repentance should be taught in a story form like the one of the prodigal son. For example:

Kamau had only one son whose name was Karanja. Kamau loved his son very much, but one day when his father was working on the farm, Karanja stole all his father's money and run away. When Karanja spent all the money, he started feeling pain for what he had done. His clothes became rags, he had no where to live and no food to eat. He was afraid to return to his father, because he knew his sin had separated him from him.

Karanja realized that his parents and other people were not happy with his behavior. One day, he willingly decided never to sin any more. He decided to change his attitude, not only toward stealing, but also to all sins, and soon went home. After sharing with his parents them what he had decided, his parent grandly welcomed him and was he accepted back into their fellowship. He therefore had decided to change his mind and will towards sin. Thereafter, his parents would see the life of their son changed and through their continuous help, Karanja became the person they desired. In case he sins, he always confesses and asks for forgiveness from the parents and the offended person. Repentance therefore is a one time decision which changes the whole person's life that is, his mind, attitudes, will and behaviors.

It is sin which has separated us from God (Isa. 59:1-2; Hos. 5:4-7). Sin is to reject God and to refuse to do what is right before Him (Num. 15:31; Eph. 4:18, James 4:17, Rom. 14:12). Sin causes people to flee from God, and continueing in sin causes people to feel ashamed of their deeds (Gen. 4:4, 16; Jn. 3:19-20, Lk. 5:8). Sin too destroys good relationships between people, even between friends and family members (Prov. 18:19, 24:9, 14:21; James 4:1). The only solution is to turn from sin and turn to God through faith in Christ.

Prayer

The concept of prayer among the Central Bantu is biblical. Prayer is a Christian way of communicating with God, which all believers offer continually (1 Thes. 5:17, 2 Thes. 1:3, 17; Lk. 18:1). Believers ought to tell God all their problems through prayer (Matt. 6:25, 31-33). Believers must ask God for forgiveness through prayer (1 John 1:9; Mk. 11:25, James 1:6-7). All these scriptures emphasize how believers ought to be always in prayer.

Contextually, believers' prayers should be affirmed as well as corrected. Prayers are offered to God by all people, but there are prayers for God's children, those who have put their faith in Christ Jesus. We should think of a good father and his son. Why do a father and son talk together? Sometimes the father wants to share a gift, knowledge, story or something precious with his son. Sometimes a son needs a warning about something dangerous from his father. Sometimes a father might want to confirm to his son how he loves him. All these are done through talking. A father is free with a son but not with a stranger, and that is why he can give anything to his son. It is the same way with a believer who has given his or her life to Christ and becomes his child (John 1:12).

Prayer will be very effective if we are talking with God, to whom we have already given our lives, by accepting the death of His Son Jesus Christ (1 Pet. 5:7). We should put our faith in Christ so that we may talk to Him in a child-father relationship. In this relationship, we request everything from the Father in the Name of Jesus, and we will receive (Jn. 16:23). Jesus taught His disciples how to pray, because they had already accepted Him as their Savior (Matt. 6:9-13).

Accepting Jesus

The idea of accepting Jesus as Lord and Savior is biblical, and must be reinforced among the Central Bantu believers. The thing that needs to be clarified is how one accept Christ. The notion of losing one's salvation biblically challenged and corrected.

Contextually, accepting Jesus can be presented in a parable like this one:

> In one village, there was a boy who fell in a deep pit and started crying out, Help! Help! When villagers came to help him, none of them would get inside the pit because it was deep and slippery. They looked for a long rope and lowered it in for him to hold. He held it and the helpers were able to pull him out. The boy had a choice to refuse to hold the rope but he willingly held it ready, to be saved from the pit.

Realizing the danger of living in sin, accepting Jesus as Savior is an individual choice. One has to accept that he or she cannot save himself, and therefore he needs help (Titus 3:5). When a person accepts Christ, he is saved, and will want to keep following, obeying and listening to the voice of Christ (Jn. 10:27-30).

Transformation

According to the field research, believers talk of salvation as leaving the old way of life and adopting a new life style. By this, we have noted they mean abandoning behaviors such as drinking beer, insulting others, or committing adultery. Thus, when one is not involved in these behaviors, he or she is morally transformed and he or she is saved.

The concept of moral transformation is biblical. In his writing to the Corinthian church, Paul stated that: "Neither the sexual immoral nor idolaters nor adulterers ... nor thieves ... will inherit the kingdom of God. This is what some of you were. But you were washed, you were sanctified, you were justified in the name of the Lord Jesus Christ and by the Spirit of our God."[433]

---

[433] 1 Corinthians, 6:9b-11(New International Version).

This means that believers in Christ should be different in their behaviors from other people in the community. Their moral behaviors should be seen and desired by every body. But before moral behaviors, people must express their faith in Christ, and good morals will follow thereafter.

Contextually, teaching about moral transformation should be affirmed but corrected among the people of our study. The emphasis should be first putting one's faith in Christ and through the help of the Holy Spirit; one will seek to bear the fruit of the Spirt. By doing so, it is dealing with what causes those bad morals, that is the sinful nature in every human being. A good contextual illustration such:

Some times a mouse might be dead inside a house and to an extent, under a bed. After a few days, it starts stinking and its smell in the whole house causes everybody to have a stomach-ache. The solution is not to spray good perfume or air freshener in the house but to find a dead mouse and throw it away. By dealing with the root cause of the smell, the problem will be solved. Putting one's faith in Christ, therefore, will solve bad morals in a Christian. Thus, one should change from the old way of life, accept Jesus Christ in his life so as to live new life in Him (2 Cor. 5:17).

Gospel Tract 2

As we communicate the gospel to non-believers, we should utilize the following outline, in all the areas of the gospel proclamation.

God's Creation

Parable: There was a rich man who had a beloved son. All that he had was for his son. The man used to enjoy having fellowship and friendship with his son. The man had trusted his son so much that he had shown him where he used to keep all his property, including money. One day when the man was working on the farm, his son stole his money and ran to another country. The son used all the money with prostitutes, and after a short time he had nothing to eat or anywhere to stay. In spite of all troubles it was impossible for him to return to his father. The son was afraid of his father because of the wrong he had done against him, because it had separated them completely.

The Bible tells us that the first human beings were created in God's image (Gen. 1:27, 2:22). God instructed them to obey Him and continue enjoying His presence, fellowship, peace, harmony and communion (Gen. 2:15-17). After sometime, they rebelled and willingly rejected God by obeying Satan, who deceived them and caused doubts in their lives (Gen. 3:1-7). After that, they rebelled against God and became alienated from Him (Gen. 3:10). When God visited them, they would run away from Him for they did not want to face His holiness. God, too, alienated them for He would not tolerate sin. Adam and Eve also alienated each other (Gen. 2:12) as they started accusing each other over sin.

If the person you are presenting the gospel to can read the Bible for himself, let him do so. Use illustrations and concepts from his context, which reflect his level of understanding. Encourage the listener to ask questions as a way of participating, and illustratively answer them. Remember, Jesus' method of presenting, the gospel was using people's contexts, and their level of understanding.

Then say: Sin has separated us from God. Isa. 59:1-2, Hos. 5:4-7. What is sin? Sin is to reject God and to disobey Him. It is to cut ourselves away from his fellowship, harmony and peace and start pursuing our own desires (Num. 15:31, Eph. 4:18). Sin has its consequence, which is death (Rom. 6:23).

Human sin

Adam and Eve deliberately and willingly rejected God and became sinners against Him (Gen. 3:1-7). Through them, their children also became sinners, not only by birth (nature) but also by practice (Gen. 4:1ff – Cain and Abel). Sin followed their generations up to this day. Human beings continued rejecting God and continued distancing themselves from Him.

Because of sin, human beings are far from God's fellowship and communion, and they cannot reconcile themselves with Him (Isa. 59:2). Sin has separated people from God and has broken their relationship that is, peace, harmony and acceptance from Him (Isa. 59:1-2; Hosea 5:4-7).

The person to whom you are presenting the gospel might ask: What is sin? Sin is to reject God and to break His requirements, that is, willingly not obeying Him and refusing to accept what He says, that human beings are all sinners (Num. 15:31; Eph. 4:18-19; 1 Jn. 3:4). Sin is to refuse to do what is right (Jam. 4:17; Ps. 14:3; Rom. 14:23). There is no one who is right before God because "all have sinned and have fallen short of the glory of God" (Rom3:23).

Remind the person that God created us in His own image, but when our first parents sinned against God we were all separated from Him, and this will be forever (Gen. 1:26; Isa. 29:13; Col. 1:21; Jer. 2:5; Isa. 64:7). Sin twisted human thinking. One cannot reason like God (Isa. 55: 8-9; Gen. 6:5; Rom. 1:21; Prov. 6:16-19). Sin made humans powerless to do what God wants them to do (Rom. 7:18; 5:6; 8:7-8). Sin causes a person to flee or escape from God and not to think about Him. Human beings are guilty and ashamed before God because of their sinful nature and sinful acts that they do (Gen. 3:8; Gen. 4:4-6; Jn. 3:19-20; Lk. 5:8). Not only does sin destroy a good relationship between God and humans but also between humans and their friends (James 4:1; Prov. 18:19; Prov. 24: 9).

Reminder. As one explains the origin of sin, he should mention that we are sinners because of our ancestors' sin, and we continue in this status because we are all sinners.

God's judgment

On this biblical truth, one can start with a "Parable" like

this one:

> There was a father who had a son whom he loved very much. One day the son willingly killed his father's only cow when he tied it out to pasture. When the father realized that his son had deliberately killed the cow, he was so angry that he whipped the son very hard. The son was whipped because of what he had done. This does not mean that the father did not love the son but, it was the son who had decided to be wicked, and his father did not tolerate that act. The son had acted against the will of his father.

The Bible says that God is love, and out of His loving nature He loves us. Because of our sin, we are all under His judgment. Though God loves us, He does not love the sin in us. He rejects our sin and hates it (1 Cor. 6:9-10; Gal. 5: 19-20; Jn. 3:16; Rom. 3:23). Because of our sin, whatever we do even if it looks good, does not please God (Isa. 1:11; Jer. 6:20; Matt. 23:23). This can be illustrated with the good things that people do in the culture. All the good works done by a sinner do not please God at all.

The Bible says that we are people who always disobey God, but He still loves us in His Son (1 Jn. 4:10; Jn. 3:16; Rom. 5:8). Because God is holy, He can not look at our sins (Habak. 1:13; Ps. 5:4-7). Though we are sinful, in His love God still calls us to come to Him (Isa. 1:16-18; Matt. 11:28-30). However, because of our sin and sinful nature before holy God, we still await God's dreadful judgment (Heb. 2:2-3, 9:27, 10:26-27, Rom. 1:31-32).

A gospel presenter must convey clearly that the wages of sin is death (Rom. 6:23) and the gift of God is salvation (eternal life). He can briefly illustrate this with a story as follows:

> There was a hen that laid six eggs in the bush. When one day she was away, a snake came and ate one egg and to deceive the hen replaced it with one of it's own eggs. The hen wondered many times why one of her eggs was different from the others, but she did not care much. She kept on sitting on them until they

hatched. Eventually the snake's egg hatched, but as a little snake it did not harm the chicks. The little snake was a friend of all the chicks, and the hen loved him. The neighboring hens kept on telling the chicks' mother to kill the snake but she refused. The little snake grew up with the chicks and became very big. When one night the hen and her chicks were sleeping, the snake woke up slowly and ate all of them.

Application. Whose fault was that? Of course, it was hen's. The wages of sin is death. The hen never thought that the snake would one day kill her and her family. Indeed, it is dangerous to keep on nursing our sinful nature and yet God is telling us that we should repent and accept His Son. The wages of nursing our sin is death, God's judgement over us.

God's way to escape judgment

All people are sinners and as such, are spiritually dead. One can tell Kamba story:

A mother's ten-year-old boy was playing outside their home. The child wandered down a path toward the forest where he was attacked by a dangerous twelve-foot-long python. At the child's screams the mother came running from the house. Other villagers rushed to the place where the python was strangling the child. The men ran off to get weapons to kill the python. The boy screamed even louder. So his mother jumped on the huge python and, with her bare hands, forced it to release the child. Both the mother and her son went free. Where there is love, nothing is impossible.[434]

Out of His love, God prepared a way to escape His eternal judgment (separation from Him - Jn. 14:6). In His deep and Fatherly love for sinners (Jn. 3:16), He desires us to live with Him forever

---

[434] Joseph Healey and Donald Sybertz, *Towards an African Narrative Theology* (Nairobi: Paulines Publications Africa, 2000), 71.

(1 Jn. 4:9-10). He does not want us to be eternally separated from Him. His plan is to eternally rescue us from damnation (Eph. 1:4).

Jesus is like the boy's mother who willingly rescued the boy from danger. He suffered on behalf so that we may escape God's everlasting wrath. Jesus suffered so that we may live forever. Because of His love for us, Christ died for our sins (1 John 4:10).

God's love for sinners can also be illustrated with Bantu day to day experiences especially a story of a burning house:

> Once upon a time in one Kikuyu village there was a mother who had a small child called "Munyaka" (translated in English as good luck). One day Munyaka had a slight headache. His mother left him lying in bed in the house and went into one of her near-by neighbors's house to ask for medicine.

> While she was still at her neighbors' house, suddenly she saw flames coming from her own grass thatched house, where her son was sound asleep. The mother run as fast as she could in order to get Munyaka out of the house before the flames reached him. As she was removing the boy from the bed, her arms and legs were severely burned, and her whole body was singed. Fortunately Munyaka was removed from the house without a flame touching him. As Munyaka grew older his friends would make fun of his mother and say: "Why isn't your mother pretty like our mothers? Why is she so disfigured? Why does she have scars over her whole body?" Even Munyaka began to despise his mother and make fun of her.

> One day when Munyaka was alone with his mother, he asked her: "Why are you so disfigured and not pretty like my friends' mother?" Munyaka's mother replied to him: "My son, I am disfigured and have scars all over my body because of you. I am not pretty like the other mothers

because of you." Then she explained to Munyaka everything that had happened.

From that day on, Munyaka realized how much her mother loved him and how much she had done for him. He continuously would tell his friends: "My mother loves me more than your mothers love you. She is the nicest mother in the whole world."[435]

Application. Munyaka's mother was a "savior" to her son. Out of her deep love for him, she risked her own life and saved him from death. This is like what Jesus Christ did so that to save us from eternal death (John 3:16, 18-19ff).

A communicator can also use an illustration of a bridge which people use to cross over a river. If there is no bridge, the person cannot cross over and therefore, his life is in danger. With this view in mind, God prepared the way of the cross so that we can cross over from our dangerous sins through the death of His Son on the cross to Him. The way of the cross is to know and receive Him and be reconciled back to God's fellowship and communion (Jn. 5:24; Eph. 1:11, 2:3-5). We are able to know the way to eternal life through the way that He has prepared (1 Jn. 5:13; Rom. 8:16). This only one way is Jesus Christ (Jn. 14:6, Isa. 53:6).

Instead of our dying for our sins, Christ died in our place so that we may live (Isa. 53:5-6; Rom. 5:6, 8). This is the unique way that God has prepared for us. His Son Jesus came to remove the judgment that was against us for our sins (Jn. 14:6; Acts 2:38-39; Col. 2:13-14).

In this core of the gospel, the communicator must clearly connect Isa. 53:1-12 (which we have already discussed) with the death narratives of the gospel and the Pauline summary of the

---

[435] The writer has borrowed and modified this story from Joseph Healey and Donald Sybertz, 70-71.

same (1 Cor. 15:3-5). He must stress that Christ's death was the final sacrifice for our sins. He can mention how sin in the Old Testament was removed from people, and how Jesus Christ's blood was superior to that of goats and calves. Through His final and ultimate sacrifice, whoever repents of his sin and confesses it to Christ, He cleanses once and forever.

Not only did Jesus die on the cross, He was resurrected on the third day and appeared to many. He was put to death for our sin, but God raised Him again for our justification (Rom. 4:25). Through His resurrection, He gave us hope that even when we die, we will be resurrected.

What should we do?

A question of how one should escape from danger is asked by everybody. No one wants to be in danger. Illustrate this question with a story:

> Once upon a time there was a community of rats in a certain village in Africa. In one particular house a big and mean cat terrorized the rats. They decided to work together and build a small but strong hole that they could easily enter, but the bigger cat couldn't. After finishing and testing the hole the rats, were well pleased with their team work and cooperation. But then at a community meeting one rat said: "The cat himself can't go into the whole, but he can still catch us as we enter and leave the hole. Who is going to tie a bell around the cat's neck to warn us when he is approaching? What should we do?" Everyone was silent. All were afraid. No one was ready to sacrifice himself or herself to tie the bell.[436]

Application. The rats needed someone to catch the cat, to tie a bell on him, but no one sacrificed himself to do that. We cannot save ourselves. We cannot escape from God's eternal condemnation and death unless there is someone courageous

---

[436] Joseph Healey and Donald Sybertz, 113.

enough to help us. There must be someone willing to face death on our behalf and even to risk his life to save us, all but who is this Person? Jesus is the only Person who did that (John 3:16).

Again, with this question, one can also give a quick parable:

One man went hunting in a thick forest. As he was walking very tired and hungry, there came a big lion before him. He realized that his life was in danger and because he wanted to save himself, he ran and climbed up a tree. The man did not have any one with him to save him from the lion. As the lion was trying to get him, a tourist arrived with a gun and killed the lion. He put him in his truck and escorted him to his home.

Application. We are unable to save ourselves (Titus 3:5). We invent ways that we think can save us, but it only make matters worse. We must agree with God that we are sinful people, and repent of our sins (Rom. 2:4). Then read John 5:24 " I tell you the truth, whoever hears my word and believes Him who sent me has sternal life and will not be condemned; he has crossed over from death to life." Affirm to the person that we cannot save ourselves from God's judgment (Tit. 3:5; Eph. 2:8-9). Our self invented ways cannot save us (Prov. 14:12; Matt. 7:13; Phil. 3:4-5, 7).

Explain the meaning of repentance: discuss it as a way of turning from sin and its evil practices, and of by faith turning to God through accepting the death of Christ for our sin so that we may be reconciled back to God. We are saved by faith, "for by grace you are saved through faith; and that not of yourselves, it is the gift of God" (Eph. 2:8). Jesus died to pay the penalty of death for our sin. If we accept this for ourselves, God then considers us righteous because of Christ's death for us (Rom. 3:21-26).

It is only by believing, by faith, in our heart, that Jesus died for our sins, receiving Him in our lives, confessing our sins before Him that we will escape judgment (Rom. 10:9-10). When one does this, he or she is no longer under God's judgment because he has been saved and is in Christ (Rom. 8:1; Jn. 3:18). The one who believes in Jesus (Son of God) has eternal life (Jn. 3:14, 15, 36).

Indeed, after the person receives Christ, the person who is presenting the gospel has to assure the new believer that he has eternal life (1 Jn. 5:11-13). A repentant sinner is now a child of God and has a Father - child relationship with Him (Jn. 1:12; 1 Jn. 3:1-2). What then shall one do? The person must hear Jesus' words, believe that God sent Him to die for his sin, repent of his sin, accept the death of Jesus as payment for his sin and become a child of God.

After accepting Christ

After the person accepts salvation which Christ offered on the cross, the presenter of the gospel should talk about God's forgiveness, reconciliation and new life in Christ (2 Cor. 5:17). This can be illustrate with the story of the prodigal son (Lk. 15:11-32). The loving reconciliation between the father and the estranged son was followed by a great feast of celebration and rejoicing, which is the same way God the Father is happy when one sinner comes back to Him. His gift of salvation, redemption and eternal life is the most precious gift of all time. "But to all who receive Him, who believe in His name, he gave power to become the children of God."[437] After the person accepts Christ, discipleship towards the Scriptural view of kingdom living begins.

[437] John 1:12 (*New International Version*).

Chapter 7

CONCLUSION

This chapter reviews the purpose of this study and its research findings, outlining some concluding remarks, drawing missiological implications, advancing ministry recommendations, and suggesting further research.

The purpose of this study was to seek contextual means to enhance the faith, hope and joy of the Bantu population through a contextual teaching of the Christian doctrine of salvation, by highlighting the tensions between Bantu cultural and traditional religious beliefs of salvation and Biblical views, alleviating the fears that many Central Bantu believers have concerning loss of salvation. Moffat College students and staff, as well as graduates serving as pastors are challenged to see the urgency of fulfilling the great commission by witnessing to true Biblical views of salvation and making authentic disciples of Christ by establishing true worshiping churches.

According to the research reported in this study, many Central Bantu Christians do not have a Biblical understanding that all human beings are sinners by nature. They describe sin as something negative that is done by people either toward God or other people. Ignorant that sin resides in the human mind and attitudes, Bantu Christians view sin as behavior that displeases God or other humans. They do not understand Biblically what a believer is, nor do they understand the expected, observable attributes of believers. Salvation is perceived either as a gift from God or as attained individually through human effort. Many believers do not know the Biblical view of assurance of salvation nor what it means to be "in Christ." Due to their high view of culture, as the research reveals, the syncretic Bantu view of salvation mingles Biblical concepts with cultural, religious ideas. Many believers do not understand the Biblical basis of salvation, nor do they know its theological meaning. The reason of this confusion about the doctrine is because of the Bantus' wide experience in cultural, traditional religious beliefs before and following conversion.

Remarks and Recommendations

The central question behind this project revolves around how the salvation of Christ can be taught effectively and relevantly to the rural Central Bantu in Kenya. The research showed clearly that the Central Bantu misunderstand the Biblical meaning of salvation and hold to a view that is clearly synctetic.

Having clearly understood who the Central Bantu are, what they historically believed about salvation, their current views of salvation, the fact remains that their perception of the doctrine is syncrestistic. Many of the components that make "salvation" are human cultural focused and, they are cultural religious based. "Salvation" is attained (they believe) through their own effort and is material. Though God is understood as the supreme source of salvation, they believe there are other sources of salvation. The concept of the biblical basis and theological meaning of salvation is highly emmeshed with their cultural or religious concepts. Thus, the believers' understanding of salvation is syncretic. However, the time has come to contextualize the gospel and teach it to the Bantu. As we do this, we must be careful to keep our teaching biblically sound and theologically accurate. Then, Bantu people will experience a shift in their knowledge about salvation, behaviors, attitude, and in their belief system.

Based on this study, to reach the Central Bantu population with the biblical gospel of salvation that is contextualized, several things are required:

1. Pastors need to be educated on how to contextualize the gospel of salvation. Bible College lecturers and pastors need to adopt their soteriological terms (relevant to the cultural concepts) when they teach and affirm the gospel of salvation to the Central Bantu people.

2. Bible College lecturers and pastors need to seek substitutions and equivalents for some dominant cultural elements of cultural beliefs and practices. Eternal and spiritual dimensions of salvation must be presented as hope and joy in Christ.

3. In the churches, the teaching should take place in small group settings so as to provide more relaxed and free interaction, free discussions, questions and reflection.

Christians of other communities can modify some of the contextual principles and methods of this study and use them to witness to the animistic communities of the world. However, when this study is implemented, the Central Bantu will experience shift in knowledge such that, they will embrace the Biblical meaning of salvation hence, it will change their entire life. Through contextual teaching of salvation, the Bantu will experience shift in their attitudes and values such that, they will accept Christ in their lives and have faith and hope for the eternal life with Him. The Bantu Christians will seek enthusiastically to witness the saving power of Christ on the cross, bringing the Bantu population into a joyful hope in Christ. Through Christian witness of the gospel, the true believing and worshipping churches will be established within the Bantu cultures and, in the neighboring communities.

BIBLIOGRAPHY

Books

Adeyemo, Tokunboh. *Salvation in African Tradition*. Nairobi: Evangel Publishing House, 1979.

Adoff, Deissman Paul: *A study in Social Religious History*. New York: Harper and brothers'Publication, 1957.

Alan, Richadson. *An Introduction to the Theology of the New Testament*. New York: Harper and Brothers Publication, 1958.

Alexander, J.A. *The earlier prophecies of Isaiah*. New York: Wiley & Putnam, 1970.

Anderson, Neil. *Living Free in Christ*. Ventura: Gospel Light, 1993.

Attridge, H. W. *The Epistle to the Hebrews: A Commentary on the Epistle to the Hebrews*. Philadelphia: Fortress, 1989.

Baker's Dictionary of Theology. Grand Rapids: Baker Book House, 1960.

Bancroft, Emery. *Elemental Theology*. Grand Rapids: Zondervan publishing House, 1960.

Barclay, William. *Crucified and Crowned*. London: SCM Press Limited, 1989.

_____. *The Mind of St. Paul*. New York: Harper and Brothers, 1975.

Barnes, A. *Notes on the Old Testament: Isaiah*. Grand Rapids: Baker Books, 1964.

Barnhart, Horndike. *The World Book Dictionary A-K*. Chicago: World Book, 1963.

Baron, D. *Rays of Messiah's Glory*. Grand Rapids: Zondervan, n. d.

Barrett, G. S. *A Devotional Commentary: The First General Epistle of St. John*. London: The Religious Track Society, n.d.

Berkhof, L. *Systematic Theology*. Grand Rapids: Eerdmans, 1979.

Best, W. E. *Regeneration and Conversion*. Houston: South Belt Grace Church, 1975.

Birks, T. *Commentary on the Book of Isaiah*. London: Church of England Books society, 1878.

Boice, James Montgomery. *The Gospel of John*. Grand Rapids: Zondervan Publishing House, 1979.

Bornkamm, G. *Nouveau Testament: Problems " Introduction*. Geneve: Editions Labor, 1973.

_____. *Jesus of Nazareth*. London: 1960.

Bradshaw, Bruce. *Bridging the Gap: Evangelism, Development and Shalom*. USA: MARC, 1993.

Brown, Colin. "*Forgiveness,*" *Dictionary of New Testament Theology v. 1*. Grand Rapids: Zondervan Publishing House, 1975.

_____. *1 & 2 Corinthians: New Century Bible*. Greenwood: The Attic Press, 1971.

Bultman, Rudolf. *Jesus: Mythologie et Demythologisation*. Paris: Seuil, 1958.

Primitive Christianity: In its Contemporary Setting. Philadelphia: Fortress Press, 1955.

_____. *Theology of the New Testament.* New York: Charles Scriber's Sons, 1955.

Calvin, John. *Commentary: Harmony of the Gospels.* Grand Rapids: Eerdmans Publishing Company, 1949.

Chafer, Lewis Sperry. *Systematic Theology.* Dallas: Dallas Seminary Press, 1950.

Cohn, Haim. *The Trial and Death of Jesus.* New York: KTAV Publishing House, Inc, 1977.

Colquhoun, John. *Repentance.* London: The Banner of Trust, 1965.

Conzelmann, H. *The Theology of St. Luke.* London: Faber, 1960.

Cowles, H. *Isaiah: with Notes.* New York: Appleton and Company, 1869

Creswell, John W. *Research Design: Qualitative and Quantitative Approaches.* London: Sage Publications, 1994.

Cullmann, O. *The Christology of the New Testament.* London: SCM Press, 1963.

Culpepper, Robert H. *Interpreting the Atonement.* Wake Forest: Eerdmans Publishing Company, 1966.

Douglas, J. N. D. Ed. *The New Bible Dictionary.* New York: Doubleday, 1992.

Driver, Brown and Brings. *A Hebrew and English Lexicon of the O. Testament.* Oxford:

University press, 1907.

Erickson, J. Millard. *Salvation: God's Amazing Plan.* Wheaton: Victor Books, 1978.

Evans, Williams. *The Great Doctrines of the Bible.* Chicago:

Moody Press, 1968.

Farrar, F. C. W. *The Early Days of Christianity*. New York: Funk 7 Wagnalls, 1983.

_____. *The Life and the Work of St. Paul*. New York: Dutton and Company, 1893.

Freedman, David N. Ed. Anchor Bible Dictionary. New York: Doubleday, 1993.

Gilliland, Dean S. *The Word Among Us*. Word Publishing Press, 1989.

Godet, F. *Commentary on the First Epistle to the Corinthians, v. 2*. Grand Rapids: Zondervan Publishing Company, 1957.

Gration, J. A. "*Conversion in a Cultural Context. International Bulletin*. V. 7, No. 4, October 1983.

Gray, G. *The Book of Isaiah, vol. 1: International critical commentary*. New York: Scribener's Sons, 1912.

_____. *A Critical and Exegetical Commentary on the Book of Isaiah*. New York: Scribener's Sons, 1912.

Grudem, Wayne. *Systematic Theology: An Introduction to biblical Doctrines*. Leicester: InterVasity Press, 1994.

Hamlin, E. John. *A Guide to Isaiah 40-66*. London:SPCK, 1979.

Healey, Joseph and Sybertz Donald. *Towards an African Narrative Theology* (Nairobi: Paulines Publications Africa, 2000).

Hegre, T. A. *The Cross and Sanctification*. Minnesota: Bethany Fellowship, 1969.

Hengstenberg, E. *Christology of the O. Testament and a commentary on Messianic predictions Vol.2*. Grand Rapids: Kregal, 1956.

Herman, Ridderbos. *Paul: An Introduction to His Theology*. New

York: Eerdmans Publishers Company, 1975.

Hesselgrave, David R. *Communicating Christ Cross-Culturally*. Grand Rapids: Zondervan Press, 1978.

Hindson, Edward E. *Isaiah's Immanuel*. U.S.A. Presbyrerian and reformed, publications Comp. 1978

Hodges, Zane C. *Absolutely Free*. Dallas: Redencion Viva, 1989.

Hoekeman, Anthony. *Created in the Image of God*. Grand Rapids: Eerdmans Publishing

Company, 1988.

Horne, Charles M. *Salvation.* Chicago: Moody Press, 1971.

House, Paul R. *Old Testament Theology*. Downer Grove: InterVasity Press, 1999.

Howe, Revel L. *Man's Need and God's Action*. Greenwich: The Searbury Press, 1954.

Hunter, A. M. *Gospel and Apostle*. SCM Press Ltd., 1975.

Idowu, Blaji. *Olodumare: God in Yoluba Belief.* London: Clower and Sons, 1962.

Interpreter's Bible Dictionary, Vol. 5. New York: Abingdon, 1956.

Jeremias, J. *New Testament Theology*. London: SCM Press, 1971.

Johnson, Patrick. *Operation World*. Carlisle: Om Publishing Company, 1993.

Jong-Youn, Lee (ed). *The Mission Theology of Paul*. n.p.: 1994.

Kabetu, M. N. *Kikuyu: Customs and Traditions*. E. A. Literature Bureau: PCT Press, 1966.

Kenyatta, Jomo. *Facing Mt. Kenya*. Nairobi: Heineman Ed. Books, 1938.

Kiehl, Erich H. *The Passion of our Lord*. Grand Rapinds: Baker Book House, 1990.

Killel, R. *Great Men and movements in Israel*. New York. Macmillan, 1929.

Kimamba, Icharia. *The Eastern Bantu People: Survey of East African History*. Nairobi: E.A. Publishing House, 1968.

Kraft, Charles H. *Communication Theory for Christian Witnesses*. New York: Orbis Books, 1991.

_____. *Communicating the Gospel God's Way*. Pasadena: William Carey Library, 1979.

Kummel G. Werner. *The Theology of the New Testament*. Grand Rapids: Abingdon Press, 1973.

Ladd, G. W. *The Theology of the New Testament*. New York: Abingdon Press, 1974.

_____. *A Theology of the New Testament*. Grand Rapids: Eerdmans Publishing Company, 1974.

_____. *Theology of the New Testament*. London: Lutterworth, 1974.

Latourette, Kenneth. *A History of Christianity Vol. 2*. Harper and Row: 1975.

Lindblom, Joh. *A study on the Immanuel section in Isaiah*. Lund: Lund CWK Gleerup, 1957.

Lowen, A. Jacob. *Culture and Human Values*. Pasadena: William Carey Library, 1957.

M. Herbert. *Interpreting Isaiah: The Suffering and Glory of the Messiah*. Grand Rapids: Zondervan Publishing House, 1985.

MacArthur, John. *Confession of Sin*. Chicago: Moody Press, 1986.

_____. *The Gospel According to Jesus*. Grand Rapids: Zondervan, 1988.

Macclaren, A. *Exposition of Holy Scriptures: Isaiah chapters 1-18*. New York: Hodder Stouchition, 1906.

Manson, T.W. *The Saying of Jesus*. London, SCM Press, 1964.

Martin, R. P. *New Testament Foundations. Vol. 2, Revised Ed.* Grand Rapids: Eerdmans, 1986.

Mauchline, J. *Isaiah 1-39*. New York: Macmillan, 1962.

Mbiti, John. *Bible and Theology in African Christianity*. Nairobi: Oxford University Press, 1986.

_____. *Concept of God in Africa*. London: SPCK, 1970.

_____. *The African Religions and Philosophy*. London: Heineman, 1969.

Mcdonald, H. D. *The Atonement of the Death of Christ*. Grand Rapids: Baker Book House, 1985.

_____. *Forgiveness and Atonement*. Grand Rapids: Baker Book House, 1984.

_____. *Living Doctrines of the New Testament*. Grand Rapids: Zondervan Publishing House, 1972.

McGavran, Donald A. *Understanding Church Growth*. Grand Rapinds: Eerdmans Publishing Company, 1990.

_____. *The Bridge of God*. New York: Friendship Press, 1955.

McGrath, Alister E. *Justification by Faith*. Grand Rapids: Zondervan Publishing House, 1988.

Media and Message: A Resource Book on the Use of Media in Evangelism. World Evangelistic Fellowship: Paternoster Press Ltd. 1989.

Morris, Leon. *The Cross in the New Testament*. Grand Rapids:

Eerdmans Publishing Company, 1965.

_____ *The First Epistle of Paul to the Corinthians: Tyndale Bible Commentary Series*. New Testament Series, v. 7. n.d.

Moyer, Larry. *Free and Clear: Understanding and Communicating God's Offer of Eternal Life*. Grand Rapids: Kregel Publication, 1997.

Murray, John. *Redemption Accomplished and Applied*. Grand Rapids: Eerdmans Publishing Company, 1987.

Muthiani, Joseph. *Akamba from Within*. New York: Exposition Press, 1973.

Muriuki, Geoffrey. *A History of the Kikuyu, 1500-1900*. Nairobi: E.A. Publishing House, 1968.

New Bible Dictionary. Grand Rapids: Eordmans, 1953

Ndeti, Kivuto. *Elements of Akamba Life*. Naironi: E.A. Publishing House, 1972.

Nida, A. Eugene. *Customs and Cultures*. New York: Harper and Brothers, 1954.

Nixon, Leroy (Transl). *The Gospel According to Isaiah*. Grand Rapids: Eerdmans Publishing Company, 1953.

Nygrey, Anders. *Commentary on Romans*. Chicago: Mody Press 1947.

Orelli, C. *The prophecies of Isaiah*. Edinburgh: T.&T. Clark, 1895.

Orr, James. *The International Standard Bible Encyclopedia*. Michigan: WMB Publishers, 1952.

Owen, John. *The Forgiveness of Sin*. Grand Rapids: Baker Books, 1977.

Packer, J. I. *New Dictionary of Theology*. Leicester: InterVasity

Press, 1988.

Padilla, Rene. *Mission Between the Times: Essays on the Kingdom*. Grand Rapids: Eerdmans Publishing Company, 1985.

Parker, T. H. L. *Calvin's Commentaries: The Gospel of St. John Ch. 11-21*. Grand Rapids: Eerdmans Publishing Company, 1961.

Pascal, Blaise. *Pensee*. Baltimore: Benguine, 1966.

Payne, J. B. *The Theology of the Older Testament*. Grand Rapids: Zondervan Publishing House, 1962.

Phillips, J. B. *Making Men Whole*. New York: The Macmillan Company, 1953.

Picirilli, R. E. *Paul the Apostle*. Chicago: Moody Press, 1986.

Pink, A. W. *The Doctrine of Salvation*. Grand Rapids: Baker Book House, 1975.

Pringle, William. *Commentary on the Book of the Prophet Isaiah*. Grand Rapids: Eerdmans, 1948

Taylor, Vincent. *Forgiveness and Reconciliation*. London: Macmillan and Company LTD, 1956.

Radmacher, Earl D. *Salvation*. Nashville: Word Publishing Company, 2000.

Ridderbos, H. *Paul and Jesus*. np. 1958.

Rimmer, Harry. *The Purpose of Calvary*. Grand Rapids: Eerdmans Publishing Company, 1939.

Ryrie, Charles. *Basic Theology*. USA: Victor Books, 1987.

_____. *Biblical Theology of the New Testament*. Chicago: Moody Press, 1959.

_____. *The Holy Spirit*. Chicago: Moody Press, 1965.

Scherer, James and Stephen B. Bevans (ed.). *New Directions in Mission and Evangelization 1*. New York: Orbis Books, 1994.

Shorter, Aylward. *Prayer in the Religious Traditions of Africa*. Nairobi: Oxford University Press, 1975.

Simmons, Thomas Paul. *A Systematic Study of Bible Doctrine*. Russell: 1955.

Simpson, A.B. *Isaiah*. Harrisburg: Christian Publications, n.d.

Smalley, A. William (ed). *Reading in Missiological in Anthropology*. Pasadena: William Carey Library, 1978.

Smedes, Lewis B. *Union with Christ*. Grand Rapids: Eerdmans Publishing Company, 1983.

Smith, Donald K. *Creating Understanding*. Grand Rapids: Zondervan Publishing House, 1992.

Smith, G.A. *The Book of Isaiah*. New York: Harper and Brothers 1927, Vol. 1.

Smith, Ryder. *The Bible Doctrine of Salvation: A Study of the Atonement*. London: The Epworth Press, 1946.

Steffen, Tom A. *Reconnecting God's Story to Ministry: Crosscultural Story Telling at Home and Abroad*. La Habra: Center for Organization and Ministry Development, 1996.

Strong, Hopkins. *Augustus Systematic Theology v. 1*. New Jersey: Fleming H. Company, 1970.

_____. *Systematic Theology*. Philadelphia: The Judson Press, 1912.

Terry, John Mark, Smith, Ebbie & Anderson, Justice. *Missiology: An Introduction to the Foundations, History and Strategies of World Missions*. Nashville: Broadman & Homan Publishers, 1998.

Theological Dictionary of the New Testament Vol. 9. Grand Rapids: Eerdmans Publishing Company, 1974.

Thiessen, Henry. *Introductory Lectures in Systematic Theology.* Grand Raoids: Eerdmans Publishing Company, 1949.

Unger Bible Dictionary. Chicago: Moody Press, 1973.

Van Engen, Charles (ed). *The Good News of the Kingdom.* New York: Orbis Books, 1993.

Vine, W. E. *An Expository Dictionary of the New Testament Word.* New Jersey: Fleming Revell Company, 1966.

_____.*First Corinthians: Local Church Problems.* Grand Rapids: Zondervan, 1961.

_____. *The First and the Last.* London: Pickering & Inglis, n.d.

_____. *Isaiah's prophecies, promises, warning.* London: Oliphants, 1953.

Vischer, Lukas. *Reformed Witness Today.* Seoul: PTS, 1982.

Von Rad, G. *Old Testament Commentary.* New York: Harper & Row, 1965.

Walvoord, John. *Jesus Christ Our Lord.* Chicago: Moody Press, 1991.

Wareig, Earnest C. *The Evangelism of Jesus.* New York: The Abingdon Press, 1918.

Waterhouse, Steven. *What Must I do to be Saved?* Amarillo: Westcliff Press, 1995.

Webb, Barry. *The Message of Isaiah.* Leicester: InterVarsity press, 1996.

Westermann, C. *Elements of the Old Testament Theology.* Atlanta: John Knox, 1982.

Willy, H. Orton & Culbertson, Paul T. *Introduction to Christian*

Theology. Kansas City: Beacon Hill Press of Kansas City, 1994.

Wilson, R. Mcl. Hebres. *New Century Bible Commentary*. Grand Rapids: Eerdmans / Marshal Morgan & Scott, 1987.

Wordsworth, W.A. *The prophecies of Isaiah the Seer*. Edinburgh: T.&.T. Clark,1939.

Young, E. *Studies in Isaiah*. Grand Rapids: Eerdmans, 1954.

Young, Hwa. *Mangoes or Bananas? The Quest for an Authentic Asian Chtistian Theology*. Oxford: Regnum Book International, 1997.

Journals and Periodicals

Castro, Emilio. "Mission Today and Tomorrow." *International Bulletin*. V. 5, No. 3, July 1981.

EAJET. 1982, V.2, No. 1, 12. 1987, V. No. 2, 30.

Halverson, Richard C. "Methods of Personal Evangelism," *Christianity Today,* Oct. 28, 1966.

Hibert, Paul. "Critical Contextualization." *International Bulletin of Mission Research*, 11, No. 3 (July 1987).

Kroeker, Peter J. "Development and Mission." *Mission Focus. V. 15, No. 2.* June 1987.

Simon, Arthur. "Bread for the World: Clear Command, Complicated Task." *International Bulletin. V. 5, No. 1.* January 1981, 22.

Strom, Donna. "Cultural Practices - Barriers or Bridges?" *EMQ* (July 1987).

Wan, Enoch. "Jesus Christ fro the Chinese: A Contextualized Reflection." *CATW*, Nov. 2000.

World Council of Churches. "Mission and Evangelism - An Ecumenical Affirmation". *International Bulletin. V. 7, No. 2*, April 1983, 13.

Unpublished Works

Contextualization. "Class Lecture," Western Seminary, Spring 1999.

Christ and Salvation. "Class Discussions." Moffat College of Bible. July, 1997.

Duffy, David K. "A Study of Confession of Sin in Relation to the Context of 1 John." Capital Bible Seminary, *Thesis*, 1980, Microfilm.

Gehman, Richard. "Ancestor Relations Among three African Societies in biblical Perspective." Fuller University: Microfilm International, 1975.

Hebrew I and II, "Class Lectures," North Park Theological Seminary, Fall, 2001, Spring, 2002.

Interpreting New Testament 1, "Class Notes," North Park Theological Seminary, Fall, 2001.

Introducing People to Jesus Series. n.d. n.p., 15.

Isensee, Ralph H. "The Meaning and Significance of Metanoeo and Metanoia." *Thesis*, 1951.

Johnson, Lewis. "The Complete Sufficiency of the Union with Christ." *Bibliotheca Sacra 120.* (Jan.-March 1963), 16.

Jung, Wolfgang E. "Contextualization in the OT and NT and its Applications." Grace Theological Seminary, *Thesis* 1993. Microfilm.

Kineman, Larry E. "The Lord's Supper: Meaning and Practice in the NT and in the Christian Churches of Christ." Anderson University, *Thesis*, 1988. Microfilm.

Launstein, Donald H. "The Theological Concept of the Gospel According to St. Paul." *Th.D. Dissertation,* Grace Theological Seminary. 1969.

Nelson, Craig W. "Confession and Repentance in Neh. 9." Grace Theological Seminary,   *Thesis*, 1984, Microfilm.

"Statement of Faith: United Church of Canada and the Korean Methodist Church," *Tabor Heights Bulletin*, Portland OR, Oct. 2002.

Strongmberg, Jean (ed.). "Mission and Evangelism: An Ecumenical Affirmation / A Study Guide for Congregation" NCC of USA, 1983.

Tabor Heights United Methodist Trinity Sunday Worship Bulletin. "Sermons of John Wesley," June 15, 2003.

Thieme, Robert B. "Union with Christ." Portland: Research Exchange Network, 1987. Microfilm.